RETHINKING ENGLISH HOMICIDE LAW

Rethinking English Homicide Law

OXFORD
UNIVERSITY PRESS

General Editor's Introduction

The law of homicide has a high profile in the criminal law and in public policy. Indeed, such are the extremes of emotion and controversy it evokes that successive governments since the 1950s have shied away from promoting legislation to re-shape what is, for several reasons discussed below, an unsatisfactory structure of legal responses. In this volume six leading scholars from England and Wales discuss possible paths for reforming major aspects of our law of homicide. The authors make reference to the approaches of other legal systems, but the emphasis is upon debating the principles on which the English law should be grounded. The book's foremost aim is to initiate a serious re-thinking of this important field of criminal law, in the hope that a reinvigorated and better informed debate, and even a new legislative structure, will ultimately result.

ANDREW ASHWORTH

Contents

The Contributors

C. M. V. Clarkson is Professor of Law at the University of Leicester, and was Head of the Law Department from 1996–9. He is co-author of Clarkson and Keating's *Criminal Law: Text and Materials*, 3rd edn. (1998), author of *Understanding Criminal Law*, 2nd edn. (1997), and co-editor (with Rod Morgan) of *The Politics of Sentencing Reform* (1995). He has written several articles on criminal law, sentencing, and the conflict of laws.

Nicola Lacey is Professor of Criminal Law at the London School of Economics. She is the author with Celia Wells of *Reconstructing Criminal Law*, 2nd edn. (1998), co-author of Fraser and Lacey, *The Politics of Feminism*, and is also the author of *State Punishment* (1988) and *Unspeakable Subjects: Essays in Feminist Legal Philosophy* (1998). She has written extensively on the criminal law, criminal justice, and legal theory.

R. D. *Mackay* is Professor of Criminal Policy and Mental Health at De Montfort University Law School, Leicester. He has carried out several empirical research projects into responses to mentally disordered defendants in the criminal process, criminal law and penal system. He is the author of *Mental Condition Defences in Criminal Law* (1995), and has written or co-written many articles. He is a member of the Parole Board.

Martin Wasik is Professor of Criminal Justice, School of Law, University of Keele. Among his publications are *Emmins on Sentencing*, 3rd edn. (1997) and the recent volume (with Gibbons and Redmayne) on *Criminal Justice: Text and Materials*. He has written widely on the criminal law, computer law, criminal justice, and sentencing. He edits the sentencing section of Blackstone's *Criminal Practice*, and is chairman of a new statutory body, the Sentencing Advisory Panel.

Celia Wells is Professor of Law at Cardiff Law School. Among her books are *Corporations and Criminal Responsibility* (1993), *Negotiating Tragedy: Law and Disasters* (1995), and (with Nicola Lacey) *Reconstructing Criminal Law*, 2nd edn. (1998). She has written many articles on aspects of the criminal law and of medical law. She has recently taken over as co-editor of *Legal Studies*.

William Wilson is Reader in Criminal Law at Queen Mary and Westfield College, London, and is the author of a major text on *Criminal Law: Theory and Doctrine* (1998). Among his publications are articles on the law of murder and on intention, and he has also written or co-written several articles on criminal law theory. He is currently working on a new book on 'Wrongdoing and Responsibility'.

The Editors

Andrew Ashworth is Vinerian Professor of English Law in the University of Oxford. The third edition of his *Principles of Criminal Law* (1999) has been published recently and, in addition to books on *The Criminal Process*, 2nd edn. (1998) and *Sentencing and Criminal Justice*, 3rd edn. (2000), he is working on a co-authored text on human rights and criminal proceedings.

Barry Mitchell is Reader in Criminal Justice at Coventry University. He has completed various empirical studies on homicide, including studies for the Home Office and for the DPP's Department, and is currently researching the investigation and prosecution of homicides. He is the author of *Murder and Penal Policy* (1990), and has written several articles on criminal law, especially on matters relating to homicide.

Table of Cases

Table of Legislation

(I) UK Legislation

(II) International and Foreign Measures

1

Introduction

ANDREW ASHWORTH AND BARRY MITCHELL

This volume contains six essays by leading academic lawyers on the English law of homicide. The volume was conceived for what might be described as a political purpose, that is, to relaunch debate on the future of the English law of homicide. Trials for murder and manslaughter still attract great public attention, and the study of those branches of criminal law occupies a central place in university criminal law courses that belies the relative rarity of homicides in practice. Yet the shape of English homicide law remains partly in the grip of a statute passed amid passionate debates about capital punishment, and partly governed by common-law doctrines that have never received parliamentary attention. The development of the law has been left largely in the hands of the senior judiciary: even if it is thought satisfactory that the dividing lines between the most serious offences in the criminal calendar are drawn by judges rather than by Parliament, there are limits to what can be achieved by them. The structure of the offences cannot be altered by judicial decision, and it seems to be accepted that partial defences cannot be abolished or introduced in that way either.[1] Most of those concerned with the operation of the law recognize the need for change. Of reform proposals there has been no shortage—notably the Fourteenth Report of the Criminal Law Revision Committee in 1980,[2] whose recommendations are incorporated in the draft Criminal Code of 1989;[3] the report of the Select Committee of the House of Lords in 1988–9;[4] and the Law Commission's report on Involuntary Manslaughter in 1996.[5] But there has been no legislative action, and the prospects for any general reform of the law of homicide (as distinct from a decision to legislate on one element, such as the proposed offence of corporate killing) do not seem great.

One primary purpose of this volume is to rekindle debate on some of the major issues in the law of homicide, with a view to reawakening interest in

---

[1] See e.g. Lord Lloyd of Berwick in *Clegg* [1995] 1 AC 482, 499–500.
[2] *Offences Against the Person* (1980) (Cmnd. 7844).
[3] Law Commission, *A Criminal Code for England and Wales* (Law Com. no. 177) (1989), cll. 54–64.
[4] House of Lords, *Report of the Select Committee on Murder and Life Imprisonment* (H. L. Paper 78, 1989).
[5] Law Commission, *Legislating the Criminal Code: Involuntary Manslaughter* (Law Com. no. 237) (1996).

a broad reform initiative. To engage in these tasks productively is no easy matter. Academic criminal lawyers, whose work involves research into, writing about, and teaching the law, are well placed to engage in debate about the structure of the law and the reasons for and against change. But it might be argued that the law of homicide, with its unusually high public profile, can only be altered if there is public and political acceptance of the details of the proposed reform, and therefore that a volume of academic essays is likely to be too remote from the fray. These public and political perspectives are not neglected in this volume: both in this Introduction and in the essays that follow there is discussion of the proper relationship between the shape of homicide law and 'public opinion', and indeed there is keen analysis of what passes for 'public opinion' and of what evidence can be regarded as reliable. Of the eight authors contributing to this volume, one (Barry Mitchell) has conducted empirical research into public views about the law of homicide and the distinctions it should embody, and another (Ronnie Mackay) has been a member of the Parole Board for several years and has ample experience of reviews of life-sentence prisoners.

The differing experience of our authors leads on to another point. Some politicians, civil servants, or members of law-reform bodies have been known to ask what the academic view is on a certain issue. There have also been occasions when it has been said that the publication of one or two academic articles critical of a proposal from the Law Commission or some other body 'weakens' the proposal, because it suggests that it is controversial and not securely based. But academics are not a homogeneous group who chose their career because they hold the same views as others. On the contrary, the academy contains individuals who hold a wide range of views, and who approach problems from a variety of perspectives. Thus there are groups or tendencies within academic criminal law—for example, one might label some as subjectivists, others as objectivists, some as critical scholars, others as contextualists, and so forth. The authors of this volume do not share a single approach to the subject matter, save that they have agreed for present purposes to think and to write about the project of reforming the law of homicide. This diversity of approach should be celebrated at an intellectual level, in so far as it is evidence of academic independence. But the law itself has to take a view, and one set of reform proposals needs to be put forward as the most appropriate, the least objectionable, or the 'best fit'. That leads on to deeper questions about the standards by which appropriateness and 'fit' should be judged, and much of this introductory chapter is concerned with those issues.

At several points in the essays below, the argument turns to major issues of principle that affect the criminal law generally. Some of these run into questions of moral philosophy, such as the extent to which either criminal liability or sentencing ought to be based on 'moral luck' (as where death results unexpectedly from a person's act or omission). This Introduction will pursue some of those issues, whilst also exploring the legal and political context of homicide law (notably, the mandatory penalty for murder, and the role of the jury in criminal trials). What will not be found, either in the Introduction or in the essays, is a detailed examination of the existing English law of homicide. That is available in the leading textbooks, and the essays look to possible futures more than to the past or the present. Nor is it claimed that the book is comprehensive in its coverage of the law of homicide, and there are several categories of killing (for example infanticide, suicide pacts, killings in self-defence, euthanasia) which are not dealt with here. Nor does the volume aim to provide a review of previous law-reform recommendations or the laws of other jurisdictions, although there are discussions of comparative law on several specific issues. The aim of the volume is to explore some of the central questions of principle and structure that need to be tackled if a satisfactory law of homicide is to be designed.

Drafts of the six essays were presented at a conference in Oxford in January 2000, having been circulated in advance, and there was extensive and stimulating discussion. The editors are grateful to Chris Gane, Roger Leng, Ian Dennis, and Malcolm Davies, each of whom kindly agreed to give oral comments on a particular paper in order to launch the discussion. Special thanks go to Lord Justice Buxton, who not only chaired the conference with wit and good humour, but also made several astute comments and interventions which enriched both the conference and this volume. The conference received generous financial support from the British Academy and the Society of Public Teachers of Law, for which we and over forty colleagues who attended it are most grateful.

A. CONCERNS ABOUT THE EXISTING LEGAL STRUCTURE

Criminal homicide is a comparatively rare occurrence in England and Wales; in a country of over 50 million people, there are around 750 offences initially recorded as murder or manslaughter each year, and only 450–500 convictions.[6] But the relative rarity of such homicides should not be used as an excuse for ignoring the need to reform the law. Some have argued that criminal homicide is a unique form of offending in so far as it represents a wrong done against a 'higher authority'.[7] Whatever view one takes of this, homicide has a strong claim to be (at least) one of the most serious crimes. Instead of prescribing a maximum penalty, as is the usual practice, the law specifies a mandatory sentence for convicted murderers. The need for the criminal justice system to respond to its most heinous offences in a principled and rational manner is unaffected by the volume of offences.

---

[6] Home Office, *Criminal Statistics, England and Wales 1997* (1998) (Cm. 4162), ch. 4.
[7] See e.g. G. P. Fletcher, *Rethinking Criminal Law* (Boston, Mass., 1978), ch. 5.

The existing law of homicide in England and Wales can be summarized briefly. The offence of murder carries a mandatory penalty of life imprisonment, and a person is liable for murder through causing a person's death, whether by act or omission, either with intent to kill or with intent to cause grievous bodily harm. That liability to conviction for murder may be reduced to manslaughter if the killing stemmed from provocation, diminished responsibility, or a suicide pact. These are commonly referred to as forms of 'voluntary manslaughter'. If a person causes another's death without the intent necessary for murder, there may be liability to conviction for manslaughter if it is shown that the defendant was subjectively reckless as to death or grievous bodily harm, or grossly negligent as to death, or that the death resulted from an unlawful and dangerous act of the defendant's. These are commonly referred to as forms of 'involuntary manslaughter'. All offences of manslaughter carry a maximum penalty of life imprisonment, and it will be evident that the offence covers cases of killing that are almost serious enough for a murder conviction, as well as some cases in which the culpability is relatively low on the scale. Among the other homicide offences in English law are causing death by dangerous driving, and causing death by careless driving when intoxicated, both of which have a maximum penalty of ten years' imprisonment.

One of the reasons for drawing a distinction between the two offences, as murder and manslaughter, is probably that it is thought fair to label degrees or types of homicide separately, although for many years we have had a single offence of manslaughter which encompasses two rather different types of homicide, the 'voluntary' and 'involuntary' forms described above. From time to time the suggestion is made that English law should go further and merge the two offences into one, which would carry a maximum penalty of life imprisonment, and would leave the trial judge to reflect the gravity of the homicide in the sentence.[8] Reform bodies, however, have resisted this[9] and, indeed, the existing English view is, at least at a superficial level, one which has been adopted in several other Western jurisdictions.[10] However, the laws of those other countries vary considerably in the number of offences recognized, in the factors which characterize the worst homicides, and in the interpretation of basic concepts. Some, for example, do not recognize provocation and/or diminished responsibility as a valid (partial) excuse; some attach weight to what are seen as good or bad motives; and others regard the method of killing as significant in determining the offence category.

English law has reached its current state largely in a piecemeal fashion,

---

[8] See e.g. Lord Kilbrandon in *Hyam* v. *DPP* [1974] 2 WLR 607, 640; and Lord Hailsham in *Howe* [1987] 2 WLR 568, 581.

[9] e.g. Criminal Law Revision Committee, n. 2 above, para. 15.

[10] For a description of the structure of homicide law in several other countries see House of Lords, n. 4 above, app. 5.

as a result of gradual evolution. Reviews have tended to focus on specific aspects of homicide, such as murder[11] and involuntary manslaughter,[12] and the only general review of homicide law is now rather dated.[13] However, there is objective evidence of discrepancies between the law in theory and the verdicts reached in the courts,[14] and part of the explanation for it may be a lack of satisfaction amongst lawyers, judges, and the public, who then try to correct what they perceive to be shortcomings within the law. For many years the separation of murder from manslaughter was based in part on an untested assumption that it met with general public approval,[15] but more work is necessary before we can accurately gauge the precise extent to which ordinary people support the law.

B. THE PENALTY FOR MURDER: THE CART BEFORE THE HORSE?

The principal statute in the English law of homicide is the Homicide Act 1957, and the structure of that statute was much influenced by the decision to separate some capital murders from other non-capital murders. That separation ceased in 1965 when the death penalty was abolished, but since then the mandatory sentence of life imprisonment has continued to exert significant effects on the structure of homicide law. Because judges have no discretion when sentencing for murder, this means that the only possible approach to a case for which the mandatory penalty is manifestly inappropriate is to reduce the offence to a lower category (usually manslaughter). This is the reason often given for the category of 'voluntary manslaughter': thus the Homicide Act provides that killings in circumstances of diminished responsibility, provocation, or a suicide pact fall into this lesser category, even though the intent required for murder was present. Even with this distinction, the category of murder still includes cases which lie a considerable distance apart in terms of heinousness—one might contrast a deliberate contract killing with a killing in a pub brawl in which a chair or ashtray is used as an impromptu weapon on the victim's head.

It is not simply that judges are obliged to pass the same sentence on offenders with significantly different degrees of culpability. Distinctions of culpability are drawn, but they are drawn behind closed doors by the Home Secretary and his advisers, who have the responsibility for determining the release date of adults sentenced for murder. Although the European Court of Human Rights has in recent years found the United Kingdom in breach of the Convention for its law on discretionary life-sentence prisoners and on young offenders detained during Her Majesty's Pleasure for murder, it has

[11] Ibid. [12] See Law Commission, n. 5 above.
[13] Criminal Law Revision Committee, n. 2 above.
[14] See e.g. B. Mitchell, 'Distinguishing Between Murder and Manslaughter' (1991) 141 NLJ 935–7, 969–71. [15] See Criminal Law Revision Committee, n. 2 above, para. 15.

declined to find the mandatory sentence for adult murderers to be in breach of either Article 5 or Article 6 of the Convention.[16] This is despite the fact that the length of detention is effectively set by a politician, the Home Secretary, who is plainly not an 'independent and impartial tribunal' within the terms of Article 6. It is a source of concern that those convicted of the highest offence lack the regular access to a court (which, for these purposes, includes the Parole Board) that is available for those serving discretionary life sentences.

As mentioned above, for these and other reasons there has been a succession of recommendations that the mandatory penalty of life imprisonment should be abolished—notably, in recent years, the Select Committee of the House of Lords on Murder and Life Imprisonment,[17] and the Lane Committee on the Penalty for Murder.[18] Little has been said about the consequences of this, in terms of the range of determinate sentences that might then be passed by the courts for offences of murder. The assumption is that a tariff would be developed, with guidance from the Court of Appeal, which would be compatible with lengths of sentence handed down for other serious offences.

Should debate about the future of the law of homicide take for granted the continuation of the mandatory penalty for murder? As a matter of practical politics it seems unlikely that there will be change in the next few years, since the current government has made clear its desire to keep the mandatory penalty and the power it concentrates in the hands of the Home Secretary. The public and political reaction to any proposal for change is hard to predict. Empirical research in October 1995 indicates a good deal of public support for life imprisonment—in the form of natural life—for those cases which are viewed as the most serious.[19] Predictably, though, there appears to be no clear consensus as to the characteristics of these homicides. Nevertheless, if the mandatory penalty were abolished, public acceptance of the new system might well be determined by the sentences handed down in

---

[16] Decisions that have brought about changes in English law include *Thynne, Wilson and Gunnell* v. *UK* (1990) 13 EHRR 666 on discretionary sentences of life imprisonment and *T. and V.* v. *UK* [2000] Crim LR 187 on detention of young murderers during Her Majesty's Pleasure; cf. *Wynne* v. *UK* (1994) 19 EHRR 333 where the European Court held that the mandatory sentence of life imprisonment for murder removes the offender's right to liberty for the rest of his life, because of the seriousness of the offence, and that it is therefore not objectionable for a politician rather than a court to decide whether he may be released at an earlier point. Nevertheless pending legislation under which tariffs for those under 18 years would be set by the trial judge in open court, the Home Secretary proposed that the Lord Chief Justice review the tariffs of all defendants convicted of murder as juveniles and currently detained at H.M.'s pleasure. The Home Secretary would set new tariffs following the L.C.J.'s recommendation in existing and future cases, the recommendation being made in open court: see Practice Statement (Juveniles: Murder tariffs) *The Times*, 9 August 2000.   [17] See n. 4 above.

[18] *Report of the Committee on the Penalty for Murder* (chairman, Lord Lane) (Prison Reform Trust, London, 1993).

[19] B. Mitchell, 'Public Perceptions of Homicide and Criminal Justice' (1998) 38 Br J Crim 453.

individual cases—an unusually low sentence might fuel opposition to the change, even if corrected by means of an Attorney General's Reference to the Court of Appeal. In the context of this volume it is important that the analysis is not restricted by assumptions about the continued presence of the mandatory penalty; this applies particularly in the sphere of sentencing, where (as Martin Wasik shows in his essay) there would be a need for considerable development if the mandatory penalty were abolished.

Two other points need discussion, however. Firstly, there is the question whether the structure of the law really is so dependent on the penalty for murder. It may or may not be true historically that the desirability of avoiding the mandatory penalty was the reason why the Homicide Act 1957 declared that killings that would be murder except for the existence of diminished responsibility, provocation, or a suicide pact, should be classified as manslaughter. However, the penalty is not the only significant issue. There is also the label to be applied. One might argue that it is morally and socially appropriate to convict, say, a provoked killer of an offence less than murder, in recognition of the mitigating circumstances under which the killing occurred. One might further argue that, if juries were not presented with this possibility, they might nevertheless try to find some (probably less satisfactory) way of avoiding a murder conviction. Where the law offers two or more grades of liability for causing the same consequence, and especially where the offences have such a high profile as murder and manslaughter, it is surely wise to exploit that gradation in order to reflect significant differences in culpability. Versions of this argument are found in several places below.

The second and final point on the penalty for murder concerns the determination of how long an individual offender should serve in prison. The Home Secretary controls these decisions at present, and it has been argued that this is unsatisfactory for various reasons—not least because, for example, the Home Secretary is a politician, and there is no hearing. If murder cases were treated as, or might include, discretionary sentences of life imprisonment, then courts would set a tariff period and this would bring a significant part of the sentence-fixing operation into a public forum. After the expiry of the tariff period, release would then be in the hands of the Parole Board, which means that the actual release date would still be set by a tribunal at a later date. Under the present 'mandatory' system, these decisions remain in the domain of the Executive, and a power that courts normally have in criminal cases is absent in murder.

C. WHICH DISTINCTIONS OUGHT TO BE REFLECTED IN THE LAW?

At present there are two principal offences of homicide, murder and manslaughter, underpinned by various other offences such as infanticide and causing death by dangerous driving. We have already noted that the label 'manslaughter' encompasses two different species of offence—'voluntary manslaughter', which amounts to mitigated murder, where the requirements for murder are present but there is also evidence of provocation, diminished responsibility, or a suicide pact; and 'involuntary manslaughter', where the requirements of murder are not present and the culpability may be considerably lower. One could clearly argue that voluntary and involuntary manslaughter ought to be separated as different offences; but it is interesting to note, as Martin Wasik demonstrates in his essay, that such a separation would not create a hierarchy of offences for sentencing purposes, since the sentence for some crimes of involuntary manslaughter (that is those falling just short of murder) would be considerably higher than most sentences in cases of provocation or diminished responsibility. The argument for separation would be one of labelling rather than one of sentencing.

Questions of labelling raise the issue of parameters. What is to be the touchstone of appropriateness in labelling? This is a general question in criminal law. For example, it is well known that it would be possible to draft a single offence to cover theft and deception, but it was decided to retain separate offences and separate labels. There may be a moral distinction between thieving and deceiving, and it is a distinction that people may expect to be reflected by the law, but we have little hard evidence on that. It is certainly possible to create a single offence of criminal homicide: but, quite apart from the fact that a single undifferentiated offence of homicide would transfer power away from juries to judges and the Parole Board, it is unlikely that people would want such an undemonstrative and uninformative law. Indeed, there is evidence that people expect the law to draw finer distinctions than that: a survey in England and Wales revealed very strong support for separate offences to reflect perceived variations in the nature and gravity of homicides. Much less clear, however, is the precise number of offences; participants in the survey found the exercise difficult but, if anything, they appeared to favour a minimum of two offences.[20] Here we should discuss the issue in terms of principle and policy: what should determine whether we should have one, two, five, or seven offences of homicide? Apart from the distribution of decision-making power, and also the capabilities of decision-makers (too many alternatives might confuse juries), what other considerations should determine the label?

One attractive principle is that offences should be labelled separately where this reflects a morally and socially significant difference, either in degree of culpability or in the context of offending. Part of the attractiveness of the principle is, of course, its vagueness. The reference to moral and social significance propels us into a dark area: is there consensus on the

---

[20] Ibid.

significance of many of the factors that might arise in homicide cases? Various questions need to be answered if progress is to be made in this area, and some of them tend to be obscured by broad references to 'public opinion'. It is important to distinguish the opinions of people who are questioned as part of a well-conceived survey, from 'public opinion' in the shape of answers to unsophisticated yes/no questions, and then again from the views put forward by the popular press or some politicians in the name of public opinion. So far as possible it is the first kind of public opinion that has a claim to be considered when reshaping the law of homicide, and there are very few British surveys that measure up to the required standard. The task of eliciting reliable data which also offers explanations for responses across a reasonably comprehensive range of issues almost inescapably warrants more than one lengthy interview with each respondent. Much care is necessary in the use and definition of terminology, and the minimum sample size needed to justify comments about public sentiment throughout the country naturally makes the task very costly as well as time-consuming.

When the results of a well-conceived survey emerge, the next question is how much weight should be given to them. There is evidence of considerable abhorrence of child killings,[21] even where there is no intent to kill, the reasons for which include the child's helplessness, defencelessness, loss of life expectancy and, where the killer is an adult, the idea that there has been a breach of trust—that all adults have an important welfare duty towards children. The definition of 'child' might be debatable,[22] but there is an argument based on social revulsion and welfare for treating child homicides as particularly serious. Ought the law to reflect this? To answer that question we must consider the issues of principle that ought to shape the law of homicide, and even the most carefully elicited public opinion must be scrutinized by reference to its rationality. Can the category of child killings be identified as distinct, on defensible moral grounds, from other forms of killing? For example, if it is the vulnerability or helplessness of the victim that makes people regard these killings as more culpable, are there not other killings (for example of the elderly or disabled) that ought to be classified similarly? If it is the fact that the killing of a child deprives the victim of a whole lifespan, does that mean that killings of the elderly should be regarded as less culpable or harmful because they do not have as long to live? If killing in X circumstances is held to be worse than killing in Y circumstances, the reasons need to be scrutinized and then compared with reasons relied upon elsewhere in the law of homicide, and perhaps in criminal law generally.

---

[21] Ibid.

[22] Unpublished findings from qualitative research undertaken in July–October 1998 suggest that sixteen would be the favoured upper age limit; see B. Mitchell, 'Further Evidence of the Relationship Between Legal and Public Opinion on the Homicide Law' [2000] Crim LR (forthcoming).

What detailed questions of labelling need to be resolved? Many of these appear in the remainder of the book, but a number of particular points can be signalled here. Firstly, given the extent of the variations in the factual circumstances and moral culpability in homicides, should there be more than two principal offences? As we have seen, in existing law the offence of manslaughter is divided into two forms (voluntary and involuntary) with differing requirements, and each of those may be committed in different ways. Should the label 'manslaughter' be applied to both, or would it be better to confine that label to a more distinct group of homicides and to devise fresh labels for other lesser forms of homicide (as, for example, Chris Clarkson argues below)?

Secondly, much of the debate about the structure of the existing law has focused on the lower boundary of murder, that is, where to draw the culpability line between murder and manslaughter. As senior members of the House of Lords have recognized, those convicted of murder do not necessarily represent the most reprehensible killers.[23] Some of them deserve neither the stigma of being labelled a murderer nor the mandatory life sentence. This may be due in part to the definition of murder, particularly the fact that neither the defendant nor an ordinary prudent individual need have anticipated death.[24] Moreover, the legal definition of <u>intent</u>—which has a crucial bearing on the existing boundary between murder and manslaughter—is arguably still far from satisfactory, notwithstanding a series of appeals spanning twenty-five years or so.[25] In addition, considerable reservations have been expressed about the wisdom of relying solely on the cognitive concept of intention as the appropriate means of selecting the worst kinds of unlawful killing.[26] Moreover, William Wilson argues that labels and offence-differentiation may perform functions other than marking the relative seriousness of offences: in his essay, he demonstrates that a different wrong is involved in deaths resulting from attacks, and argues that this should be marked by the use of the distinct label, 'murder'.

Thirdly, is it appropriate to keep the various forms of mitigated murder separate, or should we contemplate a single form of mitigated murder that

---

[23] e.g. in *Hyam* v. *DPP*, n. 8 above, 640, Lord Kilbrandon commented: 'It is no longer true, if it was ever true, to say that murder as we now define it is necessarily the most heinous example of unlawful homicide'; and in *Howe*, n. 8 above, 581, Lord Hailsham remarked: 'Murder, as every practitioner of the law knows, though often described as one of the utmost heinousness, is not in fact necessarily so, but consists in a whole bundle of offences of vastly differing degrees of culpability, ranging from brutal, cynical and repeated offences like the so-called Moors murders to the almost venial, if objectively immoral, "mercy killing" of a beloved partner.'

[24] The arguments for and against the GBH rule are set out in A. Ashworth, *Principles of Criminal Law*, 3rd edn. (Oxford, 1999), 270.

[25] See e.g. W. Wilson, 'Doctrinal Rationality after *Woollin*' (1999) 62 MLR 448; and A. Norrie, 'After *Woollin*' [1999] Crim LR 532. Naturally, these concerns as to the meaning of intent apply to many other crimes apart from murder.

[26] See e.g. R. A. Duff, *Intention, Agency and Criminal Liability* (Oxford, 1990).

does not require the law to define provocation, or diminished responsibility, or intoxication, but rather provides that any killing that satisfies the definition of murder and yet proceeds from extreme emotional or mental disturbance should be classified as a lesser offence? There may be certain pragmatic arguments in favour of a general category of mitigated murder, but there is a strong counter-argument based on labelling. It is that partial defences such as diminished responsibility and provocation are fish from different kettles and ought to be kept morally separate. But this claim assumes a coherence in the doctrine of provocation that might not exist. It is one thing to argue that, whatever people's differences in character, the law should expect them to exercise reasonable self-restraint in the face of provocation—at least to the extent of not launching a serious physical attack on another. It is quite another thing to draw a defensible line between those personal characteristics of the defendant that may properly be taken into account in such cases, and those characteristics (if any) that ought to be left out of account. The English courts, perhaps sensitive to the argument that the law is unduly influenced by male perspectives on emotion and anger,[27] have delivered conflicting judgments on this crucial issue of 'characteristics'.[28] Some of those decisions have diluted the objective condition in provocation considerably, by allowing account to be taken of the abnormal mental condition of defendants.

In her essay Celia Wells argues that there really is no sustainable distinction in practice between the two sets of 'characteristics' mentioned above. How should that argument be assessed? The paradigm case of provocation is surely some distance from the paradigm case of diminished responsibility, but there is a middle area where the two notions come so close as to be barely distinguishable, in the eyes of some. Celia Wells poses poignant questions about the distinctions relied upon in some of the decisions, and about the ability of the existing legal structure to accommodate some of the issues she raises. Moreover, in existing law there is no sharp distinction between provocation and diminished responsibility as partial defences: it is possible to plead them as alternatives, or for a court to find both of them proved.[29] In his essay Ronnie Mackay argues that in principle the two defences should not be regarded as mutually exclusive. However, he would see them as part of a general restructuring of the law that would find a place for a realistic and workable defence of insanity—ensuring that those suffering from acute forms of mental disorder are acquitted of homicide altogether, rather than

[27] See e.g. D. Nicholson and R. Sanghvi, 'Battered Women and Provocation: the Implications of *Ahluwahlia*' [1993] Crim LR 728; A. McColgan, 'In Defence of Battered Women who Kill' (1993) 13 OJLS 508.

[28] The split decision of the House of Lords in Morgan Smith, on 27 July 2000, is unlikely to have settled the matter; see further J. Horder, 'Between Provocation and Diminished Responsibility' (1999) 9 King's College LJ 143.

[29] See R. D. Mackay, 'Pleading Provocation and Diminished Responsibility Together' [1988] Crim LR 411.

convicted of manslaughter on the ground of diminished responsibility. He would retain the doctrine of 'diminished' to deal with lesser forms of mental abnormality, but would rid it of the various conceptual and drafting confusions from which section 2 of the Homicide Act 1957 suffers.

A fourth labelling issue raises the politically awkward question of how to deal with mercy killings. It seems that there is a reluctance to admit openly, by creating a separate category, that cases of mercy killing are dealt with on different principles than other cases that fulfil the definition of murder. The fear is that there would be staunch opposition in Parliament and from the media for any explicit relaxation of the law. So we continue with the implicit relaxation of the law, usually manifested by psychiatrists stating that the mercy killer was suffering from an abnormality of mind at the time. The prosecution will often accept a plea of guilty to manslaughter by reason of diminished responsibility, there is no trial, and the sentence is light. But such an outcome is a travesty of fair labelling, since in some such cases the defendant is not suffering from any mental abnormality. The label is an affront to the mercy killer, who is often as calm and collected as can be, in the face of abnormal suffering by the deceased (often a close relative or friend). It is an inaccurate label in many cases, and therefore an inappropriate one. If pragmatism really does demand this gross mislabelling so as to avoid political embarrassment, we should be clear exactly why principle is being compromised.

A fifth issue of labelling concerns what has been termed 'the principle of correspondence'—the principle that the fault element required for an offence should have, as its object, harm of the same degree of seriousness as that which the offence punishes. In bald terms, if murder is the offence, an intent to kill (and nothing less) ought to be the specified fault element. In his essay William Wilson argues that, whatever views might be held by members of the public,[30] there is a sound moral reason for going beyond the correspondence principle and maintaining a wider fault element for murder. He locates this sound moral reason in a line of argument found, in slightly different forms, in the writings of John Gardner[31] and Jeremy Horder.[32] Its foundation lies in the notion of attack: one who makes an intentional attack on another's bodily safety should not be judged according to a slide-rule with exact degrees of blame tracking exact degrees of foresight, but ought to take responsibility for wider (though not disproportionate) consequences of that attack, even if they were not foreseen. This is

---

[30] On which see B. Mitchell, 'In Defence of a Principle of Correspondence' [1999] Crim LR 195 and, more fully, id., nn. 19 and 22 above, suggesting that many members of the public would expect a murder verdict to be based on a serious, life-threatening attack rather than some lesser assault.

[31] Most clearly in 'Rationality and the Rule of Law in Offences against the Person' (1994) 53 CLJ 502.

[32] e.g. in 'A Critique of the Correspondence Principle in Criminal Law' [1995] Crim LR 759.

not pure constructive liability, the argument goes, because a person who intends a mere assault would not be held guilty of murder. It is a more limited and rational response to a person who intentionally sets himself against another's interests, limited in the sense that it requires fault of the next least degree of harm. Thus William Wilson argues that a version of the GBH rule can be defended on this basis; in a similar way, and on similar moral grounds, Chris Clarkson would wish the law of homicide to distinguish between homicide by gross negligence and homicide resulting from an intentional assault by some violence less than grievous bodily harm. He too draws upon the notion of attack as expressing a distinct wrong.

Some will doubt whether, even in this more restricted form, the claim that the user of force has 'changed his normative position' vis-à-vis the victim is a compelling reason for concluding that he should therefore be held criminally liable for consequences that were unexpected and unforeseeable, and labelled a murderer. Why should the degree of criminal liability turn on the chance outcome rather than on what the perpetrator intended or knowingly risked? It is hardly convincing to reply that a person who chooses to use violence 'makes his own luck', because that begs the question. Why should the law adopt that approach for offences of violence, in preference to the rival principle that defendants should be judged on what they intend, or knowingly risk, or (even) are grossly negligent about?

A final point about labelling concerns the reasons why one might wish to affix different labels. Many of the issues mentioned above are not reflected in the labels for other offences: provocation, recklessness as distinct from intention, and mental abnormality falling short of clinical mental disorder, are rarely reasons for convicting of a lesser offence. This is partly because in many parts of the criminal law there is not a hierarchy of offences—although there has long been a hierarchy of non-fatal offences, and neither the legislature nor the courts of England and Wales have exploited this to give effect to qualified defences.[33] Such a hierarchy has been used to facilitate the grading of homicide offences, and indeed could be expanded. Substantial differences in culpability might be reflected by different offence labels: at present the law distinguishes killings with intent to kill or to cause grievous bodily harm from other killings, whether reckless or grossly negligent, and Chris Clarkson argues that the latter two ought to be labelled separately. Another ground for separate labels might be the context of the killing, which leads Clarkson to argue for separate offences of corporate killing and causing death by dangerous driving—not that such offences are more or less serious than other forms of homicide, but that the circumstances in which they are committed may warrant a distinct label. The arguments for and against this are discussed in his essay

---

[33] Cf. the laws of other Commonwealth jurisdictions, such as the Griffith Code of Queensland and Western Australia.

below. A further reason for separate labels may be to distinguish different grounds for mitigating what would otherwise be a murder: thus it was argued above that a general category of 'mitigated murder' might trample on important moral distinctions by lumping together the genuinely provoked killer with the unprovoked mentally abnormal killer, for example. What is clear about these varied reasons for separate labels is that they do not always relate to gradings of seriousness. Thus, if one follows Clarkson's argument, causing death by dangerous driving might properly be sentenced more severely than grossly negligent killing or some cases of killing by attack. Thus substantial differences in culpability ought to be reflected in different offence labels, but there are also other strong reasons for separate labelling.

D. Partial Defences and Degrees of Responsibility

Provocation and diminished responsibility, along with other forms of justification and excuse such as self-defence and duress, may be thought to have a role to play in mitigating murder. Where the killing is in self-defence, the existing law takes an 'all or nothing' approach; once the defendant goes beyond reasonable force he is liable to conviction for murder,[34] and the fact that he acted in self-defence (albeit excessively) is legally immaterial. This approach was upheld by the House of Lords in *Clegg*,[35] although Lord Lloyd seemed to favour a compromise verdict of manslaughter. Nevertheless, the Government subsequently expressed the view that, whatever force there is in such an argument, it is outweighed by the complexity that it would introduce to the law.[36] The law adopts a tougher approach where the killing was committed under duress, rejecting either a full or a partial defence based on necessity, duress, or duress of circumstances. However, there is a forceful argument that, subject to certain safeguards, the law should show some sympathy to those who kill in such circumstances.[37] Again, research suggests that members of the public take a very different view from that of the law—indeed, the only real uncertainty seems to be whether they would prosecute the killer for any offence at all, let alone murder.[38]

If elements of excuse and justification are to be given some weight in the legal process in homicide cases, should they make their presence felt at the conviction or sentencing stage? Part of the problem, as Nicola Lacey points out in her essay, is that their relevance varies—for example, provocation

---

[34] *Palmer* v. *R.* [1971] AC 814.   [35] See n. 1 above.
[36] *Report of the Interdepartmental Review of the Law on the Use of Lethal Force in Self-Defence or the Prevention of Crime* (Home Office, London, 1996).
[37] See J. C. Smith, *Justification and Excuse in the Criminal Law* (London, 1989), 73–9.
[38] See Mitchell, n. 19 above, 457, 458.

seems to go to grading or perhaps labelling, whereas diminished responsibility operates as an exemption without apparently influencing the question of gravity. Nevertheless, the rationale for partial defences or mitigating factors calls for an examination of the nature and extent of a defendant's responsibility for, in homicide, causing death. The capacity theory prima facie implies a strong case for a broad range of partial defences to murder, but it raises practical difficulties of meaningful assessment and its hints of determinism surely threaten the traditional normative nature of the law's judgments and evaluations. Thus, we might look instead to some form of the hitherto less fashionable character theory, and in her essay Nicola Lacey considers the claims of a restricted version of it, in the form of a 'reasons' approach. Here the legal spotlight would fall on what the defendant's conduct reveals in the light of the circumstances and context in which it occurred. If that conduct is founded on reasons which are consistent with good citizenship, the defendant should be at least partially if not wholly exonerated. Some potential excuses, such as involuntary intoxication, appear not to sit comfortably with this theory, and there may be some doubt about the extent to which there always exists a clear notion of what is socially approved (that is, fulfilment of the rule-of-law requirements of certainty and consistency seems rather dubious). Moreover, Lacey's approach would necessitate a more finely graded criminal law, which required juries to make quite detailed choices among a number of alternatives. But Lacey argues that, if this is what the social function of criminal law requires, it is what we should aim to achieve.

There is a second, quite separate issue about responsibility which has traditionally been raised in relation to diminished responsibility but which surely ought to affect other pleas such as provocation. This stems from the obvious fact they are founded on the idea that a person's responsibility can be reduced: these defences imply a sliding scale of responsibility, and that an individual's whereabouts on the scale should indicate the extent of legal liability. This is not uncontroversial: some have argued that responsibility is only susceptible to a simple distinction—a person either is responsible for her actions or she is not; there can be no 'halfway house'.[39] However, there can surely be degrees of culpability, and there is every reason to use the structure of homicide to allow expression to be given to those degrees.

E. JURY TRIAL AND FACT-FINDING

Once the debates about labelling and the separation of offences have been conducted, one must return to the practicalities of jury trial and consider

---

[39] e.g. A. Kenny, 'Can Responsibility be Diminished?', in R. G. Frey and C. W. Morris (eds.), *Liability and Responsibility: Essays in Law and Morals* (Cambridge, 1991).

whether there are pragmatic reasons for modifying the scheme that has been decided to be the most appropriate on grounds of principle. If it were decided, say, that there is a case for eight different legal categories of homicide (for example: murder; killing upon provocation; killing during mental abnormality; killing by excessive force in self-defence; killing under duress; reckless killing; grossly negligent killing; killing as a result of an attack), in addition to infanticide and others such as corporate killing and causing death by dangerous driving, there is an obvious question about whether this proliferation of categories would tend to complicate trials to an extent that risked obfuscating juries, to the detriment of the fair administration of justice. It matters not whether defendants or the prosecution might be expected to benefit, or that the 'benefits' might be unpredictable, if it were thought on good evidence that the risk of inaccurate verdicts would increase.

Let us suppose that good evidence pointed in the direction of an unwelcome increase in the risk of inaccuracy. The obvious response would be to consider some simplification of the categories, assuming that no radical reform of the jury system (for example the judge retiring with the jury) is likely in the short term. Returning to the notional list of eight categories in the last paragraph, one might combine cases of mental abnormality with those of duress; one might combine cases of provocation with those of excessive defence; and one might combine cases of reckless killing with those of killing by attack. If this were thought insufficient to clarify proceedings and promote accurate verdicts, one might argue for a single broad category of mitigated murder that encompasses provocation, mental abnormality, duress, and excessive defence—perhaps along the lines of the American Model Penal Code's (MPC) category of killing during extreme emotional or mental disturbance.

Any drift in this direction raises three objections that need to be confronted, even if they are not thought conclusive. Firstly, we must be clear that the sacrifice of more communicative labels is acceptable. Labelling arguments cannot be dismissed as academic musings: we have noted that labels may matter to the public, both on and off juries, and may also matter to defendants. Thus we have argued that the paradigm provoked killer occupies a different moral position from the paradigm mentally abnormal killer, and that to lump them together blurs important moral distinctions. If pragmatism drives us towards a single category of 'mitigated murder', this is a communicative loss. Secondly, a move from specific labels to broader categories may also result in a rule-of-law deficit. Thus in existing law there are statutory provisions on provocation and diminished responsibility, which have been interpreted in subsequent judicial decisions. A broad category such as killing during extreme emotional or mental disturbance would blur the boundaries considerably: all would turn upon the evidence of the degree of disturbance in the case, to be determined by medical evidence or by inference from the circumstances, and all manner of different conditions might be included, or excluded. The boundaries of existing categories would doubtless be broken, and it would not be necessary to show that a person was provoked at all, let alone reasonably provoked, if it appears that control was lost to some extent. A (partial) answer to this would be that any rule-of-law protections provided by statutory and judicial definitions are largely illusory anyway. Thus Celia Wells's argument is that there is little practical point in pursuing separate categories in view of the historical tendency for them to become distorted and even to merge (which could be said of the recent trends in provocation and diminished responsibility).

All of this brings us to the third objection. In the absence of separate categories for provocation or duress, for example, there would be a significant procedural deficit in that evidence on these matters might not be relevant at trial, unless needed to establish the degree of emotional disturbance experienced by the defendant, and in order to give the judge sufficient information on which to pass sentence the matters would have to be ventilated in a *Newton* hearing, before sentence, where standards of evidence and presentation might be less exacting than at the trial. Again, it is not relevant to speculate in whose favour this lowering of standards might operate. Assuming that the idea of a broader qualified defence to murder of this kind were to be fully accepted, so that provocation would disappear as a distinct legal doctrine, the questions to be addressed are whether provocation (or duress) should still be relevant to sentence, and, if so, how the procedural requirements of *Newton* hearings can be sharpened suitably.

Returning to the functions of the jury, there is the further question of its normative role. One hears of instances of 'jury nullification', where a jury takes a decision that effectively nullifies a legal distinction or judicial direction, and thereby exercises a normative judgment. But there are also examples of the law deliberately placing considerable normative discretion in the hands of the tribunal of fact. The primary example is perhaps dishonesty in theft, where magistrates and juries often have the power to decide, by applying what are termed 'the current standards of ordinary decent people', the effective reach of the criminal law. It would be possible to expand this approach within the law of homicide. Gross-negligence manslaughter already has a test that culminates in the question whether 'the conduct of the defendant was so bad in the circumstances as to amount in the jury's judgment to a criminal act or omission'. The test of provocation contained in clause 58 of the draft Criminal Code culminates in the question whether in all the circumstances the provocation was 'sufficient ground for the loss of self-control', which leaves the normative issue firmly in the hands of the jury. Clause 56 of the draft Criminal Code takes the same approach to diminished responsibility, the test being whether the mental abnormality was 'a substantial enough reason to reduce the offence to manslaughter'.

Now it might be argued that the need for rule-of-law protections is not great when we are considering qualified defences to murder. No citizen should place reliance on these doctrines when acting, since the law's simple injunction is: 'you must not kill'. However, there is another important aspect of the rule of law, and that is consistent decision-making. It would surely be objectionable if some juries accepted, for example, the homosexual advance defence in provocation whereas others refused to contemplate it. Within the doctrine of provocation lie several normative issues (including matters such as identity and gender, highlighted by Celia Wells) that should not be open to resolution by prejudice, ignorance, or other inappropriate means. Some will consider this to be a powerful argument in favour of both retaining a distinct doctrine of provocation and retaining a legal framework for determining what factors should and should not be taken into consideration. But the counsel of despair, or reality, is that the resulting legal distinctions tend to become blurred and self-contradictory (as Celia Wells contends in relation to provocation) and that juries are likely to follow their own lights anyway. But if there is to be a choice between sharing the power and responsibility between judge and jury (by requiring juries to select a verdict from among several alternatives, thus assisting the judge in passing sentence) or concentrating considerable power in the hands of the judge (by leaving few choices to the jury), then there is an argument for trying to draw juries more into decision-making. As Nicola Lacey argues, the criminal law here is performing an important social function, for which the institution of the jury seems well fitted. If the reply to this is that in practice there are problems in jury trials, the path of principle is to direct attention to solving those problems rather than to give up on the jury.

F. Subjectivity, Certainty, and Moral Resonance

In the foregoing paragraphs we have referred to the importance of upholding 'rule of law' values in any reformulation of the law of homicide. We have also recognized that there are limits to this in practice: there are few topics on which we can formulate a clear and certain test which will yield just results in all or even most cases. That does not remove the principle of maximum certainty as a goal, but it does require a realistic appraisal of practical possibilities and warns against any tendency to claim that the principle is being respected when it is not.

One of the benefits of adopting a subjective principle of criminal liability is that it should yield fairly specific and certain tests. Thus the current mental element for murder—intention to kill or cause grievous bodily harm—ought to achieve a fairly high degree of certainty and of conformity to rule-of-law values. That high degree is lowered in some cases, however, because of the judges' approach to defining intention, and in particular their refusal to affirm that foresight of virtual certainty amounts to intention. The House of Lords again had the opportunity to make an unambiguous statement in *Woollin*,[40] but it failed to do so, and held that where foresight of virtual certainty is proved a jury is entitled to find that the defendant intended death or grievous bodily harm. This form of words harbours considerable uncertainty. It can be read as suggesting that courts may only find intention where the defendant foresaw the result as certain, and thus as a tightening of the law.[41] On the other hand, it can be read as preserving the possibility that a court might decide that a defendant did have the relevant foresight of virtual certainty but should not be held to have intended the result. Since such a conclusion could only be reached by the intervention of some factor not explicitly declared in the legal rule, it follows that the courts may have retained an amount of 'moral elbow-room' which, like the Scots test of 'wicked recklessness', leaves a gap to be exploited, at least in cases of foresight rather than direct intention. Such a gap may allow the tribunal to load into its decision all manner of prejudicial or other extraneous factors.

In law this gap could be closed, simply by defining intention in terms of either purpose or foresight of virtual certainty (although 'virtual' inevitably leaves some scope for judgment). But that would not conclude the issue of subjective standards and certainty, because there is the further question whether the law can be formulated so as to use only subjective concepts (with a high degree of certainty) and yet capture the necessary moral distinctions. A simple 'intent to kill' formula would narrow the definition and enhance certainty, and might also claim a 'moral fit' with public opinion. When invited to say what characterizes their perception of the most heinous homicides, a significant proportion of respondents referred to premeditation, but on further clarification they identified an intent to kill. When asked to comment on the adequacy of an intent to cause serious harm (without more), respondents were very hesitant and many seemed intuitively unhappy that such a fault element should suffice for murder.[42]

An alternative approach would be to broaden the definition of murder as Scots law does—the test of 'wicked recklessness' allows various moral and social distinctions to be reflected, at least in categorizing a killing as murder or culpable homicide. However, in doing so it sacrifices 'rule of law' values to too great an extent. One could preserve those values and yet specify that killings which stem from terrorist motives, or where the victim is a child or a police officer, should be classed as murder if there was an intention to cause serious injury. Alternatively, one could widen the test still further, as William Wilson proposes in his essay, so as to convict those who kill and who intend to expose another person, without lawful excuse, to a

---

[40] [1999] AC 92; and see n. 25 above.   [41] Wilson, n. 25 above.
[42] See Mitchell, n. 22 above.

serious risk of death. This, in Wilson's view, both captures the nature of the wrong in murder and satisfies the certainty principle.

Both this proposal, and the reliance of the existing law on the *Woollin* definition of intention, leave open the distinct possibility that extraneous factors might enter into decision-making at crucial points. What little knowledge we have of jury discussions suggests that there are occasions on which prejudicial assumptions dominate the jury's approach to its task, whether explicitly or implicitly. It may be difficult to exclude these from any sphere of judgement, homicide no less than others, and the remedy lies in changes to the jury system rather than in changes specific to the law of homicide. But some of these extraneous factors may stem from more basic moral assessments of right and wrong, which are not reflected in the law. For example, Celia Wells shows that the notion of loss of self-control used in provocation cases encompasses a wide variety of emotional states, some of which seem to fall well outside the natural meaning of the words. Provocation cases also raise questions about the idea of self-protection and its role, especially in cases where an abused woman kills her partner when he is resting or sleeping. There is no legal category that reflects the moral assessment of such cases—certainly not the doctrine of provocation, strictly construed, and probably not self-defence, strictly construed.[43] Public-survey research indicates considerable support for self-preservation as a wholly or partly acceptable ground for deliberately killing another (although this includes both cases classified as self-defence and those classi-fied as duress, which English law presently excludes from homicide cases).[44] And what of revenge? One of the primary categories of murder, recorded annually in the Criminal Statistics, is 'revenge killings'. But since a revenge killing is usually one that follows on something done by the victim to the offender, exactly how should revenge killings be distinguished from provoked killings, on a moral plane? The unsatisfactory concept of loss of self-control hardly seems equal to the task. Lapse of time is not a sure indicator, at least if one considers many of the cases now held to fall within the doctrine of provocation. Are reflection, planning, and premedi-tation the kinds of factor that generate the distinction? Can we say that someone who reacts without reflection to an adverse act may be categorized as 'provoked', whereas someone who has time for reflection commits a revenge killing (and therefore murder)? Questions of this kind suggest that some of the basic moral distinctions underlying the law of homicide are not clearly resolved, either in principle or in practice. Only if they were could one begin to discuss the way in which legal categories ought to reflect them.

[43] Cf. McColgan, n. 27 above.   [44] See Mitchell, n. 22 above.

2

Murder and the Structure of Homicide

WILLIAM WILSON*

I. INTRODUCTION

In this Chapter I consider the options for reforming the law of murder, with particular reference to the desirability of restructuring the upper boundary between murder and manslaughter. I have limited discussion to what categories of unlawful killing should be murder. It is rather artificial to cut up the analytical cake in this way but for obvious reasons it would be inappropriate for me to attempt a scheme of liability for homicide as a whole. For similar reasons I make only passing reference to matters relating to defences and sentencing although it is hard to imagine, for example, a satisfactory reform of homicide which did not have the mandatory sentence as a central topic for consideration.

The changes I advocate are ones which sit more easily with our doctrinal traditions than those currently favoured by the Law Commission, and which respect the reality of our moral culture. They represent an attempt to redraw the boundaries between murder and manslaughter slightly so that they form a more coherent whole. I favour codification because, while the distinction between murder and manslaughter is the outcome of casuistic determinations based in changing moral and social judgments, it is the duty of the elected legislature to ensure that these judgments are cogent and just. However, by working within the common law's own range of options as far as possible, it affords the possibility that domestic law might develop some of its own solutions rather than be beholden to a possibly reluctant legislature.

The basic premise informing the discussion, and which dictates the emphasis of the Chapter,[1] is that murder and manslaughter are to be understood as

* Thanks are due to Antony Duff, Mike Redmayne, Stephen Shute, and the participants at the 'Rethinking Homicide' Conference for their help and criticisms.
[1] I am referring, in particular, to my relatively scanty treatment of the options of merging the two offences on the one hand and creating further differentiation within murder on the other.

involving distinct wrongs rather than different degrees of the same wrong. This has a social basis to which the common-law tradition is particularly sensitive, and is perhaps best captured in the opposition of two moral prohibitions. These are, respectively, the 'do not kill' and the 'do not endanger others' prohibition. The modern tendency in most common-law systems is to require breaches of the former to involve a manifestation in action of the killer's contempt for the value of life. Domestic law has taken a different course. It separates the action part of murder (an act of serious violence) from the consequence (death). Given that homicide liability attaches to an *event* (the fact of death) rather than a *way of behaving* it pitches the substantive standards required to avoid responsibility with maximum moral clarity: 'Do not intentionally inflict serious violence on another. If you do and they die as a result you are guilty of murder.' Critics of the English system complain that the absence of a 'contempt-for-life' or comparable requirement pulls in conduct-choices which may result in unfair labelling.[2] Supporters argue that by setting the causal ball rolling in this distinctive way such killers lose the right to abjure full responsibility for the consequences. As long as we are clear that what we are looking for is a distinct wrong rather than a distinctive level of culpability, representative labelling can be satisfied. Here, I call this 'rough justice': it is the ethical substratum to the traditional common-law notion of implied malice with which the domestic system, almost uniquely, has kept faith.

English law's attempt to use intentional physical violence or its equivalent as marking the boundary line between murder and manslaughter has otherwise been at the expense of some doctrinal rationality, however, by ridding doctrine of the capacity to designate as murder certain cases of 'wicked' risk-taking which fall little short of murder's paradigm case. In the concluding sections I argue for the incorporation of two particular cases of risk-taking into a reformed English model. Both are logical extensions of the 'rough justice' package. The first involves cases where the defendant *directly* intends to expose another to mortal danger. The second involves a 'sanitized' form of felony-murder by which recklessness sufficient for liability in manslaughter becomes sufficient also for murder where it occurs in specified criminal contexts. I argue further for an explicit distinct structure of liability, comparable in conception to accessorial liability, in cases of murder by omission, where traditionally there has been something of a mismatch between the paper rules and the practices of courts and legal officials.

---

[2] In *Powell* [1998] 1 Cr App R 261, 269 Lord Steyn, criticizing GBH-murder, said 'the present definition of the mental element of murder results in defendants being classified as murderers who are not in truth murderers'.

II. GRADING AND LABELLING

It is a commonplace to observe that murder is a more heinous killing than manslaughter. What is less commonplace is the attempt to analyse wherein its heinousness lies.[3] Is it largely a question of grading so that, for example, murder represents a particularly bad breach of a single prohibition? Or is it largely a question of labelling, such that murder and manslaughter represent breaches of separate prohibitions?[4] Whichever view we take on this issue, and I favour the separate-prohibition approach, dividing murder into different grades of seriousness, such as occurs in the United States, is not a solution which many would advocate for the domestic system. The ambition typically prosecuted here is of making a more cogent linkage between offence labels and the social obligations which underscore them rather than creating yet further grounds for differentiation.[5] No doubt certain killings, say those involving extreme cruelty, infant victims, or police officers, encompass moral depravity of such gravity that they seem to cry out to be treated as special cases, not least for protectionist reasons.[6] However, the view taken here is that this does not require resort to special substantive homicide categories.[7] Offence labels should focus our opinions about wrongdoing rather than simply instantiate such opinions in doctrine. Even to practised lawyers the complexity of opinion-derived provisions such as that found in the Pennsylvanian Penal Code threatens to submerge whatever intrinsic rationality its provisions may embody.[8] Offence labels should help people make moral sense of the world and excessive 'particularism' may confound that aim.[9]

The possibility that the murder–manslaughter divide is primarily a question of grading adds fuel to the argument in favour of abandoning the

---

[3] In the United States, at least, the consensus holds rather that it is a particularly bad breach of a single obligation. See e.g. G. Fletcher, *Rethinking Criminal Law* (Boston, Mass., 1978) and L. Weinreb, 'Homicide: Legal Aspects', in S. Kadish (ed.), *Encyclopaedia of Crime and Justice* (New York, NY, 1983), 855.

[4] Cf. P. H. Robinson, 'Should the Criminal Law Abandon the Actus Reus–Mens Rea Distinction?' in S. Shute, J. Gardner, and J. Horder, *Action and Value in Criminal Law* (Oxford, 1993), 187, 208 and S. Shute et al., ibid., 14; and see Nicola Lacey's helpful discussion, Chapter 5 below.

[5] Comparable provisions apply in a number of European jurisdictions, notably Germany, Italy, Malta, Spain, Switzerland, and Turkey.

[6] See B. Mitchell, 'Public Perceptions of Homicide and Criminal Justice' (1998) 38 Br J Crim 453.   [7] Cf. The MPC, Proposed Official Draft (1962), s. 210.6.

[8] See S. Kadish and S. Shulhofer, *Criminal Law and its Processes* (Boston, Mass., 1995), ch. 5.

[9] This is in no way to oppose Gardner's view, first articulated in 'Rationality and the Rule of Law in Offences against the Person' [1994] 53 CLJ 502, that important moral differences between different forms of action should figure in offence labels. R. A. Duff rightly identifies an 'attack on another's life' as being the distinctive element of wrongdoing in murder; see id., *Intention, Agency and Criminal Liability* (Oxford, 1990), 112–13. Cf. Clarkson, Chapter 6 below.

attempt to realize a differentiated conception of criminal homicide.[10] The arguments against a unified law of homicide have been well rehearsed elsewhere.[11] The strongly held view here is that it is glib to suppose that the difficulties involved in creating cogent and watertight boundaries between murder and manslaughter can be solved by removing the boundary itself with degrees of moral wickedness reflected in sentencing rather than the offence label or extensions to the range of defences.[12] Conviction-labels are as important as justice in the distribution of punishment.[13] These labels instantiate and reflect a pre-juridical method of categorizing anti-social deeds, which method reflects, more or less precisely, the reality of our moral culture. At its simplest that culture has sought to identify a particular class of killings which separates itself from the pack of unlawful killings by the unique quality of the deed from which it issues. At a basic level it judges that killing by risk-taking is the breach of a different moral obligation than murderous killings—the implication being that murder is a form of deliberated wrongdoing like stealing, lying, or committing adultery. At the conceptual level it is largely for this reason—that murder is *sui generis* and is not merely the apex of a sliding scale of culpable homicides—that the mandatory sentence is usually justified. Its unique character generates its distinctive punishment. To destroy life is to forfeit the right to life or, in its modern version, the right to a life *in society*.

III. DIFFERENTIATED MODELS

A. The Law Commission Model

The simplest model capable of sustaining a differentiated law of homicide might be expected to follow the example of the draft Offences Against the Person Bill 1998 and produce three grades of offences with a fault element degrading from intentional/purposive killing (say murder) to (subjective) recklessness (say manslaughter) to negligence (say negligent killing).[14] Such an approach would address the present judiciary's concern to keep murder and manslaughter distinct while presenting a clear basis for constituting

---

[10] See e.g. Lord Kilbrandon in *Hyam* v. *DPP* [1975] AC 55, 98.

[11] See generally House of Lords, *Report of the Select Committee on Murder and Life Imprisonment* (HL Paper 78–1 of Session 1988–9), vol. 1, 27–37; Criminal Law Revision Committee, *Working Paper on Offences Against the Person* (1976), paras 3–11.

[12] An attractive *via media* is provided by the Swedish Penal Code where, by s. 2, it is for the judge to decide by reference to a scheme of mitigating and aggravating criteria in line with the MPC whether the relevant killing should be labelled and punished with maximum severity.

[13] Which is why we have of course, in addition to manslaughter, various crimes of reckless endangerment.

[14] Such a proposal has the support of the Law Commission in *Legislating the Criminal Code: Involuntary Manslaughter* (Law Com. no. 237) (1996).

murder on the highest rung on a ladder of graduated offences against the person.[15] Given this overall context it is possible, as Martin Wasik assumes in his Chapter, that similar considerations will figure in future reform initiatives.[16] There are undoubted benefits which would attach to this. From the pragmatic point of view, given that the mandatory sentence is likely to be with us for the foreseeable future, restricting murder to its focal instance will significantly reduce the occasions for implementing the mandatory sentence and with it much penal injustice.[17] Moreover, a charge of murder (intentional killing) would contain the doctrinal seeds of the lesser offences thus allowing the jury to return alternative verdicts, without complication, where intention was not proven.

Nevertheless, I hope that such a model would be rejected. The common law's refusal to use intention to mark the boundaries between the offences is no meaningless historical accident. Unlike other crimes constituted by intention, such as theft, where the starting point for criminal liability is something the actor has done—an appropriation of property—rather than the occurrence of an event, the actor's conduct rarely signals his purpose. Often death is a side effect, perhaps undesired, perhaps unforeseen, of the execution of other purposes. The evidence discloses an intention to cause someone serious injury or an intention to frighten or perhaps no intention at all beyond 'doing one's own thing' but it may disclose nothing which could convince a jury beyond reasonable doubt of an intention to kill. It is inevitable and desirable, under these conditions, that the fault element in murder should stretch outside its focal case to accommodate these cases of unprovable intention where the defendant's conduct crosses an appropriate threshold of culpability.[18]

Substantive considerations are also weighted against such a model. In large measure they are driven by the evidential problems described above. If it is generally impossible to prove intention in its focal sense then the fault element must transmute into something which can be proved.[19] Accordingly, the common-law fault element is satisfied upon proving the actor 'as good as' intended to kill,[20] and with it is compromised the idea

---

[15] See M. Wasik, 'Form and Function in the Law of Involuntary Manslaughter' [1994] Crim LR 883.

[16] The Select Committee of the House of Lords notes that the Law Commission and 3 of the 21 judges who expressed an opinion were in favour of it. Of the 12 member states replying to a questionnaire from the Council of Europe the majority had a law of criminal homicide which used intention as the characterizing mental element of the most serious offence. These include Denmark, Germany, Luxembourg, Norway, Spain, Switzerland, and Turkey. See House of Lords, n. 11 above, app. 5.

[17] Since GBH-murder obviously figures strongly in the number of convictions.

[18] See Fletcher, n. 3 above, 256–9.

[19] It is also inevitable that rules of evidence operate to ease the prosecution's burden; *DPP v. Smith* [1961] AC 290.

[20] See n. 30 below. Cf. *Hyam v. DPP*, n. 10 above. Most other jurisdictions extend murder beyond the core concept of direct intentional killings, at least in the limited sense of treating knowledge of practical certainty as a form of intention. And in a number of countries an intentional killing is merely a synonym for what we call voluntary homicide. The Netherlands e.g.

that murder is a form of killing characterized by a unique mental element. Characterizing murder should be seen, then, as an interpretative task rather than a matter of concepts on the one hand, or distilling the public mood from public-opinion surveys (however cogently fashioned) on the other.[21] The practical background to the interpretative exercise is that murder is a label with huge symbolic importance which would be reduced almost to vanishing point were the murder label to be restricted to its paradigm case.[22] The merit of the common-law approach to homicide is that it has attempted to achieve practical solutions to these problems of categorization and thus organize the relatively disparate moral responses taken to different types of killing.

B. THE COMMON LAW

It is widely thought that the common law, in keeping with its casuistic development, offers no unified scheme of liability. However, apart from the English model, which will be tackled separately, most such systems have as their basic ethical core the appropriateness of treating as murderers those who manifest contempt for the value of life.[23] This emphasis can be seen reflected in a number of doctrinal features of the common-law system, not least in its adoption of an extended form of intention. In GBH-murder the influence of the contempt-for-life ethic is manifested in the gradual drawing together of the two forms of implied malice, namely the intention to cause grievous bodily injury and the intention to expose another to a serious risk of death. Typically, this is done by requiring the intended injury in cases of GBH-murder to involve a serious risk of death and for such risk to have been foreseen.[24] Although such an approach is not in favour in England it has been widely adopted elsewhere.[25] The modern profile of murder's other

includes among the categories of intentional killing conditional intent which is defined as indifference as to whether death will occur or not. Fletcher, n. 3 above, 325, notes that both Soviet and German law defined intention in a similarly broad fashion to include cases where the defendant intentionally engages in life-endangering activity and in so doing 'reconciles himself' or 'makes peace' with the likelihood of death.

[21] Cf. Mitchell, n. 6 above.   [22] See n. 17 above.

[23] Until *Hyam*, n. 10 above, this was also perceived to characterize murder in domestic law.

[24] The New Zealand Code is typical. By s. 167(b) it is murder 'if the offender means to cause the person killed any bodily injury that is known to the offender to be likely to cause death and is reckless whether death ensues or not.' This provision has been interpreted to require a conscious appreciation *at the time the acts were committed* that death was likely. Lack of awareness due to not troubling to consider the likelihood of death or due to rash instinctive reaction, such as characterized *Woollin* [1999] AC 92 or *DPP v. Smith*, n. 19 above, would not satisfy this fault element. The MPC has taken an altogether different approach by excluding GBH-murder and submerging cases where the defendant intends to cause serious injury in the more general fault element of extreme recklessness.

[25] *R. v. Piri* [1987] NZLR 66; *Harney* [1987] 2 NZLR 574. For discussion, see A. Simester and W. Brookbanks, *Principles of Criminal Law* (Wellington, NZ, 1998), 452–4.

fault forms, felony-murder, and murder by risk-taking, also disclose this ethical imprint.

1. FELONY-MURDER

The ethic is seen most obviously in the retreat from felony-murder. The common law treated homicide committed in the course of committing a felony as murder, whether or not actual malice was present. Where it survives, as it does in a majority of American states,[26] the courts have limited its scope in a number of ways not least by the requirement introduced by English courts that the felony, or its manner of commission, be such as is 'known to be dangerous to life and likely in itself to cause death'.[27] The view is now widely held that felony-murder is inconsistent with the modern basis of murder liability in that it is out of step with the principles of correspondence and of subjective fault. Its destiny is to be submerged, it is thought, in a cogent notion of murder by excessive (subjective) risk-taking.[28]

A dissenting opinion holds that this approach is misconceived and that historically the retreat from felony-murder has owed more to a concern to reserve murder for the most culpable of unintended killings. Once one has decided to inflict a harm of a given gravity one crosses a moral threshold which disables one from denying responsibility for the consequences although these may be more serious than those intended or foreseen. Indeed, in English law felony-murder's remnants are, arguably, still to be found in the unrefined GBH-murder rule.[29] It is rough justice, but still justice, for those who kill intending only grievous bodily harm to be labelled a murderer. It will be suggested below that there are grounds for mounting a revival of a form of felony-murder in other contexts such as rape or armed robbery to help plug the gap left in domestic law by the wholesale abandonment of risk-taking as murder's fault element.

2. MURDER BY EXTREME RECKLESSNESS

More broadly, most common-law jurisdictions have kept faith with the idea that if murder is to express denunciation for the manifestation in action of a person's contempt for life then particularly culpable forms of risk-taking

---

[26] The French Penal Code allows felony-murder to aggravate intentional killing. The other systems allow for felonies to aggravate but only if it is done to facilitate or conceal the ancillary felony (i.e. not accidentally).

[27] *Serne* (1887) 16 Cox CC 311; *People v. Washington* 62 Cal. 2d 777. Other common strategies include: requiring the underlying felony to be independent of the homicide; requiring the felony to be one of a certain type; and strict interpretation of the rule of proximate cause.   [28] Fletcher, n. 3 above, 302–3.

[29] It is noteworthy that under New Zealand Law intending GBH is explicitly constituted, albeit in an extended form, as a type of felony-murder; Crimes Act 1961, s. 168(1)

must qualify as murder's fault element.[30] Characterizing such conduct has proved problematic, however.

(i) Risk-centred approaches

Risk-centred approaches to the construction of liability for murder emphasize the nexus between degrees of responsibility and degrees of fault. The higher the likelihood foreseen the more the outcome expresses the actor's choice and hence the greater the culpability attached to the decision to court the risk.[31] For both these reasons the actor's state of mind is comparable in terms of moral culpability to the intending actor. It goes without saying that the higher the degree of risk courted the closer that comparability becomes which leaves a question mark over whether foresight of high probability or even practical certainty[32] should be the relevant standard. Accordingly, Stanley Yeo recommends a strict risk-centred approach as the basis for a schematic approach to criminal homicide. Although conceding that degrees of moral heinousness do not directly translate into a correlative degree of risk-taking he insists, quite plausibly, that if murder and involuntary manslaughter are limited to the most reprehensible killings the fuzzy edges between the two will not create substantial injustice.[33]

Some consider definitional imprecision to be in any case a positive merit.[34] As murder is a construct of social morality its elements must reflect that morality, which argues in favour of giving juries a say in the labelling of unjustified risk-taking leading to death, as is already the case with manslaughter.[35] Such reasoning might be more convincing were it not for the widespread absence in common-law systems, at least, of sentencing discretion in murder, and if consistency of treatment was not considered a key principle of criminal justice. Whether someone has committed murder is not a matter of opinion. As Lacey argues in Chapter 5 below, it is a matter of satisfying an offence definition with a relatively high degree of specificity. The obvious danger is that a risk-centred approach serves simply

[30] 'Properly limited, (murder by recklessness) includes only conduct about which it might be fairly said that the actor "as good as" intended to kill his victim and displayed the same unwillingness to prefer the life of another person to his own objectives'; Weinreb, n. 3 above, 860.

[31] The usual connection made is that courting high risks is less easy to justify and renders it easier to draw the inference that the actor was reconciled to the outcome: 'There is a great difference in moral and social content between (a person who believes a consequence is probable and one who believes it only possible).' (Jacobs J. in the Australian case of *La Fontaine* (1976) 136 CLR 62, cited in S. Yeo, *Fault in Homicide* (Sydney, 1997), 65.)

[32] This is the position adopted by the Indian Code.

[33] Yeo, n. 31 above, 147, gives as a preferred model the Indian Code, where the cut-off point between murder and manslaughter lies between death foreseen as practically certain and death foreseen as very likely, and between intending 'mortal injury' and intending life-threatening injury.

[34] J. Horder, 'Intention in the Criminal Law—A Rejoinder' (1995) 58 MLR 678, 687.

[35] *Adomako* [1994] 3 All ER 935.

to allow expression for, rather than refine and focus, the jury's moral judgment.[36]

(ii) Attitude-centred approaches

Historically the common law has sought to characterize risk-taking constitutive of murder as turning upon the defendant's attitude rather than on degrees of probability. To convert recklessness sufficient for manslaughter into that sufficient for murder the nature and context of the risk-taking must be such, on traditional tests, as to display an 'abandoned and malignant heart' or a 'depraved heart, devoid of social duty, and fatally bent on mischief'. This approach has continued to be influential in the United States. Examples commonly given of such conduct include firing a gun into a moving vehicle or an occupied house, firing in the direction of a group of persons, and failing to feed an infant knowing it was starving to death.[37]

The importance of this formulation is that it expresses the (commonly held) view that the concepts of 'intention and recklessness do not, of themselves, appear to be sufficiently well focused to mark out those killings which are the most heinous. The law must resort to some kind of moral and social evaluation of conduct if it is to identify and separate out the most heinous killings.'[38] Couched in language which suggests that a central characteristic of the deed in murder is the nature/character of the killer these tests almost perfectly represent, if regrettably without clarifying, what it is about the 'murderer' which we find so appalling. Murderers, in the focal sense, show themselves to be a peculiar kind of person, uncomprehended by civilized society. Shooting into a train carries a small risk but it is a type of risk-taking which causes us to question the shooter's humanity.[39]

Indifference. The Model Penal Code (MPC) reflects the ambition to differentiate murder and manslaughter by all matters germane to moral culpability[40] Context is accounted for by a feature which is central to a cogent notion of recklessness and is embraced by the MPC,[41] namely justifiability. Since risk-taking is endemic in social life the judgments we make about whether a person is reckless or not turn upon whether the risk was worth taking or not. Attitude is accounted for by the use of 'indifference'

---

[36] It is this basic uncertainty which has prevented the House of Lords from seeing a way through the problem of a single fault element (recklessness) governing liability for two separate offences.

[37] Weinreb, n. 3 above, 860. W. La Fave and A. Scott, *Criminal Law* (St Paul, MN, 1978), 541–5.

[38] A. Ashworth, *Principles of Criminal Law*, 3rd edn. (Oxford, 1999), 273. See also Fletcher, n. 3 above, 274.

[39] This helps explain the continued influence of the forfeiture argument in the United States where the death penalty is still retained.

[40] It designates as murder a criminal homicide committed purposely or knowingly; or recklessly 'under circumstances manifesting extreme indifference to the value of human life.' (s. 210.3)   [41] S. 2.02(2)(c).

as a moral index of the type of recklessness required. To be reckless is not necessarily to be indifferent. Indifference adds moral gravity to the concept of recklessness by distinguishing between those who take unjustified risks (of death) out of ignorance, inadvertence or an unrealistic optimism and those who do so because they 'could not care less' whether the risk materializes.[42]

In the opinion of many, however, the MPC also fails satisfactorily to deliver the kind of definitional precision which could support a rational system of blame and punishment. When does unjustified risk-taking manifest 'extreme' as opposed to 'ordinary' indifference? What, moreover, does indifference add, in terms of culpability, to the fact that the actor, knowing that death was risked nevertheless, without reasonable excuse, went ahead and took it?[43] The answer must be that the Code does not require, apparently, the accused to *be* indifferent in the sense of one who consciously shrugs his shoulders as he courts danger. Extreme indifference is an attitude which 'manifests' itself in the way the defendant behaves rather than a cognitive state.[44] At its simplest it means there was no social value attending the actor's conduct capable of sustaining an arguable case that the actor harboured the same respect for life as the rest of us.

A further refinement, in support of indifference as the touchstone of murderous risk-taking, has lent significance to the quality of indifference displayed. It has been argued that less blame attaches to those whose indifference derives from their lack of knowledge as to what the outcome of their risk-taking will be (knowledge deficit) and someone who cares so little that he would not adjust his behaviour even if he did (value deficit).[45] On this view Mrs Hyam would be guilty of murder if it could be shown that she would not have changed her plan whatever her degree of foresight and manslaughter if her decision to court the risk of death was taken because she had simply 'lost the plot'.

The strength of this approach is that it succeeds in capturing an elusive analytical element implicit in the very unanalytical notion of the 'depraved heart' or attitude.[46] A willingness to run risks is not the same as being reconciled to their outcome. It is the latter attitude which displays more forcefully the moral hallmark of the murderer—the person who is 'happy' to take whatever consequence fate throws up and who, therefore, 'as good

---

[42] This is the form commonly taken by recklessness in rape; see e.g. Lord Hailsham in *Morgan* [1975] 2 All ER 347, 357. See also Lawton LJ in *Kimber* (1983) 77 Cr App R 225, 230.

[43] Criminal Law Revision Committee, 14th Report, *Offences Against the Person* (1980) (Cmnd. 7844), para 26.

[44] Cf. Duff, n. 9 above, 160 et seq.; K. Huigens, 'Virtue and Criminal Negligence' (1998) 1 Buffalo Crim LR 431, 434–9.

[45] B. Mitchell, 'Culpably Indifferent Murder' (1996) 25 Anglo-Am LR 64–86.

[46] Or in the notion of 'wicked recklessness'. See further pp. 31–2 below.

as intended' to kill.[47] What it fails to do unfortunately is to provide a secure evidential and moral basis for the differentiation. It is surely wrong, for example, that the threshold degree of moral blame suitable for murder is so heavily weighted towards value deficit. Should it really make a difference to the judgments of blame that we would visit on Mrs Hyam that she hoped her victims would escape serious injury when she had taken pains to assure herself that her rival was in the house before setting it alight? The fragility of this distinction between knowledge and value deficit is both illustrated and compounded when we consider the type of evidence which will be needed to distinguish the two types of indifference: 'the judge should direct the jury to examine the evidence for anything to suggest that the accused did care, or that he hoped the risk would not materialize.'[48] How a judge should direct a jury and how a jury would respond to a case such as *Hyam* in which the point of the dangerous activity was *to make a point* to a (necessarily) living person while at the same time showing an utter disregard for the dangerousness of the medium of that message is not seriously considered.[49]

Wicked Recklessness.   Scots law contains its own version of the American depraved-heart doctrine. Murder is 'constituted by any wilful act causing the destruction of life, whether intended to kill, or displaying such wicked recklessness as to imply a disposition depraved enough to be regardless of consequences'.[50] The fault element in Scots law, by contrast with the domestic system, engages directly with the notion of moral heinousness. Largely because of this correspondence between murder at the juridical and social level, murder doctrine is widely thought to work satisfactorily in Scotland by contrast with English law where the absence of a wicked-recklessness equivalent causes doctrinal tension and instability.[51]

Despite these considerations[52] the view taken by successive reform bodies is that 'wicked recklessness' is too imprecise a concept to sustain a differentiated law of homicide. Lord Goff, a supporter of the Scots model, has tried to shore up such imprecision by recasting 'wicked recklessness' as 'indifference'. His attempt not only failed to capture the full richness of the former but was also essentially ill conceived.[53] An attitude of indifference

---

[47] See n. 30 above. As Mitchell, n. 45 above, 75, puts it, 'the only difference between the value-deficit killer and the killer with oblique intention is that the former thinks that death may occur while the latter believes it is inevitable'.   [48] Mitchell, n. 45 above, 79.

[49] For further discussion of this point, see pp. 39–43 below.

[50] Macdonald, *Criminal Law*, 5th edn. 89, cited by Lord Goff in 'The Mental Element in the Crime of Murder' (1988) 104 LQR 30.

[51] See e.g. Goff, n. 50 above; A. Norrie, 'Oblique Intention and Legal Politics' (1989) Crim LR 793, and see further below.

[52] And the fact that it is surely 'desirable that the crime of murder should be the same both North and South of the river Tweed' (Goff, n. 50 above, 47).

[53] G. Williams, 'The *Mens Rea* for Murder: Leave it Alone' (1989) 105 LQR 387.

may well constitute risk-taking as heinous beyond the threshold suitable for manslaughter, but so also may any other attitude—say drunkenness, anger, or lust which would prompt a jury to conclude that the defendant's reck-lessness was 'as wicked and depraved as the state of mind of the deliberate killer'.[54] Scots law clearly recognizes this whatever its other limitations. The distinctiveness of the Scots approach is that it renders explicit the idea that the concept is a moral judgment that we apply to certain cases of risk-taking rather than a conscious thought process which accompanies it. The chal-lenge set by the Scots, and indeed the American, model is to create a struc-ture of liability which withstands the 'too imprecise' complaint, but which nevertheless captures what it is about the attitude accompanying, and/or context of, unjustified risk-taking which can push it through a higher threshold of wrongdoing.

C. The English Model: Rough Justice

English judges have long been embarrassed by the apparent mismatch between the definition of murder and the corresponding basic obligation. If, as it appears, the scope of the 'do not kill' prohibition is unclear criminal doctrine must clarify that scope rather than incorporate its 'fuzzy edges'. The choice has been conceived as being between a definition of murder which excludes many which our untheorized moral sensibilities would designate as murderers, and a definition which would include some which those same sensibilities would designate only as 'manslayers'. In executing its choice English doctrine steers a path between the common law and the simple model favoured by the Law Commission. In line with the latter the bound-ary between the two offences is drawn by intention and there is no room for felony-murder. In other respects domestic law departs from the simple model[55] in including as murder's fault element the intention to cause serious injury,[56] although significantly it also parts company with those common-law jurisdictions which define 'serious' injury as life-threatening injury.[57]

1. Reckless Killings

Recklessness has been progressively removed from the fault profile of murder in a number of House of Lords cases culminating in *Woollin*.[58] The House of Lords here approved the following direction in cases where the simple direction would not be appropriate:

---

[54] G. H. Gordon, *The Criminal Law of Scotland*, 2nd edn. (Edinburgh, 1978), 735–6.
[55] Australia also follows this approach; see Yeo, n. 31 above, ch. 3.
[56] *R. v. Cunningham* [1981] 2 All ER 863.
[57] See e.g. the Codes of New Zealand, Australia, and India, and nn. 24, 33, 55 above.
[58] [1998] 4 All ER 103.

Where the charge is murder and in the rare cases where the simple direction is not enough, the jury should be told that they are not entitled to find the necessary intention, unless they feel sure that death or serious bodily harm was a virtual certainty (barring some unforeseen intervention) as a result of the defendant's actions and that the defendant appreciated that such was the case. The decision is one for the jury to be reached upon a consideration of all the evidence.[59]

This decision marked a conclusive break with other common-law jurisdictions by removing any leeway previously available to the jury to convict of murder on the basis of foresight falling short of moral certainty. In this it is widely approved for removing the uncertainty characterizing previous formulations, which in its application if not its form still hankered after the common-law model.[60]

2. INTENTIONAL KILLINGS

On the face of it *Woollin* appears to instantiate the standard test of intention.[61] On this analysis intention now comprises two states of mind, namely: (a) acting for the purpose of bringing about a consequence whether as an end-in-itself or as a means to achieve another end; or (b) acting in the knowledge that the consequence is virtually certain, whether or not that consequence was desired as an end-in-itself or as a means to an end. It may well be that the House of Lords presumed that this is what they were doing. What they actually said, however, was something quite different. Following the example set in the earlier cases of *Moloney*,[62] *Hancock*[63] and *Nedrick*[64] we are told what intention is not—appreciating a consequence to a lower degree of risk than that of virtual certainty—but not what it is. We are not told that the jury must find intention wherever there is foresight of virtual certainty but that they are not entitled to find intention without it. As such the definition of intention continues to fall between the two stools of direct intention and the standard definition which includes foresight of moral certainty as an alternative form.

3. EVALUATION OF THE DOMESTIC MODEL

The abandonment of recklessness as a fault element and the continued existence of GBH-murder appear to stand in opposition to the developmental logic of the common law, which is that murder is differentiated from manslaughter by a fault element which in all its forms expresses the actor's contempt for the value of life. As such it can be argued that by promoting the values of certainty and consistency the values of doctrinal rationality

---

[59] N. 58 above, 113.   [60] Cf. Norrie, n. 51 above.

[61] See J. C. Smith's note on the case at [1998] Crim LR 890.

[62] [1985] AC 905.   [63] [1986] AC 455.   [64] [1986] 3 All ER 1.

have been forfeited. By 'rationality' in this context is meant the process by which the scope of our social obligations is successfully articulated in rules. Specifically it is thought that there is a mismatch between the social meaning attached to the offence-label 'murder' and the persons designated 'murderer' by doctrine and it is this mismatch which a reformed homicide should strive to eradicate.

Murder under the English model is often criticized as being both under- and over-inclusive.[65] It is under-inclusive by finding no place for the terrorist or Mrs Hyam. Lord Steyn justified under-inclusiveness by the fact that 'below murder there is available a verdict of manslaughter which may attract in the discretion of the court a life sentence'. This is a notably disappointing solution to the difficulties involved in creating a rational basis for differentiation. As argued earlier, conviction-labels are as important as justice in the distribution of punishment. They identify distinctive wrongs underscored by corresponding social obligations.

It is over-inclusive by condemning some we might prefer to stigmatize as manslayers (murder by GBH/cases of imperfect justificatory motive) or not stigmatize at all (cases of indirect intention involving perfect justificatory motives). The response taken in *Woollin* to 'over-inclusiveness' was no more convincing. The problem posed by good motives is accommodated by continuing the fudge sustained by *Hancock* and *Gillick*[66] which resists denoting all cases of foresight of virtual certainty as cases of intention. *Woollin* contains, it should be noted, no explicit suggestion that the judicial approach in either *Adams*[67] or *Gillick* has been disapproved. Indeed Lord Steyn took pains to emphasize that trial judges understand that the *Nedrick* direction is not automatically to be given in cases of 'indirect' intention.[68]

Effectively, then, *Woollin* sustains two complementary, if inconsistent, methods of constructing the fault element in murder. In cases involving dangerous activity disclosing no social value the fault element includes acting for the sake of a consequence (death/GBH) and acting in the knowledge that a consequence (death/GBH) was virtually certain. In cases involving a justifying motive trial judges may prefer to stress that they are entitled but not bound to find intention where there is foresight of virtual certainty and that they should make their determination on a consideration of all the evidence. Or they may give a direction which excludes the standard test of intention. This equivocation is the result of knowledge of virtual certainty having been designated a form of intention rather than recklessness and of the sustained absence of a workable generalized justificatory defence capable of exculpating those whose

---

[65] See generally Fletcher, n. 3 above, 267. Cf. W. Wilson, 'Doctrinal Rationality after *Woollin*' (1999) 62 MLR 448; A. Norrie, 'After *Woollin*' [1999] Crim LR 532.

[66] [1986] AC 112.   [67] [1957] Crim LR 365.

[68] N. 58 above, 112; and see Wilson, n. 65 above.

conduct is morally inconsistent with the criminal intention required by the offence definition.[69]

Lord Steyn also confirmed that the House of Lords are uncomfortable with GBH-murder and perhaps, under appropriate circumstances, may be emboldened to make changes.[70] If it is abandoned, and there is a suggestion that it may be on the judicial agenda,[71] how might it be replaced? The obvious replacement is the refined common-law notion of implied malice, namely an intention to inflict injury so serious as to put the victim's life in peril. Various reform bodies have also recommended the 'beefing up' of the present notion of implied malice. Thus the Criminal Law Revision Committee,[72] the Law Commission[73] and the Select Committee of the House of Lords on Murder and Life Imprisonment[74] have recommended that the mens rea for murder should include an intention to cause serious injury when accompanied by an awareness that life would thereby be endangered. As will be suggested in the next section, such a requirement misses the point of implied malice.

IV. RETHINKING THE STRUCTURE OF HOMICIDE: EXTENDING ROUGH JUSTICE

Each of the models of liability considered so far take it as a basic premise that criminal homicides are appropriately differentiated according to tests which respectively emphasize degrees of responsibility or moral heinousness. It has been suggested that schematic approaches which attempt to provide a scientific sliding scale of responsibility with cut-off points dictated by degrees of risk/degrees of risk foreseen are not conducive to creating a tight nexus between blame and cognition due to contextual variables such as motive, manner of commission, and so on. The common-law model shows itself more sensitive to the complex nature of the moral judgments which characterize our assessment of different types of killing but errs on the side of an over-exclusiveness which fails to draw a bright line between murder and manslaughter. The domestic model largely avoids this problem by excluding from the definition of murder all cases of risk-taking

---

[69] As it was, given that *Woollin* involved an undeliberated killing of an infant by its angry parent there was no scope in the domestic system to acknowledge that knowledge of virtual certainty was the fault element in murder subject, say, only to certain specified exceptions where the defendant's action was justifiable apart from the fact of death.

[70] '(Murder) is a species of constructive crime . . . This feature of the law of murder may have contributed to the problems which courts have experienced with mens rea in murder. But unless the House of Lords or Parliament have occasion to revisit this point the sufficiency of an intent to cause serious harm is the basic assumption upon which any analysis must proceed.' (n. 58 above, 107).

[71] See the reference to 'the House of Lords', ibid.   [72] N. 43 above, para 28.

[73] Law Commission, *A Criminal Code for England and Wales* (Law Com. no. 177) (1989), Draft Criminal Code Bill 1989, cl. 54(1).   [74] N. 16 above, para. 71.

unaccompanied by an intention to cause serious injury. In this it is often criticized for not linking liability for GBH-murder to the foresight of death.

A. ROUGH JUSTICE: THE GBH-MURDER RULE

Recently, Jeremy Horder has encouraged us to take a more positive view of the English model.[75] The fairness of punishment, under this approach, is not a function of the foresight or attitude of indifference, and so on, of the defendant which accompanies his voluntary conduct. Rather, it is a function of the moral implications of his intending to violate an interest of the victim for purposes of assigning moral and criminal responsibility. Although this is not a new idea its particular strength lies in the fact of its conclusions being deduced from an historical examination of largely mainstream doctrine; the same doctrine, in fact, which has led others to criticize the domestic model.

Horder argues that a distinct merit of the domestic system is its rejection of the idea that judgments of correct labelling outside murder's focal cases are tied to degrees of foresight. On the contrary, it is not unfair to censure for an unforeseen harm (death) where that harm is not disproportionate to the harm (GBH) intended. This kind of rough justice is not merely to be tolerated by a rational system of blame and punishment on pragmatic evidential grounds; it is demanded by it for substantive reasons. Taking responsibility for our actions means that we must take responsibility for the (not disproportionate) consequences of, and circumstances surrounding, our actions since they are implicit in the very concept of action. Implied malice is not then a weak compromise with the contempt-for-life model but rather evinces a moral rationality all of its own and informs, overlaid with a requirement of proportionality between harm intended and harm punished, the doctrinal components of all crimes of violence stretching from psychic assault all the way up to murder. If the intention to assault sustains liability for section 47[76] but not section 20 of the Offences Against the Person Act 1861, and the intention to inflict bodily injury sustains liability for section 20,[77] the same principle of fairness allows the intention to cause grievous bodily harm to sustain liability for murder, given that a lesser intention (to cause bodily injury) sustains liability for manslaughter.[78]

Taken as a whole, this is a plausible restatement of the ethical foundation of the English approach to crimes of violence. Critics have insisted, however, that its adherents are committed to the existence of a rather under-theorized

[75] J. Horder, 'Two Histories and Four Hidden Principles of Mens Rea' (1997) 113 LQR 95.
[76] *Roberts* (1971) 56 Cr App R 95.
[77] *Mowatt* [1968] 1 QB 421; *Savage* [1991] 4 All ER 698.
[78] See Horder, n. 75 above, 107, on why manslaughter is not bitten by the proportionality requirement.

moral bridge between crimes involving different wrongs and levels of wrongdoing.[79] If there is a bridge it is one which has been 'cobbled together' for reasons of expedience rather than in response to and in furtherance of cogent principles of criminal justice.[80] The idea is rejected that there are thresholds of blame which are so loosely connected to the constituent elements of the crimes themselves.[81] While we may be disposed to insist that the authors of violence take the 'rough with the smooth' a problem left uncatered for is the matter of representative labelling. Both murder and manslaughter will arguably be diminished as offence labels and in their symbolic importance if doctrine strays too far from their paradigm cases. The rough-justice model allows a murder conviction in cases where no realistic threat to life is posed and where, far from intending to kill, the defendant intends not to kill.[82] In such cases, at least, it is arguable that the defendant's intended harm is different in kind as much as degree from that for which punishment is sought. As a matter of labelling-propriety, it seems to follow, therefore, that a *restructured* law of homicide should pay particular attention to how murder, outside its paradigm case, differentiates itself from manslaughter, given that manslaughter's own paradigm case includes a death attributable to an act of violence falling short of mortal injury. The first and obvious requirement is a cogent notion of serious bodily injury which satisfies the proportionality requirement otherwise than, at present, by default.[83]

One solution offered to this problem of representative labelling is to define serious injury in such a way as to require the injury intended to pose some objective risk of death. Examples of GBH-murder defined in this way include the Indian Code, where the fault element is 'the intention of causing bodily injury to any person' and the bodily injury intended to be inflicted 'is sufficient in the ordinary course of nature to cause death'.[84] By contrast with the subjectivist versions detailed above there is no requirement that the

[79] Ashworth, n. 38 above, 85–6.

[80] In 'On the General Part of Criminal Law' in R. A. Duff (ed.), *Philosophy and the Criminal Law* (Cambridge, 1998), 226–9, John Gardner sketches the beginnings of such a bridge. Commenting upon the phenomenon of 'unselfconscious' intentional success worthy of full moral evaluation e.g. in art, sport, or literature he insists: 'All that is needed to meet the requirement of intentional success (as, say, an artist) is that a person intend, under some description, to perform the actions that go up to make the activity in which she succeeds' (227–8). Assuming we agree and the 'under some description' makes it easy to agree, this provides an obvious moral link between homicide (the outcome) and inflicting GBH (the action), but a further step is still necessary to convince Ashworth and the like that murder is the correct homicide form.

[81] '(The public) wish to see some link between the harm for which the defendant is held responsible and what the law describes as his mens rea. The correspondence principle provides one.' (B. Mitchell, 'In Defence of the Correspondence Principle' [1999] Crim LR 195, 201.)

[82] Commonly cited examples include practices such as kneecapping adopted by criminal organizations for purposes of punishment.

[83] As J. Horder appears willing to concede in 'Questioning the Correspondence Principle: A Reply' [1999] Crim LR 206, 213.   [84] S. 300(3).

defendant be aware that the injury he intends is mortal.[85] This coheres with the moral thrust of the rough-justice approach. It is what one intends rather than what one foresees which forms the basis of one's responsibility for what occurs. As long, then, as the injury intended is sufficient ordinarily to cause death, for example a blow on the head with an iron bar, a savage beating, or a knife wound to the thorax, liability is incurred. On the practical side, such a formulation pre-empts defences rooted in an attitude of culpability, say rage or intoxication, which is morally comparable to actual foresight and generally obviates evidential problems, particularly in cases of spontaneous, instinctive acts of aggression.[86]

The difficulty posed by such compound tests is that they add little by way of moral or conceptual clarity to the notion of implied 'malice'.[87] The key task, for purposes of fair labelling, is to cut up the murder–manslaughter cake in a way which renders the two wrongs meaningfully distinct and makes it clear exactly how citizens must behave to avoid the relevant prohibition. The simplest way of doing so is to ensure that the harm to be intended for murder is the gravest non-fatal harm bearing its own distinct offence label—which at present is grievous bodily harm. What is clearly important is that grievous bodily harm is defined with sufficient precision for this purpose.[88] Given all the various variables, substantive, procedural, and evidential, which contribute to case outcomes in criminal trials, rough justice is the most we can and should aspire to.

A perhaps more serious problem is that the rough-justice model fails fully to sustain the standard justification for a differentiated homicide, which is that there are certain classes of killing which distinguish themselves from the pack of unlawful killings by the unique heinousness of the deeds which cause them. While the intention to cause grievous bodily harm is clearly capable of forming part of a hierarchical framework stretching from trivial acts of violence up to killing it is less clear how, in cases such as *Hyam*, the intention to frighten or create mortal risks, without more, should contribute to this picture.[89]

In the following section I shall argue for an extended fault element to take into account two forms of risk-taking consistent with the philosophy of the rough-justice model since each involves, as does GBH-murder, a

---

[85] Cf. e.g. Law Commission, n. 73 above, Draft Criminal Code Bill 1989, cl. 54(1).

[86] The Criminal Law Revision Committee, n. 43 above, para. 33, also flirted with such a test. In similar vein the Texas Penal Code, s. 19.02(b)(2), provides that it is murder if one 'intends to cause serious bodily injury and commits an act clearly dangerous to human life that causes the death of an individual'.

[87] It was the opinion of a number of the Criminal Law Revision Committee, n. 11 above, that in most conceivable cases the proposed test would, in any event, collapse into a serious bodily injury test.

[88] Cf. the MPC, s. 210.0(3), which refers to 'bodily injury which creates a substantial risk of death or which causes serious, permanent disfigurement, or protracted loss or impairment of any bodily member or organ'.   [89] See Horder, n. 75 above, 106–11.

purposive attack upon a victim's corporal interests. In order to ensure that the extension suggested is cogent for purposes of moral evaluation and effective law-making I have constructed the discussion around a consideration of a number of hypothetical cases which, it is suggested, any reformed law must be able to accommodate. One inevitable and possibly unfortunate consequence is that it will expose precisely my own pre-theoretical conception of what classes of killer are properly designated murderers and/or treated as such. I am reconciled to the fact that many will find it over-inclusive.[90]

B. Rough Justice: Risk-taking

What principles of fairness govern the case where the harm is foreseen but there is no harm, serious or otherwise, intended or where it is impossible to prove such intention? Given that, here again, there are two offence-labels available how is the correct label assigned?

1. Intending to Expose Someone to Mortal Danger

A practical starting point for differentiation is provided by the traditional common-law model since, like the Scots model, it is heavily indebted to common-sense notions of moral heinousness, which sustain the differentiated penal response. It was suggested earlier that this approach in its various guises is unable to locate a cogent socially approved basis for determining the level of depravity required. This can clearly be discerned in the following optimistic and woolly evaluation of the American contempt-for-life approach from one of its supporters:

> ... a motorist who attempts to pass another on a 'blind curve' may be acting with such criminal negligence that if he causes the death of another in a resulting traffic accident he will be guilty of manslaughter. And such a motorist may be creating fully as great a human hazard as one who shoots into a house or train 'just for kicks', who is guilty of murder if loss of life results. The difference is that in the act of the shooter there is an element of viciousness—an extreme indifference to the value of human life—that is not found in the motorist. And it is this viciousness which makes the act (murder).[91]

A better focus to the problem of indiscriminate risk-taking essayed in this latter analysis has been provided by Lord Hailsham. In *Hyam*, he insisted that intention rather than foresight was the fault element in murder. Mrs Hyam was guilty of murder because, lacking any lawful excuse for what she did, she intended to expose her victim to the serious risk of death or

---

[90] Cf. Clarkson, Chapter 6 below.
[91] R. Perkins and R. Boyce, *Criminal Law* (New York, NY, 1982), 60.

grievous bodily harm.[92] This is both a theoretical improvement upon the unmediated moral judgmentalism of the American model and also, by not conflating moral heinousness with degrees of risk foreseen, upon Lord Diplock's intention/foresight amalgam. For Lord Hailsham risk-taking does not become the fault element in murder simply by crossing a threshold of probability, say from possible to probable. As along as it is the accused's intention to court a serious risk of death the actual degree is unimportant,[93] subject always to the overriding requirement that risk taken be unjustified.[94]

Lord Hailsham's restatement is ultimately unsuccessful[95] since he adopts a broad notion of intention which would deem a consequence intended whether it was desired or foreseen as morally certain. The result is to conflate the intentional with the reckless exposure of a person to the serious risk of death. As Lord Hailsham admits it might conceivably convict of murder the above overtaking motorist,[96] which caused him to try to shore up his analysis by requiring the act to be aimed at someone.[97] However, as Lord Bridge pointed out in *Moloney*, while this might enable the acquittal of the motorist it would also acquit those such as terrorists who aim their life-threatening acts at nobody and are designed solely for the purpose of creating terror—in short the very people which an extended fault element would be designed to catch. A more cogent solution would have been to adopt a notion of intention closer to its focal meaning of aim, purpose, or desire *and* to require the end intended to be exposure to the serious risk of death rather than, in Lord Hailsham's formulation, death or serious injury. The resulting fault element is intending, without lawful excuse, to expose another to the serious risk of death.[98]

The merit of such an approach can best be illustrated by reference to some other classic cases involving killing by risk-taking, falling either side of homicide's dividing line, namely (manslaughter) *Goodfellow*,[99] *Cato*,[100] *Hancock*

---

[92] In this it shadows traditional conceptions of implied malice whose various guises include the 'wilful exposure of life to peril' and 'an intention to do an unlawful act which is dangerous'; see generally K. J. M. Smith, *Lawyers, Legislators and Theorists* (Oxford, 1998), 132 et seq.

[93] It might be assumed to be anything above de minimis as in the Russian roulette and malignant shooter cases.   [94] Hence the 'without lawful excuse' requirement.
[95] Cf. Fletcher, n. 3 above, 272–4.

[96] Or, in Lord Hailsham's version, 'a motorist guilty of undertaking a dangerous overtaking manoeuvre on the basis of his full contemplation and knowledge of the approach of an approaching cyclist.' (n. 10 above, 78).

[97] This idea was floated by Viscount Kilmuir in *DPP* v. *Smith*, n. 19 above, 327.

[98] A 'lawful excuse' or 'without reasonable cause' qualification will be necessary to prevent the conviction of incompetent circus knife-throwers, and so on, who, while intending to expose others to the serious risk of death, provoke no substantial public disapprobation. See Section IV below for extended discussion.

[99] (1986) 83 Cr App R 23. Defendant convicted of manslaughter, having set fire to his council house in a bid to be rehoused.

[100] [1976] 1 WLR 110. Defendant convicted of manslaughter having injected his friend with what proved to be a fatal dose of heroin.

and Shankland,[101] (murder) *Hyam, Commonwealth* v. *Ashburn*,[102] *Banks* v. *State*.[103] What distinguishes Messrs Hyam and other risk-takers as *murderers* from Messrs Goodfellow and other risk-takers as *manslayers* is that the point of their action is to expose the victims to the risk of death. It is in this sense only, but crucially, that their action is victim-centred or, for want of a better expression, 'aimed at' a victim.[104] Looked at another way, which indicates how distinct in terms of moral responsibility the two attitudes are, the (merely) reckless killer acts despite the risk of death. Mrs Hyam,[105] the malignant shooter and the Russian-roulette player act because of it. If there was no risk to life attending their conduct they would not have acted in the way they did; they would have changed their behaviour. Taking the risk thus structures their conduct.[106] In this respect the test bears comparison with Mitchell's value-indifference test, which asks whether the defendant would have acted differently had he known *the outcome was to be fatal*. As explained earlier, whether or not such a distinguishing test is morally informative, what is quite certain is that proof of the relevant attitude would create substantial evidential difficulties. How could a jury ever be certain that Mrs Hyam, Mr Smith, Messrs Hancock and Shankland, the Russian-roulette player, and so on, would not have acted differently if their guardian angel had allowed them to press the fast forward button? A value-deficit test of murderous risk-taking seems destined to convict no one, or, in common with the *Hancock* test, relies for such a conviction upon jury pragmatism.[107]

---

[101] [1986] AC 455. Conviction for murder quashed, conviction for manslaughter substituted. Defendants killed motorists having dropped a lump of concrete from a road bridge onto the carriageway of a road in an attempt to impede progress. Under my proposal Messrs Hancock and Shankland would appear to be guilty of murder since, like Mrs Hyam, they appeared to intend to expose their victims to the risk of death. I realize that many may think this inflates murder too far from its paradigm case. But it should not be forgotten that the jury did convict at first instance on the basis of a *Hyam*-type direction. There may be a case for giving the jury a 'get out' clause somewhat in the manner of a reverse version of the Swedish Penal Code (see n. 12 above).

[102] 331 A.2d 167 (1975) Defendant convicted of murder in the second degree having killed his victim in the course of a game of Russian roulette.

[103] 85 Tex.Crim 165, 211 S.W. 217 (1919) Defendant convicted of murder having fired a gun into the caboose of a passing train despite overwhelming unlikelihood that he would hit an occupant.

[104] I have argued elsewhere that doctrinal coherence would be advanced if GBH-murder can be 'understood as nothing more than an historical signal locked up in criminal law doctrine that risk-taking where it is in some sense victim-orientated, may constitute the mens rea for murder.' See 'A Plea for Rationality in the Law of Murder' [1990] LS 307, 317. As has been explained earlier, Horder's work on the malice principle in English criminal law has taken this suggestion beyond the drawing board.

[105] Compare Mr Goodfellow whose purpose in setting alight his own council house was to be rehoused rather than to act hostilely to the interests of the eventual victims.

[106] Duff, n. 9 above, 110 et seq.

[107] It also bears comparison with the Criminal Law Revision Committee's fault element of 'intending to cause fear of death or serious injury and (being) aware that he might kill' which, centred upon the problem of terrorism, would not cover those such as the malignant shootist who desire to take the risk and are indifferent to the response of the victim (n. 43 above, cl. 56).

This test, by contrast, asks whether the defendant would have acted differently if told that there would be *no* risk of death (that is, that there *could be no fatal outcome*), for which the circumstantial evidence available, for or against, is likely to be correspondingly stronger.[108] So the shooter would presumably not fire into a carriage or room he knew to be empty. Mrs Hyam would presumably not/did not set fire to the house until assured of the presence of the victim. The Russian-roulette player would presumably insert a bullet if he accidentally discharged the sole bullet against the wall. The terrorist would presumably await a better opportunity to cause the terror intended. In each case, because it is the possibility of the outcome occurring rather than some ulterior agenda which structures the action taken the moral difference between intending to kill someone and intending to endanger their lives diminishes almost to vanishing point.

Apart from providing necessary focus to the contempt-for-life approach the importance of the proposed refined mental element is that it provides a cogent extension in terms of responsibility to the intention to kill and the intention to cause grievous bodily harm, namely an intention to expose someone to mortal danger.[109] As such it would neatly accommodate cases provided for by the American depraved-heart doctrine without succumbing to its emotionalism and conceptual vagueness. There are nevertheless two strong arguments which can be levelled against this extension. The first is that requiring the risk to be a serious one rather than, say, of the 'more likely than not' variety threatens to designate as murderers some whose risk-taking would widely be considered less heinous than others who would, by the same test, only be guilty of manslaughter. Compare the following examples

Case 1. M., a disgruntled bank employee, blows up the bank's Head Office at a time when the office was closed. He does not desire to expose passing pedestrians to the serious risk of death. This is not his point, which is to revenge himself on the bank by destroying its property. Nevertheless he knows that such an outcome is extremely likely, but he does not care.

Case 2. W. plants a car bomb in a busy street. Her purpose is not to kill but to create a risk of death of sufficient severity to mobilize the police and the media thus creating publicity for her political goals. To minimize the risk of death she provides a very precise bomb warning, which in 90 per

---

[108] The analysis is not that the actor intends the outcome but that he intends to subject the victim to the risk of the outcome, which requires the actor both to believe that acting in the way he intends creates the possibility that it will occur and to act on that belief; J. Horder, 'Varieties of Intention' (1994) 14 LS 335. For less cogent analyses, see G. R. Sullivan, 'Intent, Subjective Recklessness and Endangerment' (1992) OJLS 380 and, regrettably, my own 'A Plea for Rationality in the Law of Murder', n. 104 above.

[109] Malta has an alternative fault element of intending to put the life of another in manifest jeopardy; see House of Lords, n. 11 above, app. 5.

cent of cases would be sufficient to prevent loss of life. Due to the error of a bomb-disposal expert the bomb detonates, killing the latter.

It is clearly arguable that there is more responsibility, more blame and more of the 'murderer''s credentials attached to M. than to W. and yet under the refined rough-justice approach it would be the latter who would be guilty of murder. For this reason there is a strong argument either for a separate offence label, say, of causing death by intentional endangerment, or for the support of a further category of murderous *reckless* killing arising out of the commission of inherently dangerous offences. The latter option will be returned to below. The former is rejected for creating an unnecessarily complex label. Both common law and Scots law have traditionally attached the murder label to cases of wicked recklessness. Domestic law has rejected risk-taking as murder only because of an assumption that it is impossible to draw a clear line between murder and manslaughter. Those who desire to create the risk of death show contempt for the value of life and so we should not be uneasy with the appropriateness of the label, although, inevitably, given instances will not always record the degree of heinousness which we naturally associate with the label.

The second argument is that the concept of seriousness of risk is too flexible and wide ranging in any event to be morally comparable to murder's focal cases. If a person not only does not intend to kill but acts *so as not* to kill and reasonably supposes that the manner in which he is acting will not cause death it seems unsatisfactory to label such a person in the same way as someone who kills for the joy of killing. This is not rough justice. It is failed justice. The obvious response to this is that the degrees of risk foreseen must become less relevant to the ascription of responsibility when there is a purposive element. Of course they do not bear at all where the consequence itself (rather than simply the creation of the risk) is directly intended. In this latter case it would not be cogent to argue that, notwithstanding his desire to kill the victim, the actor is not guilty of murder unless the means adopted to produce the outcome were likely to achieve it and the shooter was confident of success.[110] Similarly, as can be seen clearly in the roulette example, the shooter's attitude of mind does not change with the number of bullets only the degree of risk. It is submitted that this allows us to say that the former 'as good as' intended to kill even though the risk foreseen is relatively slight.[111]

---

[110] Duff, n. 9 above, 56–7; Horder n. 108 above, 342–4.

[111] La Fave and Scott, n. 37 above, 542–3, commenting upon *Banks* v. *State*, n. 103 above, support this lack of emphasis upon degrees of risk where the defendant's conduct lacks any possible social utility. My use of 'as good as' (see n. 30 above) means that the roulette player's responsibility is little different from the pessimistic assassin since the possibility that the outcome might occur is the reason why they subject themselves to the laws of chance. Horder analyses the difference as inhering in the fact that in the former case outcome-luck, as in dice, is intrinsic to the activity in question whereas in the latter, as in darts, it is extrinsic; id., n. 108 above, 343.

2. Risk-taking in the Course of Violent Crime

It was suggested above that there might be cases of indiscriminate risk-taking which match or exceed in terms of heinousness cases where the death issues from action taken in furtherance of an actor's desire to expose the victim to the serious risk of death. It was argued that it would be generally desirable for such cases to be treated as murder if a cogent method of distinguishing risk-taking constitutive of murder from that constitutive of manslaughter could be devised.

A proposal for elevating recklessness above the ordinary is to tie risk-taking constitutive of murder into particularly heinous contexts such as the commission of dangerous felonies. In a number of jurisdictions a criminal context aggravates an intentional killing. There is no obvious reason why such a context should not also aggravate a reckless killing such that it is 'pushed' through a higher 'threshold' of blame.[112] By comparison, a person who drives dangerously to get home for tea, detonates explosives in the lawful demolition of a building or in the attempt to remove a blockage in a collapsed tunnel should expect, at worst, a manslaughter conviction. It is not unreasonable to hold that there is a basic moral distinction between risk-taking motivated by ordinary human goals and those whose attainment inherently requires action taken against the interests of another. Where the criminal context is accompanied or characterized by extremely dangerous activity, it is arguably quite fair, assuming the degree of risk taken was already sufficient for manslaughter, to set this as an appropriate threshold for liability in murder.[113] Consider the following examples, death occurring in each case, as support for such a contention:

Case 3. A., having raped V., throws her into a river to destroy evidence of his involvement.

Case 4. A., a bank robber, fires a shotgun at the feet of pursuing police officers in an attempt to evade arrest.

Case 5. A., having abducted B., keeps her imprisoned in a disused culvert. She dies as a result of the combined effect of lack of water, food, and near-freezing conditions.

Each of these cases involves the defendant in an activity which already involves an attack upon the physical interests of another. It is submitted that it should not be necessary to show further either an intention to

---

[112] I agree that there is no moral justification for treating a person as a murderer simply because he is the causal agent of the victim's death where such agency was unconnected with any decision to attack the physical interests of the victim or otherwise expose the victim to the risk of death.

[113] Whether or not the inference can be taken that the defendant was more interested in his criminal project than in the preservation of life.

cause serious injury or a specific intention to expose the victim to the risk of death. His willingness 'to go the extra distance' should suffice for murder.

The main problem here is in circumscribing the 'unholy' context. To avoid an unfocused return to the excesses of felony-murder and to maintain a clear dividing line between risk-taking as murder and risk-taking as manslaughter it is important to ensure broad parity in terms of moral heinousness with the other fault elements.[114] The simplest way of doing so, and one which would dovetail satisfactorily with GBH-murder, is to require the unlawful object to be the commission of a crime ordinarily involving an attack on or threat to the autonomy or bodily integrity of another or to involve hostile activity in evading capture or lawful arrest.[115] This would mean, say, that robbery, but not arson, could form the subject matter of the revived felony-murder[116] unless the latter was committed for a specified ulterior criminal purpose, say resisting arrest or destroying evidence. Without such a requirement a simple case of arson would too easily convert to murder.[117] Such line-drawing exercises are never satisfactory but it is probably better that whatever line is drawn is clear and morally supportable than to allow individual context to shape the range of relevant felonies.[118] A tentative prototype proposal follows:

Criminal homicide also constitutes murder when—

    1 (a) death results from the reckless exposure of another to the serious risk of death; and

    (b) D. acted either:

        (i) for the purpose of resisting lawful arrest; or

        (ii) in the execution of and for the purpose of executing any specified offence, or for the purpose of evading capture or detection following the commission or attempted commission of such offence.

    (c) The specified offences are robbery, serious sexual assault, torture, whether or not serious injury was thereby effected or intended, abduction.[119]

---

[114] The MPC goes some way towards instantiating this form of rough justice. It is not entirely successful. The acid test for the propriety of the murder label is not that recklessness and indifference (as to death) can normally be presumed from the commission of a dangerous felony. They cannot. But intending to attack another's physical interests coupled with (objectively) life-threatening behaviour renders it not unfair to punish and censure for the more serious offence.

[115] A number of jurisdictions require the offence to be one of violence e.g. South Australia; see Yeo, n. 31 above, 91–3.

[116] Canada by contrast requires the unlawful object to be an offence of mens rea; see *R. v. Vagil* (1981) 58 CCC (2d) 97.

[117] And of course many of the worst cases of arson will be captured by the former type of murderous risk-taking.

[118] For analysis of the contingent attributes of and slippage between different 'families' of crimes see Gardner, n. 80 above, 247–9.

[119] This is not intended to be an exhaustive list but rather to give a flavour of the type of situations covered.

The requirement in cl. (b)(ii) that D. be acting 'in the execution of and for the purpose of executing', rather than the more natural 'to facilitate the offence' is to minimize inflationism so as to ensure, say, that those who drive dangerously on the way to commit an offence fall outside the reconstituted felony-murder. Inevitably the requirement would protect others less deserving but, once again, the key task involved in reconstructing an acceptable felony-murder/extreme recklessness amalgam is to ensure a broad parity of culpability amongst those included.

The intended effect of these provisions would be that subject to satisfying the recklessness component of cl. 1(a) the defendants in *DPP* v. *Smith*, *Vickers*,[120] *DPP* v. *Beard*[121] and *Pagett*[122] (by cl. 1(a)(i)) and Cases 3, 4, and 5 are guilty of murder, whether or not an intention to cause grievous bodily harm can be proved. So also a defendant who, lacking express or implied malice, raped another 'to death', or caused death, say by heart failure, in the course of administering controlled torture falling short of grievous bodily harm. On the other hand the defendants in Case 1,[123] *Hancock and Shankland*, *Goodfellow*, and *Hyam* are not.[124] It must be conceded that the provision inflates murder so far beyond its core cases as to threaten the receptivity that some might otherwise have to the overall cogency of the differentiating scheme adopted.[125] This is perhaps a reason in favour of constituting this form of homicide with a separate offence label, say 'killing in the course of a felony', or otherwise leave it to be mopped up by the residual law of manslaughter.[126] As will be seen below the problem of inflationism would be compounded by my suggested fault element.

V. FAULT AND CONTEXT: VARIATION AND UNIFORMITY

The foregoing discussion has elicited the general conclusion that the intention to cause serious bodily injury and the intention to expose another to the serious risk of death are justified extensions to the paradigm case of

---

[120] [1957] 2 QB 664.   [121] [1920] AC 479.

[122] [1983] 76 Cr App R 279.

[123] Which case after all inspired the attempt to provide a fall-back fault element.

[124] Mrs Hyam and Messrs Hancock and Shankland are guilty under the alternative head of risk-taking.

[125] Research seems to indicate that the public's attitudes towards culpable killings are not as punitive as would justify treating many non-focal cases of murder as such; see Mitchell, n. 6 above.

[126] Ashworth, n. 38 above, 272, also relies on the empirical research of Robinson and Darley in arguing that the public would not consider a murder conviction deserved if an accidental killing issued in the course of an armed robbery; see P. H. Robinson and J. M. Darley, *Justice, Liability and Blame: Community Views and the Criminal Law* (Boulder, Colo., 1995). This does not damage the case that mortal risk-taking in the course of violent crime warrants being treated as murder since in the United States, where the research took place, this is murder under the contempt-for-life rather than felony-murder approach.

intention to kill murder. There are strong grounds for concluding also that reckless killings in certain criminal contexts should also surpass the relevant threshold, although here consideration has been given to the creation of a separate homicide label. No firm conclusion has yet been reached on the precise nature of the fault element to be assigned to these different categories of murder outside the case of murder by mortal risk-taking. It has been suggested that to make a clear distinction between the fault required for murder and that for manslaughter intention must, for murder by mortal risk-taking, bear its focal meaning of aim, purpose, or desire.[127] Beyond this, variation rather than uniformity is the key for providing a rational fault element.[128]

A. Intention to Kill and GBH-murder

1. Acts of Killing

For intention to kill and GBH-murder there is a strong argument in favour of adopting a broad definition of intention in the normal case where death is the result of the defendant's (positive) action. Acting with the knowledge that death is a virtual certainty is morally and conceptually indistinguishable from direct intention in most such cases. For the reasons explained earlier, however, this requires attention to be paid to cases of perfect justificatory motive, that is, where the defendant acts to uphold the hierarchy of rights and interests which the criminal law operates to defend and does so in a way which would be entirely lawful but for the circumstances which exist or the consequences which must ensue.[129] Consider, for example, the doctrinal problems posed for the successful resolution of the following hypotheticals.[130] In each case the victim dies:

Case 6. A., following a shipwreck and about to drown, snatches a lifebelt from B. who is already wearing it.

Case 7. Following an accident at sea A., a passenger on the sinking ship, attempts to climb a staircase to safety. He encounters B., another ship's passenger, who has 'frozen' on the steps blocking A.'s escape. Unable to influence B., A. forcibly pulls him from the staircase and into the briny depths beneath.

---

[127] For discussion of the lawful excuse requirement see below.
[128] See Gardner, n. 80 above, 249.
[129] For full discussion see W. Wilson, *Criminal Law: Doctrine and Theory* (London, 1998), 288–9; id., n. 65 above, 458–60.
[130] Case 6 is a variation on a hypothetical posed by Bacon. Case 7 is a hypothetical posed by J. C. Smith in *Justification and Excuse in Criminal Law* (London, 1989).

Woollin gives trial judges no general guidance on how to plug the culpability gap in such cases and, indeed, by removing some sources of ambiguity might be thought to have exacerbated the problem at least outside the medical arena. Until now the pragmatic line taken is that doctrinal rationality can be eschewed so long as they have, in the definition of intention, a flexible friend which, in appropriate circumstances can allow good intentions to take doctrinal precedence over knowledge. A restructured fault element would then need to accommodate cases of good motives in the absence of legislation creating a fully operative system of justificatory defences.

One way of doing so would be to incorporate a 'without lawful excuse' element into the definition, thereby, in effect, converting the fault element into a form of recklessness.[131] Greater specificity would be required than this to ensure that the scope of 'lawful excuses' would neither collapse into an unfocused notion of 'reasonable cause' on the one hand[132] nor be entirely exhausted by the current state of existing defences on the other.[133] It is suggested that the following definition might cover the clearest cases of lawful excuse in cases of killing by direct action.

A person does not act unlawfully (for the purpose of murder) by reason only of knowing at the time of acting that his act or omission will or may cause the death of another person if the action was reasonably taken to defend the autonomy and/or bodily integrity of the actor or another and if the other person's death would be an unavoidable concomitant of that aim rather than a means to it and the action was not taken for the purpose of harming that person.[134]

By explicitly incorporating such a provision I am not seeking to exclude an extended group of defences. Rather I am suggesting that, if direct intention is not the sole mental element for murder, there should be incorporated a cogent moral definitional correspondence between direct and indirect intention which this provision largely achieves.[135] Case 7 would appear to be covered by the provision, but not Case 6 where death is a means, rather

---

[131] *Crabbe* (1985) 156 CLR 464 discussed in Yeo, n. 31 above, ch. 3.

[132] Compare my proposal of murder by 'intending to expose another to mortal danger'. I suggest that here the legality of such conduct is *properly* determined by the jury on a 'without reasonable cause' basis; see n. 98 above. The Indian Code treats as a question of fact whether the risk-taking was, in the words of one judge 'a wholly inexcusable act of extreme recklessness' (Plowden J. quoted by Yeo, n. 31 above, 130). As Yeo concedes it affords the jury substantial discretion to exculpate for a variety of imperfect justificatory claims.

[133] Particularly in view of the fact that necessity/duress of circumstances is not currently available for murder.

[134] Cf. the Indian Code, s. 81. My thanks to Antony Duff for helping me to fine-tune this definition without committing him to assenting to its overall cogency.

[135] Whichever defences are thought appropriate may then be applied consistently to both fault forms. See A. J. Ashworth, 'The Treatment of Good Intentions' in A. P. Simester and A. T. H. Smith (eds.), *Harm and Culpability* (Oxford, 1996), 173.

than an unavoidable concomitant of, saving B.'s life.[136] B.'s relative lack of
moral heinousness could be accommodated in other ways.[137]

2. CAUSING DEATH BY OMISSION

John Gardner has reminded us that reasons differ in form as well as
content. At the level of moral evaluation we must distinguish between
action-reasons and outcome-reasons.[138] These are often conflated, leaving
some to conclude that there is no moral difference worth recording at the
level of offence definitions between, say, a stabbing and a poisoning, or
between a killing and doing something (including 'nothing') which has
death as its consequence.[139] Since in both cases there are reasons to prevent
the outcome occurring criminal doctrine should respect, through censure
and punishment, the decision of the actor not to be guided in his behaviour
by that reason. At the level of doctrine, however, action-reasons may be
constitutive of the relevant criminal behaviour. We discriminate between
ways of killing and ways of causing death. So, procuring the death of
another, if properly termed murder, is nevertheless doctrinally distinct from
murder by killing, reflecting the consideration that there are (action-)
reasons not to procure a killing which may be expected to operate independently of the (action-)reasons not to kill.[140]

   We might, then, wish to record the distinctiveness of the action-reasons
against killing by rendering homicide, by omission, a special crime. An
alternative approach would be to ensure, in the manner of derivative liability generally, a sufficient nexus between deed and outcome to warrant treating the agent as murderer. Quite apart from wishing to avoid excessive
particularism in offence labels, my preference is the latter, largely for the
common-sense reason that deeds of omission are not easily distinguishable
from deeds of killing at either the conceptual or moral level when they
approach murder's focal case.[141] Whichever approach we adopt, however,

---

[136] Cf. A. Simester, 'Why Distinguish Intention from Foresight' in Simester and Smith, ibid.,
87–99; J. Gardner, 'Justifications and Reasons', ibid., 112–14.

[137] e.g. by a defence of severe emotional disturbance.

[138] N. 80 above, 211–13, 244–9; and see J. Raz, *The Morality of Freedom* (Oxford, 1986),
ch. 6.

[139] See e.g. A. J. Ashworth, 'The Scope of Criminal Liability for Omissions' (1989) 105 LQR
424. Cf. G. Williams who follows the Gardner–Raz axis, albeit with less theoretical flamboy-
ance, in 'Criminal Omissions: the Conventional View' (1991) 107 LQR 86.

[140] Such considerations may, in extreme cases, even block the normal impetus to attribute a
consequence to the intentional action of the actor. I have in mind the absence of a murder-by-
perjury classification. J. Smith and B. Hogan, *Criminal Law*, 8th edn. (London, 1996), 355–6,
attribute this to a policy decision. This is wholly consistent with Gardner's complaint that
doctrinal variations should not invariably be attributed to higher-order moral principles, or
policy, but may simply reflect the gap which sometimes opens up in moral evaluation between
action and outcome reasons.

[141] Cf. Fletcher, n. 3 above, 634.

criminalization requires, as with accomplice liability,[142] a specially constituted fault element which is sensitive to the basis upon which we blame the
omitter, namely an evaluation of her behaviour on a balance of reasons.
This reflects the fact that we blame the omitter not simply for her failure to
prevent harm but rather for her failure to satisfy our expectations, which
demands that attention be paid both to the reasons supporting action and
to the reasons given for not acting.

The threshold question which must be asked for purposes of *general
criminalization* is not, then, the standard question whether A. desired the
victim's death or realized the inevitability (or serious risk) but whether she
ought to have prevented it given the duty owed to the victim. Criminal
doctrine must take account of many matters beyond the agent's state of
cognition pertinent to the question of 'ought'.[143] The general justification
for refusing to impose a general duty to act is commonly reckoned to be a
respect for human autonomy and a recognition that satisfying duties of
intervention would impose unpredictable burdens of uncertain scope.
Another way of saying this is that people should not be forced to do unreasonable things where 'unreasonable things' means 'things a person has not
signed up for' by virtue of their relationship with the victim, their occupa-
tion and so on. It should follow that where a duty does exist the scope of
the duty to act is similarly not unlimited but is bounded by questions of
fairness to the individual.

Case 8. D., a parent, knowing that her child will die of loss of blood if a
blood transfusion is not sought fails to do so due to a religious belief which
holds that blood transfusions are wrong.

Case 9. W., who is seriously ill, makes her husband H. promise not to seek
medical treatment for her condition although H. knows she will die without it. H. reluctantly complies out of respect for her autonomy.

Case 10. F., attempting to evade the blows of her brutal husband, H., accidentally drops V., her baby, into a pond. H. threatens F. further violence if
she rescues the child. Paralysed with fear she desists.

Case 11. F., a lifeguard, resists taking easy steps to save the life of A., B.,
and C. who are disabled by a freak wave in order to save the life of D., her
own child.

None of the decisions made in any of these cases are comparable in terms
of blame with a purposive killing. Nor is causing death on the moral

---

[142] This is not to say that accomplice-liability succeeds in this ambition but that it is a
constant doctrinal tension. Cf. I. Dennis, 'The Mental Element for Accessories' in P. F. Smith
(ed.), *Essays in Honour of J. C. Smith* (London, 1987).
[143] See generally Wilson, n. 129 above, 86–9. Arguably all omissions-based defences are of
a justificatory character.

agenda. D., W., and F. are simply being themselves warts and all and being oneself, without more, should not be the basis upon which criminal liability should be incurred, let alone liability for murder. The real concern, then, is to identify those circumstances in which an omission is excusable or ought to be excusable[144] where 'excusable' means simply that the defendant had a socially acceptable, if not necessarily praiseworthy, reason for conducting as she did.[145] At present it seems that such considerations are accommodated by adjectival law and the practices of courts and legal officials, which evince a pragmatic tendency to skate over the paper rules in cases of death following an omission. This is most clearly true in medical cases but extends more widely.[146] In *Smith*,[147] for example, a husband who failed, out of respect for his wife's wishes, to call a doctor when it was clear to him that she would die without medical attention was charged only with manslaughter when, on the test of fault then applicable, a murder charge was an obvious option. And at trial the judge directed the jury that they must give weight to the reasonableness of respecting the wife's autonomy when deciding whether he had acted reasonably in delaying the emergency call.

Further support for the existence of an inchoate balance-of-reasons approach in cases of omission comes from the widespread acceptance that a special defence of impossibility is available in cases of omission. For example, a parent who cannot swim would not be guilty of murder (or manslaughter) for failing to attempt a rescue.[148] This is generally assumed to be the omissions equivalent of the requirement of voluntariness of action. More plausibly, absent any end-directed activity, our general disposition to hold people to account for a death is unusually motive- and context-sensitive, and so it should be since agents 'by omission' take on the phenomenal attributes of 'killers' only in extreme cases. Whatever our attitude towards the non-applicability of duress to murder, for example, our moral evaluation of F.'s conduct in cases 10 and 11 is unavoidably linked to the context within which she is operating. With this in mind, it is surely inconceivable that duress would not be interpreted as negating fault in murder by omission. The mental element in murder by omission, in short, must be purpose.

---

[144] G. Hughes, 'Criminal Omissions' (1958) 67 Yale LJ 590, 606.

[145] I would not necessarily endorse the view that a balance-of-reasons approach is determinative of all matters relating to criminal liability but accept that it should be, and usually is, at least for non-regulatory crime, in the context of liability for omissions. In this latter case not only is the 'paradigm of intentional criminality . . . subverted' (Gardner, n. 80 above, 232) but also, at least partially, is the paradigm of virtue.

[146] See e.g. *Airedale NHS Trust v. Bland* [1993] AC 789; *Arthur* (1981) 12 BMLR 1.

[147] [1979] Crim LR 251.

[148] See also *Harding v. Price* [1948] 1 KB 695: one cannot report an accident one does not know to have happened; *US v. Murdock* 290 US 389: it is not a voluntary omission to file a tax return if one fails deliberately believing one has a constitutional right to avoid self incrimination. Also cases cited in Hughes, n. 144 above, and A. Smart, 'Criminal Responsibility for Failing to do the Impossible' (1987) 103 LQR 532.

More broadly, for purposes of general criminalization, the fault element for causing death by omission must be constructed quite differently to reflect our understanding that it is a duty-bearer's failure to live up to our expectations which provokes the punitive response, not his level of cognition, which, as she has not *acted* against reason, requires due regard to be paid to what is fair to expect the defendant to do given the context and her general capacity to appreciate how best to acquit herself as a morally responsible human being.[149]

B. KILLING IN THE COURSE OF VIOLENT CRIME

As discussed earlier, a common view is that a subjective test of liability is a crucial concomitant of breaches of the 'do not kill' obligation. Moreover, if this homicide category is constituted as a form of murder it is arguably crucial that a requirement of foresight is particularly necessary to prevent a form of 'double jeopardy'. If the moral threshold (for murder) is lowered by reason that risk-taking takes place in a criminal context it should not further be lowered to admit those who act oblivious to the mortal risks they run. The opposing argument is that foresight offers nothing of intrinsic moral value to the notion of unjustified and inexcusable risk-taking which inadvertence due to rage, lust, fear, intoxication, or indifference does not also add. Just censure and punishment requires only that the risk-taking be inexcusable and unjustifiable. Just as voluntary intoxication supplies the fault element for crimes of subjective recklessness so should insensitivity to risks due to lust, fear, anger, and other attitudes commonly elicited in the course of dangerous criminal activity supply the fault element for murder. The view taken here is that it is unrealistic in the heat-of-the-moment cases typically involved that the defendant's attitude will be expressed otherwise than in his action. A rapist deprived momentarily of practical reasoning capacity through intoxication or lust may well be oblivious to the risk of death provoked by his attempts to overpower his victim, but should this matter?[150] An armed robber pumped full of adrenalin may not contemplate the fearful risks to which he is exposing his pursuers when firing warning shots in their direction, but should this matter? Neither, it is submitted, is any less culpable in creating the risks to which the victim is subjected than the conscious risk-taker. What is clearly important for broad purposes of criminal justice, however, is that the fault element, given that the offence label implies exceptional degrees of moral heinousness, should relate to the outcome of death (alone) and should be

---

[149] This is made explicit in the Law Commission's most recent proposals on involuntary manslaughter. Cf. Fletcher, n. 3 above, 622–34; and J. Gardner, 'The Gist of Excuses' (1998) 1 Buffalo Crim LR 575, 593–7.   [150] Cf. *DPP* v. *Beard*, n. 121 above.

defined so as to be sensitive to the defendant's own reasoning/cognitive capacities.[151]

VI. CONCLUSION

Rationality in criminal doctrine requires a failsafe doctrinal mechanism for ensuring that censure and punishment are deserved and the degree of censure and punishment is proportionate to the degree of wrongdoing we ascribe to the defendant's conduct. It is a basic premise of criminal justice that the vehicle for appropriate censure and punishment must be doctrine rather than, for example, the moral and political response of judge and jury. The function of the different fault terms in homicide is to differentiate the offences of murder and manslaughter. Since the basic obligations are differentiated criminal justice demands that the obligation broken should be precisely identified or labelled so that blame and punishment do not exceed the scope of the defendant's wrong. The puzzle which doctrine has to settle is how to capture the obligation successfully. Is, say, as the Law Commission would have it, the distinction between murder and manslaughter reducible to the distinction between intended and reckless killings? Or are the social obligations corresponding to the wrongs involved more nuanced than this? It has been argued in this Chapter that a distinct merit of the common law and domestic models is that they reflect the fact that the wrong in murder has fuzzy edges and that murder must extend significantly beyond its paradigm case. The weakness in the former is that these fuzzy edges have elicited fuzzy doctrine. In the latter the weakness is that doctrinal clarity and simplicity have been preferred to rationality. I have attempted to provide a scheme for differentiating murder and manslaughter at the top end which is centred in murder's paradigm case of an intentional attack upon the physical interests of another.[152] Each extension to the paradigm involves such an attack in one form or another. While it may be thought that I have inflated murder too far beyond its paradigm case in certain particulars, I am comforted by the fact that the reconstituted parameters of murder differ little from those in Scotland, and in other common-law jurisdictions, are rather more precisely drawn, and are,

---

[151] Bearing in mind the Law Commission's proposals, n. 14 above, para. 5, a (very) rough prototype for such a fault element might be as follows: 'A person acts recklessly for the purpose of this section when he acts with conscious appreciation of the serious risk of death involved or whose failure to appreciate such risk manifests *his* indifference to the value of life or was otherwise inexcusable given the degree of risk to life involved, the circumstances of the risk-taking and the person's capacities to appreciate that risk.'

[152] Chris Clarkson also uses 'attack' as the signal element in that form of manslaughter relabelled as 'killing by attack'. Unlike him I prefer to use the 'moral threshold' logic to convert 'attacks of serious violence' into murder, rather than, under his scheme, manslaughter by recklessness or gross carelessness. Quaere as to whether all cases of GBH-murder would, in any event, qualify as manslaughter.

in their responsiveness to different homicide forms and contexts, less beholden to the equities or iniquities of the criminal justice system. Of course, in the 'imperfect worlds' we inhabit all this may be little comfort to those subjected to the mandatory sentence by dint of these extensions. The pragmatic response to this unhappy state of affairs is to favour restricting rather than extending the forms of murder. The Law Commission model undoubtedly scores on that front and some will prefer it for that reason. But we must also be aware that there are other grounds for pessimism than the continuation of the mandatory sentence. In particular, why should we be any more confident that this, or any other, government will find time to restructure homicide, let alone agree to *raise* the higher boundary between murder and manslaughter? If the dialogue between reformers and government concerns, rather, the desirability of *extending* the scope of murder there is surely at least an outside chance that the appropriateness of the mandatory sentence for *all forms* of murder will be considered as part of the reform package. The pragmatist must also recognize, therefore, that without such a dialogue there can be no political incentive for change. Therein lies the choice.

3

Diminished Responsibility and Mentally Disordered Killers

R. D. MACKAY[*]

Mental disorder plays an important role within the law of homicide.[1] However, it also has an equally important part to play within the broader framework of the criminal law. In this respect it is important to remember that mental disorder has no discrete role to play within the substantive law of homicide with the major exception of the doctrine of diminished responsibility.[2] This Chapter focuses on this doctrine, but before doing so the wider role of mental disorder needs be considered. An examination of the approach of other jurisdictions and an assessment of whether the diminished responsibility plea should be abolished or retained follows that section. Finally, the discussion of diminished responsibility will consider its relationship with the plea of provocation and the Chapter will conclude by considering the way forward within a reformed law of homicide.

A. The Wider Role of Mental Disorder

Murder is such a serious offence that it automatically attracts a psychiatric investigation of the accused. If this reveals that he or she is currently suffering from a psychiatric disorder, then the Mental Health Act permits a transfer from prison to a mental hospital under section 48 if there is a diagnosis of mental illness or severe mental impairment and 'that disorder is of a nature or degree which makes it appropriate for the prisoner to be detained in hospital for medical treatment and that he is in urgent need of treatment'.[3] Recent research into the operation of section 48[4] has revealed that

---

[1] J. Gunn and P. Taylor, *Forensic Psychiatry: Clinical, Legal and Ethical Aspects* (London, 1993), ch. 8, who also point out that 'The risk of homicidal attack by seriously mentally ill patients is . . . small, and the risk of suicide about a hundred times greater' (ibid., 335).

[2] There is also infanticide but this offence will not be discussed here. For a brief analysis of the Infanticide Act 1938 see R. D. Mackay, *Mental Condition Defences in the Criminal Law* (Oxford, 1995), 207–13.

[3] Mental Health Act 1983, s. 48(1).

[4] R. D. Mackay and D. Machin, 'Transfers from Prison to Hospital: An Empirical Study of the Operation of Section 48 of the Mental Health Act 1983' (2000) 40 Br J Crim 732.

during 1992, out of a total of 370 transfers, murder accounted for around 11 per cent (N=40) of the charges which triggered a transfer under section 48. More importantly, these forty charges only resulted in six murder convictions with the remaining thirty-six being dealt with in the following ways. One female defendant was convicted of infanticide, while charges in another twenty-nine were reduced to manslaughter by reason of diminished responsibility. One murder charge was withdrawn and one defendant was acquitted. The remaining three cases resulted in verdicts of insanity or unfitness to plead. These figures confirm two important points. The first is the important role which mental disorder plays in relation to the issue of criminal responsibility. The second is confirmation of the way in which diminished responsibility has eclipsed findings of insanity and unfitness to plead. More will be said about this later. However, at this stage in the discussion it seems appropriate to say more about the role of both the defence of insanity and the doctrine of unfitness to plead within the law of homicide.

The year chosen for research into section 48 was 1992. This was the same year which saw the implementation of the Criminal Procedure (Insanity and Unfitness to Plead) Act 1991. This statute enacted a series of important procedural reforms. Firstly, it mandated that both insanity and unfitness must be supported by psychiatric evidence. Secondly, with regard to unfitness it introduced a 'trial of the facts' in order to ensure that the prosecution can prove that the accused 'did the act or made the omission charged against him as the offence'.[5] Thirdly, and most importantly for present purposes, it gave judges flexibility of disposal, with the sole exception of murder charges.[6] This last point is of major importance in relation to the role which insanity and unfitness play in the crime of murder. In theory this role should be not insignificant.

The 1991 Act left the substantive law on both insanity and unfitness intact. This means that the defence of insanity continues to be governed by the *M'Naghten* Rules which essentially provide:

That to establish a defence of insanity, it must be clearly proved that, at the time of the commission of the offence, the party accused was labouring under such a defect of reason, from disease of the mind, as not to know the nature and quality of the act he was doing, or, if he did know it, that he did not know he was doing what was wrong.[7]

Similarly, the test for unfitness to plead, based on comprehending the trial proceedings, remains unaltered.[8]

Prior to the introduction of diminished responsibility in the Homicide

---

[5] Criminal Procedure (Insanity) Act 1964, s. 4A(2)(b) (inserted by the Criminal Procedure (Insanity and Unfitness to Plead) Act 1991, s. 2).

[6] Ibid., s. 5 (inserted by the Criminal Procedure (Insanity and Unfitness to Plead) Act 1991, s. 3).   [7] (1843) 10 Cl & F 200, 210.

[8] See Mackay, n. 2 above, 224–5.

Act 1957 insanity and unfitness played a vital role in avoiding murder convictions. However, since that time the use of both insanity and unfitness has been eclipsed by diminished responsibility. The reasons for this are not entirely clear; one would have expected the number of unfitness and insanity findings to remain constant, with diminished responsibility operating in a wider range of cases. But this has not happened. As Sparks puts it

The plea of 'diminished responsibility' has, in practice, partly *replaced* the plea of insanity, rather than supplementing it: and despite the nominally wider criteria of section 2, there has been no increase in the proportion of murderers excused from full punishment on account of their mental condition.[9]

The same appears to be true of unfitness with Walker also concluding 'The steady fall in both findings of "insane on arraignment" and findings of ["not guilty by reason of insanity"] has been compensated by verdicts of "diminished responsibility", *but no more*.'[10] This is perplexing. A possible explanation lies 'not only in the tactical attractions of diminished responsibility for defending counsel, but also in the preferences of medical witnesses'.[11] While there is no doubt that the elements of diminished responsibility can be more easily satisfied than those of the *M'Naghten* Rules, the continued reduction in the use of the latter in murder prosecutions could be regarded as a matter of serious concern. For what it must inevitably mean is that many of those who were formerly excused on the basis of legal insanity are now being convicted of manslaughter. The problem is compounded by the fact that the special verdict in all murder cases continues to attract a mandatory disposal of indefinite hospitalization. Small wonder then that a plea of guilty to manslaughter on the basis of diminished responsibility is regarded as more attractive.

The Criminal Procedure (Insanity and Unfitness to Plead) Act 1991 could have altered all that by giving judges flexibility of disposal in respect of murder as well as for all other offences. But in deciding not to do this it was made clear by the then Minister of State for the Home Office, John Patten MP, that the preservation of the mandatory hospital disposal for murder was 'very important for public protection'.[12] It was predicted that this refusal to extend a wider range of disposals to murder cases would be 'to continue to "force" those mentally ill defendants charged with murder to avoid unfitness and insanity by pleading guilty to manslaughter by reason of diminished responsibility . . .'.[13] Recent research indicates that this may indeed be the case. For while the number of unfitness and insanity findings has slowly

---

[9] R. F. Sparks, ' "Diminished Responsibility" in Theory and Practice' (1964) 27 MLR 9, 32 (emphasis in original).

[10] N. Walker, *Crime and Insanity in England*, vol. 1 (Edinburgh, 1968), 158 (emphasis in original).   [11] Ibid., 160.

[12] Hansard (H.C.), 1 March 1991, vol. 186, No. 67 at col. 1279.

[13] R. D. Mackay, *The Operation of the Criminal Procedure (Insanity) Act 1964: An Empirical Study of Unfitness to Plead and the Insanity Defence* (Leicester, 1991), 28.

begun to rise under the 1991 Act, with judges making full use of their new flexible disposal powers, it is clear that murder continues rarely to attract either finding. So, for example, research into the first five years of the operation of the 1991 Act reveals that murder only attracted four (9.1 per cent) out of a total of forty-four special verdicts[14] and nine (8.2 per cent) out of a total of 110 unfitness disposals.[15] In short the number of such cases remains minimal. By way of contrast the number of diminished responsibility pleas peaked at 109 in 1979 but has now fallen by over 50 per cent to forty-seven in 1997/8.[16]

Although the reasons for the decline in the number of successful diminished responsibility pleas remains unclear,[17] we need to ask whether the eclipse of unfitness and insanity in the manner referred to above is acceptable. Both of these doctrines are regarded as of fundamental theoretical importance within the criminal law. The first supposedly protects those who are mentally disordered at the time of the trial and cannot comprehend the proceedings from having to face the rigours of a criminal trial, while the second is designed to ensure that those who were legally insane at the time of the commission of the offence are not held criminally responsible. With regard to unfitness, attempts have been made to avoid the mandatory disposal in murder cases by seeking to plead diminished responsibility during the 'trial of the facts'.[18] However, the House of Lords has now ruled in R. v. Antoine[19] that this is not possible. This is hardly surprising, as a plea of diminished responsibility requires the accused to plead guilty to manslaughter. But if he has already been found unfit to plead, a prerequisite before any 'trial of the facts' takes place, then a plea of guilty has already been foreclosed. The same would seem to be true of the defence of insanity, which requires a plea of 'not guilty by reason of insanity'. In short, both require a defendant who is fit to plead. The case of Antoine graphically demonstrates the dilemma. In that case Antoine and a co-defendant killed the victim, apparently as a sacrifice to the devil. The co-accused, who was fit to plead, pleaded guilty to manslaughter on the basis of diminished responsibility; a plea which was accepted by the prosecution. Antoine however was found unfit to plead and wished to prove diminished responsibility in answer to the charge of murder which formed the basis of the 'trial of the facts'. In short, he wished to avoid a finding of murder and the

[14] See R. D. Mackay and G. Kearns, 'More Facts About the Insanity Defence' [1999] Crim LR 714, 718–19 which confirms a marked decrease in the number of murder cases.
[15] See R. D. Mackay and G. Kearns, 'An Upturn in Unfitness to Plead? Disability in Relation to the Trial under the 1991 Act' [2000] Crim LR 532.
[16] See Home Office, Criminal Statistics for England and Wales for 1998 (Cm. 4649), Table 4.7.
[17] For some tentative explanations see N. Walker, Aggravation, Mitigation and Mercy in English Criminal Justice (London, 1999), 161, 164.
[18] For discussion see R. D. Mackay and G. Kearns, 'The Trial of the Facts and Unfitness to Plead' [1997] Crim LR 644.   [19] [2000] 2 All ER 208.

mandatory disposal which would inevitably follow. In ruling that diminished responsibility was unavailable in answer to a 'trial of the facts' for murder, Lord Hutton accepted the Court of Appeal's view that 'it is not open to the jury to find the defendant guilty of murder but only that he did the act charged against him as murder ... The whole purpose ... is to protect a person who is unfit to stand trial against a verdict of guilty.'[20] While this is an admirable sentiment it means that while Antoine's co-accused was able to avail himself of a diminished plea such an approach was not open to an unfit defendant. The result for the latter is the mandatory hospital disposal. Whether this is fair is surely open to question.

This brief discussion of some aspects of unfitness to plead and insanity highlights some of the problems relating to the role of mental disorder in murder cases which will be examined in this Chapter. They may be summarized as follows. Although both unfitness and insanity protect some mentally abnormal offenders from conviction, their role in relation to murder has been and continues to be minimal. To some extent this has been exacerbated by the Criminal Procedure (Insanity and Unfitness to Plead) Act 1991 which mandates indefinite hospitalization in relation to the unfit-to-plead and legally insane who are charged with murder. The effect of this is to drive mentally disordered killers who are fit to plead into pleading diminished responsibility. This in turn means that some will be punished when they might otherwise have been acquitted, albeit on the basis of a special verdict. Is this acceptable? Indeed, should conviction and punishment ever be an option for killers who are mentally disordered at the time of the offence or should they be otherwise dealt with by means of non-penal disposals? Before these questions can be answered the diminished responsibility plea needs to be examined in greater depth.

B. The Operation of section 2 of the Homicide Act 1957

This is not the place for an exhaustive account of the law relating to diminished responsibility.[21] However, some legal analysis is required in order to set the discussion in context and to highlight some of the problems.

The first problem concerns the proper scope of the plea. Although the Royal Commission on Capital Punishment decided not to recommend the introduction of diminished responsibility, preferring instead to extend the insanity defence,[22] the Government disagreed. As a result, in March 1957 the Homicide Act was passed. The Act borrowed the notion of 'diminished

[20] Ibid., 212; [1999] 3 WLR 1204, 1214 (C.A.).
[21] For such a discussion see Mackay, n. 2 above, ch. 4.
[22] Royal Commission on Capital Punishment (1953) (Cmnd. 8932), paras. 333 and 413.

responsibility' from Scots law to give discretion in relation to the sentencing of mentally abnormal offenders charged with murder. The essentials of the plea are contained in section 2(1) of the 1957 Act, which provides:

Where a person kills or is a party to the killing of another, he shall not be convicted of murder if he was suffering from such abnormality of mind (whether arising from a condition of arrested or retarded development of mind or any inherent causes or induced by disease or injury) as substantially impaired his mental responsibility in doing or being a party to the killing.

Section 2(2) makes it clear that, as with insanity, the burden of proving this defence on a balance of probabilities rests upon the accused[23] and if the plea is successful, subsection 3 ensures a conviction for manslaughter, thus enabling the judge to exercise his discretion as to sentence.

Although initially some judges adopted a narrow interpretation of what could amount to an 'abnormality of mind' within the section, it was not long before the Court of Appeal, in the landmark case of *R. v. Byrne*[24] decided that a wider approach was called for. The crucial question was whether a sexual psychopath who had killed the victim while suffering from an impulse-control disorder was entitled to have his diminished responsibility plea left to the jury. In answering this question in the affirmative, Lord Parker CJ made the following remark, which was to have a fundamental influence on the scope of section 2:

'Abnormality of mind', which has to be contrasted with the time honoured expression in the *M'Naghten* Rules, 'defect of reason', means a state of mind so different from that of ordinary human beings that the reasonable man would term it abnormal. It appears to us to be wide enough to cover the mind's activities in all its aspects, not only the perception of physical acts and matters and the ability to form a rational judgment whether an act is right or wrong, but also the ability to exercise will-power to control physical acts in accordance with that rational judgment.[25]

The effect of this judgment was not only to permit the notion of irresistible impulse to be introduced into English law but also to allow a wide variety of less serious forms of mental condition to be brought within the scope of 'abnormality of mind'. The most extreme example of the latter is probably the way in which mercy-killing cases have been permitted to fall within section 2, with little or no real medical evidence of 'mental abnormality'.[26] In this way it has been said that 'diminished responsibility is interpreted in accordance with the morality of the case rather than as an application of psychiatric concepts'.[27] The result is that section 2 has continued to operate in a pragmatic but unprincipled manner. Certainly the courts have had

[23] See *R. v. Dunbar* [1958] 1 QB 36.   [24] [1960] 2 QB 396.
[25] Ibid., 403.
[26] See the cases discussed by S. Dell in *Murder into Manslaughter* (Oxford, 1984), 35–6. 'Mercy killing' is discussed further below, 79–80.
[27] G. Williams, *Textbook of Criminal Law*, 2nd edn. (London, 1983), 693.

little to say about the precise nature of 'abnormality of mind' other than to confirm what was said in *Byrne*, namely that the accused's mental abnormality must arise from one of the bracketed causes, and, secondly, that these causes are 'a matter to be determined on expert evidence'.[28] This paucity of judicial scrutiny as to the meaning of 'abnormality of mind' has led to a lack of guidance for psychiatrists who have to give expert evidence on the crucial issue of whether the accused's condition at the time of the killing falls within one or more of the 'four specified aetiologies [which] have no defined or agreed psychiatric meaning'.[29] Further, the two recent cases which have attempted such guidance have been criticized,[30] particularly on the basis that 'disease' within section 2 has been interpreted to refer 'to organic or physical injury or disease of the body including the brain [while] "inherent cause" . . . would cover functional mental illness'.[31] This means, firstly, that 'disease' within section 2 is much narrower than 'disease of the mind' within the *M'Naghten* Rules and, secondly, that a psychological injury would it seems no longer qualify as an 'injury' within the bracketed causes. In consequence the Court of Appeal may have unwittingly made it much more difficult for psychiatrists to bring mercy killers within the diminished responsibility plea. It is clear that all these difficulties stem from the obscurity of the aetiological causes, which as will be seen has led to suggestions that they be abandoned and replaced by a psychiatrically recognized notion.

The second problem relates to the role of the jury in diminished responsibility cases, which in turn is tied into a major procedural development effected by the Court of Appeal. When *Byrne* was decided in 1960 all diminished responsibility findings were made by a jury and Lord Parker's definition of 'abnormality of mind' was clearly premised on that fact. However, in 1968 the Court of Appeal in *Cox*[32] finally confirmed that in cases where the medical evidence all supported diminished responsibility the prosecution could accept a plea of guilty to manslaughter under section 2. Since that time it has become clear that the vast majority of cases of diminished responsibility are now disposed of without any jury involvement. Firstly, Dell in her research into diminished found that in 1976–7 only about 20 per cent of cases went to trial,[33] while more recently the Crown Prosecution Service reported that in 1986–8 'there was a total of

[28] *R. v. Byrne*, n. 24 above, 403.   [29] Dell, n. 26 above, 39.

[30] See R. D. Mackay, 'The Abnormality of Mind Factor in Diminished Responsibility' [1999] Crim LR 117, 122.

[31] *R. v. Sanderson* (1994) 98 Cr App R 335, 336.

[32] (1968) 52 Cr App R 130. For a brief history of the acceptance of pleas on grounds of diminished responsibility see *R. v. Vinagre* (1974) 69 Cr App R 104, 106–7 where it is remarked that 'in 1962 the judges decided that pleas to manslaughter on grounds of diminished responsibility could be accepted [but only] where there is clear evidence of mental imbalance.' No further evidence is given to support the assertion made about 1962.

[33] Dell, n. 26 above, 28.

178 cases where a plea was accepted by the Crown without dissent, and there were 13 cases refused by the Crown where the jury returned convictions for murder' as opposed to '18 cases where the Crown . . . refused a plea to manslaughter on the grounds of diminished responsibility and the jury returned a verdict of manslaughter.'[34] In effect this means that by 1986–8 the percentage of contested trials had fallen to 14.8 per cent. This shift in the balance of decision-making in diminished responsibility should not be underestimated. In essence what it means is that, subject to these figures remaining static, the active involvement of a jury occurs in under 15 per cent of all diminished cases and in those that are successful only around 10 per cent are returned by juries. This in turn must mean that in the vast majority of such cases the medical evidence unanimously supports such a plea, which in view of the criticisms levelled at the wording of section 2, seems somewhat surprising.

This leads to a third problem, which relates to the perceived obscurity and complexity of the wording of section 2.[35] Although psychiatrists have consistently complained about this it has nevertheless been suggested that when it comes to giving expert medical opinions about whether an accused's mental state ought to be regarded as one of diminished responsibility, less difficulty is experienced by report writers than might have been anticipated. As already indicated, although the 'abnormality of mind' factor together with the bracketed causes present psychiatrists with problems in the sense that they are not medically recognized concepts, at the very least they are not completely alien to medical thought. By way of contrast the same, it is said, is not true of the need for 'a substantial impairment of mental responsibility'. Firstly, the Butler Report remarked, that 'mental responsibility' was a phrase 'not to be found elsewhere in any statute . . . It is either a concept of law or a concept of morality; it is not a clinical fact relating to the defendant. It seems odd that psychiatrists should be asked and agree to testify as to legal or moral responsibility. It is even more surprising that courts are prepared to hear that testimony.'[36] Apart from the fact that such testimony is now rarely heard in open court, what is important to explore further is the opinion that 'mental responsibility' is not a clinical fact. While this phrase is certainly not without difficulty, research by Mitchell which elicited the views of a sample of forensic psychiatrists who had experience of preparing reports in diminished responsibility cases, reveals that rather than resort to an assessment of the accused's moral or legal responsibility they 'fall back on their real expertise and focus their attention on mental illness and personality disorder'. In short, 'they seem to

---

[34] House of Lords, *Report of the Select Committee on Murder and Life Imprisonment* (HL Paper 78–1 of Session 1988–9), vol. 2 (Oral Evidence), Pt. 1, 115.
[35] See Home Office, Dept. of Health and Social Security, *Report of the Committee on Mentally Abnormal Offenders* (1975) (Cmnd. 6244), para. 19.5 (hereafter referred to as the Butler Report).   [36] Ibid.

adopt an approach which construes "mental responsibility" in psychiatric terms.'[37] Of course, this does not mean that 'mental responsibility' is a clinical fact but it seems to support the view that, as with the bracketed causes, psychiatrists have been able to develop a medical approach towards the diminished responsibility plea.

However, this does not take account of the second problem raised in the Butler Report which relates to the use of the word 'substantial' in section 2. Here it is commented that 'The idea that ability to conform to the law can be measured is particularly puzzling.'[38] This is certainly an instance where psychiatrists can offer no real expertise. Here they cannot fall back on their clinical training as they appear to have done to make sense of the bracketed causes and the phrase 'mental responsibility'. On this occasion they are being asked to make a judgment which does not lend itself to any medical or scientific test. If ever there was a question which was one for a jury this must surely be it. Although psychiatrists should not be prevented from giving an opinion on the matter, it should be made clear that in doing so they are not exercising their clinical judgment but merely making a value judgment which can either be accepted or rejected by the jury irrespective of the medical evidence. Because this does not happen one suspects that some diminished responsibility pleas which are accepted by the prosecution might have been rejected by a jury. The obvious comparison is provocation where this does not occur. Rather, the jury always plays an active role in deciding the issues surrounding loss of self-control. The justification for this difference in approach is that the provocation plea, unlike diminished responsibility, does not involve matters of medical expertise. However, even if one accepts this line of argument the same ought to be conceded in relation to the word 'substantial' in section 2. Further, the disparity between these two pleas is exacerbated by the fact that unlike provocation the plea of diminished responsibility is an 'optional' one[39] where the burden of proof lies on the accused. This means that although it can be combined with provocation, about which more will be said later, because it is premised on a guilty-to-manslaughter plea, any defence which might lead to an acquittal cannot be run with it. The result is that in some cases the accused chooses not to run a plea of diminished responsibility in the hope of securing an unqualified acquittal. According to the Court of Appeal 'a deliberate decision by a defendant whose decision-making facilities are unimpaired not to advance before the trial jury a defence known to be available' is likely to be fatal to an appeal asking for the reception of fresh psychiatric evidence

[37] B. Mitchell, 'Putting Diminished Responsibility Law into Practice: A Forensic Psychiatric Perspective' (1997) 8 J For Psych 620, 631.
[38] Butler Report, n. 35 above, para. 19.5.
[39] See *R.* v. *Campbell* (1986) 84 Cr App R 255, 260.

in favour of diminished responsibility after a murder conviction.[40] Again this should be contrasted with provocation where the trial judge is obliged to leave such a plea to the jury provided there is some specific evidence supporting a loss of self-control irrespective of 'whether it is relied on at the trial by the defendant or not. If there is such evidence, the judge must leave the issue to the jury'.[41] It is clear that in some cases of diminished responsibility there will also be evidence of loss of self-control as it is not unusual for the defence to combine the pleas. However, if it is one of these cases where the prosecution is prepared to accept the diminished responsibility plea then the evidence of provocation will not be tested and may not be reflected in the verdict. This in turn means that there is no formal mechanism for the effect of the provocation to be considered at the sentencing stage.

The discussion above has revealed a diminished responsibility plea which operates in a largely pragmatic manner but is riddled with discrepancies and conceptual confusion. Having briefly considered some of the problems raised by the diminished responsibility plea, the next section explores the relevant experiences of some other jurisdictions.

C. COMPARATIVE ASPECTS

A number of jurisdictions have adopted a diminished responsibility plea which is modelled on English Law. Some have implemented section 2(1) virtually in its entirety. They include, for example, New South Wales,[42] the Australian Capital Territory,[43] Singapore[44] and Hong Kong.[45] However, other jurisdictions have chosen to adopt significant changes when drafting the provision that creates the plea. Of particular interest are the Northern Territory of Australia and the State of Queensland. The first has dispensed with the bracketed causes[46] while the latter has replaced the concept of 'mental responsibility' with the need for a substantial impairment of 'his capacity to understand what he is doing, or his capacity to control his actions, or his capacity to know that he ought not to do the act or make the omission . . .'[47] Both these alternatives merit further consideration. It is

---

[40] R. v. *Criminal Cases Review Commission, ex p. Pearson* [1999] 3 All ER 498, 517. Cf. R. v. *Weekes* [1999] Crim LR 907 where the accused's decision not to permit diminished responsibility to be canvassed at his trial was significantly affected by his mental illness.

[41] R. v. *Acott* [1997] 1 All ER 706, 713, per Lord Steyn.

[42] New South Wales Crimes Act 1900, s. 23A (introduced in 1974).

[43] Crimes Act, s. 14.

[44] See K. L. Penn, M. Cheang, and C. K. Tsee, *Diminished Responsibility (with special reference to Singapore)* (Singapore, 1990).

[45] Hong Kong Homicide Ordinance, s. 3.

[46] Criminal Code of the Northern Territory, s. 37.

[47] Queensland Criminal Code, s. 304A (introduced in 1961).

clear that the bracketed causes are a source of difficulty. It is also clear from the debates on the Homicide Bill that the 'parenthesis was obviously meant to limit the scope of the defence to states of mind which were recognized as pathological by psychiatrists or neurologists.'[48] However as already indicated it is equally clear that the concepts contained in the parenthesis are not so recognized within medical practice. In this context it is interesting to note that at the Committee stage of the Bill in the House of Commons it was suggested that the parenthesis should be altered to read 'however arising' but this was rejected on the basis that it would not exclude 'murderers who were merely possessed of exceptionally bad tempers'.[49] But there must surely be an easier way to exclude 'the mere outburst of rage or jealousy'[50] from diminished responsibility than to have to resort to the aetiological complexities which currently make up the parenthesis in section 2. The solution enacted by the Northern Territory of Australia leaves 'abnormality of mind' without qualification. Might this not be a simple way to improve section 2?

The second alternative of note is the way in which Queensland has replaced the concept of 'mental responsibility' with an inquiry into the 'capacity' of the accused. In doing so it more clearly focuses the enquiry on the need for a 'substantial impairment of D.'s capacity, which then results in reduced culpability that is reflected in a reduction of liability from murder to manslaughter'.[51] However, there is a danger that such a sharpening of focus would narrow the scope of the diminished responsibility plea, for example, by excluding the mercy killer whose mental capacity is unlikely to be affected in any of the ways specified in the Queensland provision.

Two other jurisdictions which are worthy of comment are Scotland and the United States of America. Scotland is of interest as the jurisdiction which first developed the diminished responsibility plea through judge-made law and where to this day it remains unaffected by statute. In his detailed discussion of the development of the plea in Scotland Gordon describes the following definition of the doctrine by Lord Allness in *HM Advocate* v. *Savage*[52] as the '*locus classicus* on the subject':[53]

. . . there must be aberration or weakness of mind; that there must be some form of mental unsoundness; that there must be a state of mind which is bordering on, though not amounting to, insanity; that there must be a mind so affected that responsibility is diminished from full responsibility to partial responsibility—in other words the prisoner in question must only be partially accountable for his actions.[54]

---

[48] Walker, n. 10 above, 151.   [49] Ibid.
[50] See E. Griew, 'The Future of Diminished Responsibility' [1988] Crim LR 75, 78.
[51] A. Ashworth, *Principles of Criminal Law*, 3rd edn. (Oxford, 1999), 289.
[52] 1923 JC 49.
[53] G. H. Gordon, *Criminal Law of Scotland*, 1st edn. (Edinburgh, 1967) 346.
[54] 1923 JC 50.

It appears that Scots law by its reference to 'bordering . . . on insanity' has adopted a narrow approach and that 'diminished responsibility is interpreted more favourably to the accused in England'.[55] Further, although the decision in *Byrne*[56] refers on two occasions to 'the borderline of insanity or partially insane' it is now clear that within the context of section 2 'reference to insanity is best avoided altogether'.[57]

Another important aspect of Scots law is the question of whether diminished responsibility has been applied to offences other than murder. Historically there are certainly suggestions from some of the Victorian cases that the doctrine was not confined to murder.[58] However, it seems clear that these cases merely mitigated punishment rather than reducing the category of the offence and in 1963 Lord Clyde opined in *HM Advocate* v. *Cunningham* that 'diminished responsibility is a plea applicable to murder. It is not open in the case of a lesser crime such as culpable homicide . . .'[59] Despite this ruling it is interesting to note that in the recent Scottish case of *HM Advocate* v. *Blake*[60] the diminished responsibility plea operated to reduce the offence of attempted murder to one of 'assault to severe injury'.[61] Clearly, this is of particular significance as the diminished plea in this case did not merely act to mitigate punishment but also altered the category of the offence charged, unlike English law where it has been ruled that the plea is unavailable in attempted murder.[62]

Turning now to the United States of America, although there has been a great deal of confusion over terminology in that country it would appear that the phrase 'diminished capacity' has been used interchangeably to represent two different pleas. They have been described as the 'mens rea' and 'partial responsibility' variants.[63] The latter mirrors diminished responsibility while in the former the defendant argues that because of the abnormal mental condition from which he was suffering at the time of the alleged offence, he lacked mens rea. This mens rea variant is not an affirmative defence but rather goes to the definitional element of the offence represented by mens rea. Although the mens rea variant has been described as 'logically straightforward and unproblematic'[64] the courts in the United

[55] J. C. Smith, *Smith and Hogan: Criminal Law*, 9th edn. (London, 1999), 214.

[56] N. 24 above, 403. See also *Walton v. R.* [1978] 1 All ER 542, 546 where Lord Keith uses the phrase 'a state of mind bordering on but not amounting to insanity' which is virtually identical to that used by Lord Allness.

[57] Smith, n. 55 above, 214. See *Rose v. R.* [1961] AC 496 and *R. v. Seers* (1984) 79 Cr App R 261.   [58] Walker, n. 10 above, 144; Gordon, n. 53 above, 336.

[59] 1963 JC 80, 84.   [60] 1996 SLT 661.

[61] In Scots law this is a form of aggravated assault often dealt with by the High Court; see Gordon, n. 53 above, 761.

[62] See *R. v. Campbell* [1997] Crim LR 495.

[63] See S. J. Morse, 'Undiminished Confusion in Diminished Capacity' (1984) 75 J Cr L and Crim 1.

[64] S. J. Morse, 'Diminished Capacity' in S. Shute, S. Gardiner, and J. Horder (eds.), *Action and Value in the Criminal Law* (Oxford, 1993), 239, 243.

States have often rejected it on the mistaken assumption that it is a form of 'partial responsibility' which should only be implemented by the State legislature,[65] while those that do accept it either limit it to the crime of murder or to so-called 'specific intent' offences.[66] Both these limitations are clearly policy-based and make little sense, for once it is accepted that evidence of mental disorder can negate mens rea, then in principle it ought to be extended to all crimes. But in much the same way as has happened in relation to the role of self-induced intoxication, principle has been sacrificed to policy. Indeed self-induced intoxication in both England and the United States has been aptly described as 'a form of *mens rea* variant'[67] for in exactly the same way the courts have chosen to limit its availability to 'specific intent' offences. In English law this is exemplified by the decision of the House of Lords in *DPP* v. *Majewski*[68] which continues to be the subject of extensive criticism. However, what is important for the purposes of the present discussion is the status of the mens rea variant in English law. It seems clear that in the United States the relationship between the defence of insanity and the mens rea variant has been of considerable concern. This certainly seems to have been a major reason why the 'specific intent' restriction has been used in that it prevents the outright acquittal of dangerous mentally disordered offenders who lacked mens rea because of their abnormal mental states. Critics of this approach have argued that such cases will inevitably be caught by the insanity defence and will also be exceedingly rare in that mental disorder will hardly ever have the effect of negating mens rea.[69] Be that as it may, it is clear that in principle if a defendant lacks mens rea then he ought to receive an outright acquittal irrespective of how dangerous he is. It is not hard to see why social-defence considerations have been used in the United States to prevent this.[70]

To return to English law, it is interesting to note that the limb of the *M'Naghten* Rules which seems to be used most frequently is the 'wrongness' limb which does not go to the issue of mens rea. However, by way of contrast there remain cases where the 'nature and quality' limb is clearly satisfied.[71] An obvious example would be insane automatism where because of an epileptic seizure or an episode of sleepwalking the accused did not know what he was doing when he committed the alleged offence. Here are clear-cut examples of lack of mens rea. But rather than lead to an ordinary acquittal on that basis English law responds by categorizing such conditions as 'diseases of the mind' which in turn result in a special verdict

---

[65] Morse, n. 63 above, 7.
[66] See generally J. Dressler, *Understanding Criminal Law* (New York, NY, 1987), 319–28.
[67] Morse, n. 64 above, 242.   [68] [1976] 2 All ER 142.
[69] Morse, n. 64 above, 244.
[70] e.g. the United States Supreme Court in *Egelhoff* v. *Montana* (1996) 116 S. Ct. 2013 has recently upheld a Montana statute which prohibits defendants from using intoxication to negate mental states.   [71] See Mackay and Kearns, n. 14 above, 722.

of 'not guilty by reason of insanity'. Arguments to the contrary have received short shrift.

In that sense it does seem as if the mens rea variant of diminished capacity which has caused so much difficulty to the American courts has no independent doctrinal role to play in English law. However, this does not mean that mental disorder has no role to play in relation to mens rea other than as part of the insanity defence. It is clear from the Court of Appeal's decision in *R. v. Clarke*[72] that if the accused's mental condition falls short of establishing that it resulted in a 'defect of reason' then a mere failure adequately to use one's full reasoning powers through absent-mindedness or confusion of thought may be used to establish a lack of mens rea. In principle this approach ought to apply to all offences but difficulties have arisen in relation to the scope of *Caldwell*[73] recklessness, which have still to be fully resolved.[74] While such cases are likely to be rare they should not be overlooked and in this connection it seems more probable that with regard to murder the diminished responsibility plea will include some cases where mens rea may have been lacking. Although it has recently been confirmed that diminished responsibility 'only comes into play where all the ingredients of murder are established against the defendant',[75] this misses the point that the vast majority of diminished responsibility pleas never come before a jury. Doubtless in some of these cases if a lack of mens rea existed the case would otherwise have fallen within the insanity defence but because of the wider scope of section 2 we cannot be sure of this. In short, the issue of mens rea is being dispensed with as a sacrifice to the expediency of avoiding the mandatory penalty for murder.

Although the mens rea variant of diminished capacity has continued to be of some importance in the United States the 'partial responsibility' variant has been much less influential and has had a chequered history. This can be well illustrated by two examples. First, the Model Penal Code (MPC) in its final draft creates an 'extreme mental or emotional disturbance'[76] doctrine which is limited to murder and seems in essence to combine diminished responsibility and provocation within the same plea. That is of particular interest as English law continues to struggle with the relationship between these two doctrines when they are pleaded concurrently (see below). However, although a number of States have adopted this particular provision of the MPC most have omitted the word 'mental' and so have restricted its scope.[77] Secondly, in the absence of a statute-based 'partial

---

[72] [1972] 1 All ER 219.   [73] [1981] 1 All ER 961.
[74] Cf. *Reid* [1992] 3 All ER 673 with *Bell* [1984] 3 All ER 842.
[75] *R. v. Antoine* [1999] 3 WLR 1204, 1214 and cited with approval by the House of Lords at [2000] 2 All ER 212. See also the remarks of Lord Hutton, ibid., 220, concerning the two limbs of the *M'Naghten* Rules.   [76] S. 210.3(1)(b).
[77] See R. Singer, 'The Resurgence of Mens Rea: 1—Provocation, Emotional Disturbance, and the Model Penal Code' (1986) 27 Bos LR 243, 292.

responsibility' defence some courts developed such a plea through judicial creativity. The most notable example came from the Supreme Court of California which in a series of cases gave the mens rea of murder an extended definition so as to reduce the gravity of the offence in circumstances where the accused's mental state would not qualify for the insanity defence.[78] In short this was the creation of a 'partial responsibility' defence 'through the judicial back door'[79] of the mens rea variant and was finally abolished in 1982[80] and replaced by the more popular mens rea variant.

It is clear from this brief discussion of 'diminished capacity' in the United States that the doctrine of 'partial responsibility' has been the subject of considerable criticism. Accordingly, it is time to examine the source of this criticism in an attempt to decide whether diminished responsibility ought to be retained.

D. SHOULD DIMINISHED RESPONSIBILITY BE RETAINED?

Ever since the enactment of section 2 of the Homicide Act 1957 the diminished responsibility plea has been subject to intense criticism. Indeed the wording of section 2(1) has been described by Edward Griew as 'elliptical almost to the point of nonsense'.[81] Griew concludes:

The wording is altogether a disgrace. Parliament has clumsily packed together two ideas. They are respectively signalled by the words 'impaired . . . mental' on the one side of the word 'responsibility' and the words 'for his acts' on the other side. The result is that the word 'responsibility' does double duty; so perhaps does 'substantially'.[82]

By compacting these two ideas of 'reduced (impaired) capacity and of reduced (diminished) liability' Griew considers that we seem to reach an equation where 'the former presumably justifies the latter by virtue of a third idea—that of reduced culpability'.[83] Although this and other criticisms have taken a number of different forms they can be split into two broad categories, namely the theoretical and the practical.

As one might expect the theoretical criticisms go to the very heart of diminished responsibility. A fundamental problem concerns the notion that responsibility can somehow be 'diminished' by mental disorder; that there

---

[78] See S. J. Morse, 'Diminished Capacity: A Moral and Legal Conundrum' (1979) 2 Int J Law Psych 271; J. Lafond and M. Durham, *Back to the Asylum: The Future of Mental Health Law and Policy in the United States* (Oxford, 1992) 39–42.

[79] P. Arenella, 'The Diminished Capacity and Diminished Responsibility Defenses: Two Children of a Doomed Marriage' (1977) 77 Col LR 827, 831.

[80] Morse, n. 63 above, 27.

[81] E. Griew, 'Reducing Murder to Manslaughter: Whose Job?' (1986) 12 J Med E 18.

[82] Ibid., 19–20.

[83] E. Griew, 'The Future of Diminished Responsibility' [1988] Crim LR 75, 81–2.

is a sliding scale of responsibility. Prior to the creation of section 2 English law adhered to a bright-line division between the sane and the legally insane, with only the latter being completely excused. But this is no longer the case. Instead we now convict mentally abnormal killers of manslaughter and permit the judge to pass a reduced sentence if he considers this appropriate.[84] However, it has been argued 'that it is *never* appropriate to base mitigation of punishment on mental disorder'.[85] There are two related issues here. The first is that those who form the mens rea of murder and proceed to perform the actus reus are all equally deserving of conviction and full punishment for that offence irrespective of 'background, mental or emotional condition, or other factors often thought to necessitate mitigation'.[86] In Morse's opinion the usual analysis of responsibility which focuses on the problems experienced by a defendant who has intentionally killed is wrong-headed. Instead the focus should be redirected to an inquiry into 'How hard is it not to offend the law?' In answering this question Morse concludes, 'So little self-control and rationality are necessary to obey the law, that when all the elements of a prima facie case are present, the person should be held fully culpable.'[87] In short, mental abnormality, not amounting to legal insanity, should have no effect on criminal responsibility. However, as Morse concedes this claim that it is easy to avoid offending, even in the subject who is mentally abnormal, cannot be proved empirically and leads on to the second issue which is that in any event the types of problem experienced by such subjects cannot be measured. This is exemplified by the decision in *Byrne*[88] where the Court of Appeal made it clear that diminished responsibility applied to those who experienced difficulty or even inability to exercise will-power to control their physical acts but at the same time conceded that 'there is no scientific measurement of the degree of difficulty which an abnormal person finds in controlling his impulses'.[89] This appears to be as true today as it was when *Byrne* was decided and has led one critic to opine:

Since the occurrence of an irresistible impulse is generally admitted to be something which cannot be established by science, it is clearly not something on which expert testimony can speak with authority. But I would go further: the difficulty in telling the difference between unresisted and irresistible impulses is not a temporary and

---

[84] This is not always thought to be appropriate: a sentence of life imprisonment is by no means a rare outcome in diminished responsibility cases.

[85] Sparks, n. 9 above, 9 (emphasis in original).   [86] Morse, n. 63 above, 30.

[87] Ibid., 30–1. More recently Morse, n. 64, 267 states, 'I still maintain that view, but for those who have more stringent requirements for responsibility, partial responsibility is clearly rational and a sensible response to it can be devised.' The suggested response 'would be simply to offer the fact-finder the option of a new verdict, "guilty but partially responsible" (GPR). GPR is a general analogue to "diminished responsibility" that applies to all crimes . . . If proven, GPR triggers a legislatively mandated reduction in sentence.' (ibid., 271).

[88] [1960] 2 QB 386.   [89] Ibid., 403.

contingent one which progress in science may remove. The notion of irresistible impulse is an incoherent piece of nonsense.[90]

More recently Morse has concluded that 'So-called volitional or control problems are generally and notoriously difficult conceptually to define and practically to apply'.[91] While this is certainly the case we now need to evaluate the question of whether these difficulties are so insuperable that diminished responsibility should be regarded as unworkable. In this context a related point is the fact that some jurisdictions have a volitional limb as part of their insanity defence. The most influential example has probably been that of the MPC which provides:

A person is not responsible for criminal conduct if at the time of such conduct as a result of mental disease or defect *he lacks substantial capacity* either to appreciate the criminality (wrongfulness) of his conduct *or to conform his conduct to the requirements of the law.*[92]

The important point to note here is that this test does not require *total* incapacity but rather is based on the need for *substantial* impairment. In that respect it bears a striking similarity to section 2 of the Homicide Act. However, while the MPC provision permits such substantial impairment to act as a complete excuse, albeit one of mental irresponsibility, the English counterpart merely permits a similar degree of impairment to reduce responsibility. Indeed, it could be argued that the English approach is preferable, subject that is to accepting that volitional impairment ought properly to be taken into account in assessing the responsibility of mentally abnormal offenders. The argument is as follows. As already indicated it is clear that there is no reliable scientific test which can tell us that on any particular occasion an impulse experienced by a mentally abnormal person was one which he could not resist. If that is the case then it can only be sensible to ask in such cases whether the difficulty which the accused experienced in controlling his impulse 'was *substantially* greater than would be experienced in like circumstances by an ordinary person, not suffering from mental abnormality.'[93] In such cases then the enquiry focuses on the degree of difficulty experienced by the mentally abnormal person in controlling his impulses not to behave in a certain manner. What is not required is any evidence that the impulses in question could not be resisted. In that sense, contrary to the approach taken by the MPC, there is no reason to excuse the defendant, as there will never be evidence of total incapacity. This then forces us to return to the original problem of whether it is right partially to excuse such a person when we accept that he 'could have helped committing his crime, despite some mental

---

[90] A. Kenny, 'The Expert in Court' (1983) 99 LQR 197, 210.
[91] S. J. Morse, 'Fear of Danger, Flight from Culpability', (1998) 4 Pysch PPL 250, 262.
[92] S. 4.01(1) (emphasis added). For discussion see Mackay, n. 2 above, 111.
[93] Smith, n. 55 above, 213 (emphasis in original).

impairment.'[94] In short, if the impulse was not uncontrollable (and we can never know this) then why reduce the gravity of the offence and permit mitigation of punishment? There is no doubt that this does present a major problem. The simple solution put forward by Sir John Smith is that 'a man whose impulse is much more difficult to resist than that of an ordinary man bears a diminished degree of moral responsibility for his act.'[95] But this is untrue, other than in respect of the 'act' of murder and while there may be practical reasons for this restriction in England, particularly in relation to the mandatory penalty, this does nothing to justify the conclusion that it is not legitimate to punish in full those who kill intentionally but at the time are volitionally impaired to a substantial degree.

Let us briefly consider one important example, namely the sex offender. It is quite clear that English law does not permit abnormal sexual urges, no matter how strong they may have been, to act as a partial excuse in relation to sexual-abuse offences. Accordingly, let us reconsider the case of *Byrne* on the basis that the perverted sexual desires from which the defendant suffered led not to a killing but to serious sexual offences. Because Byrne had killed he had a partial excuse, but in the absence of a homicide he would have had no defence, irrespective of how substantial the volitional impairment may have been. In this context it is interesting to note that the United States Supreme Court has recently used volitional control not as a vehicle to excuse but rather as a means to ensure the involuntary civil commitment of sex offenders who have served their sentences but find it 'difficult, if not impossible to control [their] dangerous behavior.'[96] In this way the Supreme Court has sanctioned the continued civil detention of dangerous sex offenders who would otherwise have to be released having served their determinate prison sentences. The important issue here is the way in which the court has used what Morse describes as 'nonresponsible dangerousness'[97] not as a means of assessing culpability but rather as a way of securing preventive detention. While English law has not yet followed this approach, the spectre of preventive detention is now present in the form of the Government's recent consultation paper on how to deal with 'dangerous severely personality disordered offenders'.[98]

It is clear from the discussion above that the question whether diminished responsibility ought to be retained has been the subject of heated debate. However, there is a related doctrine of 'partial responsibility' that has a long pedigree which may help us to explore the matter further. It is the doctrine of provocation which, like diminished responsibility, operates

[94] Sparks, n. 9 above, 16, who adds that in such cases 'there would surely be nothing unfair in punishing him in the normal way'.   [95] Smith, n. 55 above, 214.
[96] *Kansas* v. *Hendricks* (1997) 138 L Ed 2d 501, 513.
[97] Morse, n. 91 above, 265.
[98] See *Managing Dangerous People with Severe Personality Disorder: Proposals for Policy Development* (1999) (Home Office and Dept. of Health Consultation Paper).

only to reduce murder to manslaughter. The essence of the plea is that the accused was provoked to such an extent that he lost his self-control and killed. Although the level of emotional disturbance required to establish a loss of self-control remains obscure it is clear that, no matter how extreme the loss of self-control may have been, the provocation which prompted it will never act as a complete excuse. It seems to follow that as with diminished responsibility, provocation 'partially excuses' because the accused found it very difficult to control himself, not because he was *incapable* of so doing. According to Morse this means that provocation just like diminished responsibility should be abolished because 'As virtually every human being knows because we have all been enraged, it is easy not to kill, even when one is enraged.'[99] Because it is easy not to break the law 'most intentional killers deserve little sympathy'.[100] Once again however this claim cannot be empirically tested. Certainly, most of us know what it is to be enraged but it is likely that very few of us have been placed in a situation which could lead to the person who is the subject of or has instilled that rage being killed. It is once more the law's recognition that there are circumstances where the degree of difficulty in controlling one's behaviour may be so great that a 'partial excuse' is warranted. However, the differences surrounding these circumstances, as between provocation and diminished responsibility, deserve further consideration.

One of the fundamental distinctions between provocation and diminished responsibility is that while the former requires a reasonable man to have lost his self-control in similar circumstances, the latter focuses on a mentally abnormal defendant which renders any objective enquiry into loss of self-control obsolete. This has led some commentators to argue that while provocation is a 'partial excuse', diminished responsibility should be classified as a 'partial exemption' from responsibility. As Horder puts it:

Partial or complete *exemption* from liability (insanity) or from labelling as a murderer (diminished responsibility), not excuses, are what are granted to such defendants. Those who act whilst insane or while suffering from diminished responsibility are 'moral objects', persons to whom moral concern and humane treatment are due. Such people are not, though, (full) moral agents in respect of their actions: they are not persons whose action(s) can be adequately guided by moral criteria by which they stand to be judged.[101]

The difficulty with this view is that many pleas of diminished responsibility result in punishment rather than 'humane treatment' and in any event the idea of a *partial exemption* seems contradictory in the sense that, while one may be held partially responsible for an act, surely one is either totally exempt

---

[99] Morse, n. 63 above, 34.   [100] Ibid.
[101] J. Horder, 'Between Provocation and Diminished Responsibility' (1999) King's College LJ (emphasis in original).

from punishment or not. In short, it does not seem logical to speak of different levels of exemption.

It has further been suggested that while the degree of difficulty which the accused had in controlling his behaviour is impossible to measure in cases of mental disorder, this is not true of the loss-of-self-control requirement in provocation. It is here that the reasonable man test saves the day in the sense that the types of extreme circumstances which make self-control difficult are viewed as 'objective situations which are known, through common experience, to make men more or less violently angry.'[102] Two points can be made about this distinction. Firstly, as a measurement of the degree of difficulty which a person experienced in failing to control himself the objective test is of very limited help. Common experience is of very little assistance here as we simply do not know what it is like to be placed in the types of extreme circumstances which lead to a killing. This leads on to the second point which is that the law on provocation, although it continues to pay lip service to the objective requirement, has begun to dilute it by endowing the reasonable person with the personal characteristics of the accused. In so doing the law seems to be moving away from the notion that there are elements of 'partial justification' in provocation in favour of a rationale which although predominantly one of 'partial excuse'[103] also has elements of 'partial responsibility'.[104] With this in mind it is now time to consider this point more fully in the light of recent developments relating to the interrelationship between provocation and diminished responsibility.

E. COMBINING DIMINISHED RESPONSIBILITY AND PROVOCATION

As already mentioned it might have been thought that provocation and diminished responsibility were merely alternative methods of reducing murder to manslaughter. In a sense they seem to have little in common with each focusing on different requirements. For while provocation requires that loss of self-control be tested in the light of a reasonable person's response to extreme circumstances, by way of contrast diminished responsibility is premised on the need for the accused to be mentally abnormal. In that sense the two seem poles apart. However, despite the fact that a verdict on the basis of both grounds has been described as 'surely illogical'[105] it has become clear that the two pleas are not mutually exclusive. Indeed, this was made clear not long after the creation of diminished responsibility when in 1958 Lord Goddard said:

[102] Sparks, n. 9 above, 19.
[103] For discussion see J. Dressler, 'Provocation: Partial justification or Partial Excuse?' (1988) 51 MLR 467.   [104] See Horder, n. 101 above, 143.
[105] T. Morris and L. Blom-Cooper, *A Calendar of Murder* (London, 1964), 298, n. 4.

It may happen that on an indictment for murder the defence may ask for a verdict of manslaughter on the ground of diminished responsibility and also on some other ground such as provocation. If the jury returns a verdict of manslaughter, the judge may and generally should ask them whether their verdict is based on diminished responsibility or on the other ground *or both*.[106]

More recently Beldam LJ clearly endorsed this approach in *R. v. Thornton* when he remarked: 'There is no doubt that the two defences are not incompatible where the evidence which is given enables them to be combined.'[107] It has certainly become clear that combining the two pleas in this manner is not a rare defence strategy and is willingly accepted by juries in some cases. For example, an analysis of fourteen first-instance cases where the two pleas had been run concurrently revealed some common themes. Firstly, as might be expected, there was psychiatric evidence in all the cases supporting diminished responsibility. Secondly, in the majority of the cases this evidence was couched in such a way that it also referred to provocation or some similar term. Thirdly, in this way psychiatric testimony which would not normally be permitted to assist a jury[108] in its deliberations was admitted thus making it 'virtually impossible to disentangle the issues of loss of self-control, abnormality of mind and substantial impairment of mental responsibility'.[109] Indeed, the fact that the jury will be unable to keep these issues separate was conceded by Beldam LJ in *Thornton* when he said:

. . . having regard to the passages from the summing up both on provocation and diminished responsibility, . . . we would find it surprising if the jury approached the issues keeping them entirely separate. We think that, as in all such cases, the concepts of loss of self-control, abnormality of mind and substantial impairment of responsibility would have been regarded by the jury as interrelated, blending into one another, but distinguished by the essential feature that provocation produces a sudden and impulsive reaction leading to loss of control whereas impairment of mental responsibility is due to the effect of the long period of stress upon a disordered personality.[110]

It is likely that this strategy of combining the two pleas in this way has not only permitted juries to be more flexible in their decision-making by permitting them to adopt a lenient approach towards the requirements of each plea, but also that this leniency has been assisted by recent developments relating to the objective test in provocation. These developments have concerned the following crucial question. If at the time the accused was provoked to kill there is evidence that he was suffering from a mental abnormality which may have reduced his capacity for self-control, should

---

[106] *R. v. Matheson* [1958] 2 All ER 87 (emphasis added).
[107] [1992] 1 All ER 306, 315.   [108] See *R. v. Turner* [1975] 1 QB 834.
[109] R. D. Mackay, 'Pleading Provocation and Diminished Responsibility Together' [1988] Crim LR 411, 421.   [110] N. 107 above, 316.

that abnormality be classed as a 'characteristic' for the purposes of the objective test in provocation? Until recently the answer seemed to be in the negative, as was made clear by the majority decision of the Privy Council in *Luc Thiet-Thuan* v. *R.*,[111] where it was decided that the defendant's brain damage which made it difficult for him to control his impulses should not form part of the jury's assessment of whether the provocation was enough to make a reasonable man do as the defendant did. In his judgment Lord Goff expressed the concern that 'To accept the appellant's submission would . . . be to incorporate the concept of diminished responsibility indirectly into the law of provocation'.[112] Clearly, therefore, his Lordship wished to keep provocation and diminished responsibility separate by ensuring that mental conditions which might affect the defendant's level of self-control fall only within the province of the latter. However this seems to ignore the fact that when the accused relies on both defences, the cases already referred to (all bar one of which were litigated even before the decision of the House of Lords in *DPP* v. *Camplin*[113]) indicate that it was not possible to maintain a clear distinction between the two pleas. Further, the Court of Appeal had made it clear in a number of cases that it was not prepared to follow the decision in *Luc Thiet-Thuan* but preferred its own line of authority, which is clearly in favour of relaxing the objective requirement in provocation to take account of the type of mental condition which was rejected by Lord Goff as a 'characteristic'. These first instance cases culminated in *R.* v. *Smith (Morgan James)*[114] where there was medical evidence that the accused was suffering from severe depression which made him likely to have been disinhibited and more prone to injure his victim. In deciding that the proper approach was for the jury to be directed to take account of this mental state in assessing the objective requirement, the Court made reference to the fact that the accused had also pleaded diminished responsibility but that the jury had rejected it, saying:

We have not overlooked the fact that by their verdict the jury rejected the defence of diminished responsibility and must therefore have not been satisfied to the requisite standard of the [medical] evidence. On this issue, however, the onus of proof was on the appellant. On the issue of provocation it was for the Crown to satisfy the jury that the appellant had not been provoked.[115]

This draws attention to what Lord Goff described in *Luc Thiet-Thuan* as the following 'extraordinary result', namely that having failed to establish diminished responsibility the accused 'might nevertheless be able to succeed on the defence of provocation . . . on the basis that, on precisely the same evidence, the prosecution had failed to negative, on the criminal burden, that he was suffering from a mental infirmity affecting his self-control which must be attributed to the reasonable man for the purposes of the

---

[111] [1996] 2 All ER 1033.   [112] Ibid., 1046.   [113] [1978] 2 All ER 168.
[114] [1998] 4 All ER 387.   [115] Ibid., 399.

objective test.'[116] However, it is not merely the inconsistency in relation to burden of proof which gives rise to this anomaly. There is also the problem that diminished responsibility, unlike provocation, is labelled as 'an optional defence'.[117] Why is this so? It is difficult to find a coherent answer. The explanation cannot be traced merely to the fact that the burden of proving the former is placed upon the accused, as this would also make the defence of insanity optional, which is not the case.[118] All this approach does is to ensure the frequency of appeals on the basis of fresh evidence supporting diminished responsibility after the accused has been convicted of murder.[119]

It is clear from the above discussion that the line of authority supported by the Court of Appeal in *Smith* favours an approach which gives the defence every incentive to combine the two pleas. That this is so has now been confirmed by the House of Lords which recently upheld the Court of Appeal's decision in R v Smith [2000] All ER (D) 1077 by making it clear that the accused's depression ought to have been considered by the jury in its assessment of the objective test in provocation. In the course of his judgment Lord Slynn emphasized that he did not consider that the 'the existence of section 2 defining the partial defence of diminished responsibility prevents this conclusion', while Lord Hoffman opined that 'the possibility of overlap [between these two defences] . . . seems to follow inevitably from consigning the whole of the objective element in provocation to the jury'. In the light of this important decision it seems likely that the law has now advanced to a position where it can be argued that provocation and diminished responsibility are slowly collapsing or merging into one another in the sense that the clear-cut distinction which formerly existed between the two has started to disappear. Might it not be better to accept this coalescence fully in favour of a 'partial responsibility' plea, which encompasses both?[120]

F. THE QUESTION OF REFORM

It is clear from the above discussion that the role which mental disorder plays as a defence within the law of homicide is unsatisfactory. If the current law is to be improved then the following problems need to be confronted. Firstly, the plea of diminished responsibility itself is obscurely drafted which has led to repeated calls for its reform. While a rewording of section 2 might help, it would not go to the root of the problem which is

---

[116] N. 111 above, 1046.   [117] See *Campbell*, n. 39 above, 260.

[118] See *R. v. Dickie* [1984] 3 All ER 173, 178.

[119] See *Criminal Cases Review Commission, ex p. Pearson*, n. 40 above.

[120] For criticism that such an approach fails to reflect 'an ethical distinction between a partial excuse for wrongdoing (provocation) and a partial denial of responsibility (diminished responsibility)' see Horder, n. 101 above, 143.

that if the mental condition of a mentally abnormal killer can be taken into account in a murder case then why not in relation to other offences?

Secondly, and even more fundamentally, why should all such mentally abnormal killers be open to conviction for manslaughter and possible punishment? Should the law not permit some of them to have the opportunity of being excused on the basis of mental irresponsibility? This closing section will try to confront some of these important issues as well as suggesting possible reform measures.

The wording used in section 2 of the Homicide Act has few defenders and has been the subject of constant criticism. Over the years a number of reformulations have been proposed.[121] As early as 1975 the Butler Report suggested that a person should not be convicted of murder if the mental disorder from which he suffered 'was such as to be an extenuating circumstance, which ought to reduce the offence to manslaughter.'[122] The Criminal Law Revision Committee, while in broad agreement with the Butler proposal, considered it to be too lax and preferred a formula which required that 'the mental disorder was such as to be a substantial enough reason to reduce the offence to manslaughter.'[123] It is this version which found its way into the Criminal Code Bill[124] but with a technical preference for the term 'mental abnormality' rather than 'mental disorder' (although both are defined according to section 1(2) of the Mental Health Act 1983 as requiring 'mental illness, arrested or incomplete development of mind, psychopathic disorder, and any other disorder or disability of mind').

There seems little doubt that the abolition of the term 'abnormality of mind' together with the words in parenthesis in section 2 would go some way to improving the plea of diminished responsibility in so far as it would enable psychiatrists to concentrate upon an issue which is more clearly within their professional competence. At the same time, however, the phrase 'any other disorder or disability of mind' might or might not have the potential of widening the types of conditions which may be capable of supporting a diminished responsibility plea.[125] Indeed, the Criminal Law Revision Committee was concerned to ensure that their revised definition should not exclude 'some offenders who are now regarded as falling within

---

[121] Walker, n. 17 above, 192, has recently suggested replacing 'abnormality of mind' with 'an abnormal state of mind' and adding 'ill treatment' to the parenthesis. In his view this would 'demedicalise' the plea and extend it to battered women. However, while the first suggestion has much to commend it, the second seems unlikely to lead to demedicalization.

[122] Butler Report, n. 35 above, para. 19.17.

[123] Criminal Law Revision Committee, 14th Report, *Offences Against the Person* (1980) (Cmnd. 7844), para. 93.

[124] See Law Commission, *A Criminal Code for England and Wales* (Law Com. no. 177) (1989), Draft Criminal Code Bill 1989, cl. 56(1).

[125] See Griew, n. 83 above, 79, 80. This is the reason why the phrase 'except intoxication' has been inserted at the end of the definition of 'mental abnormality' in cl. 56(1) of the Draft Code so as to ensure that the transitory effects of drink or drugs would not fall within 'any other disorder of mind'.

section 2.'[126] Their particular worries concerned the depressed mercy killer 'or a morbidly jealous person who kills his or her spouse',[127] which is precisely the type of case where the 'flexibility' of section 2 might be said to work best. However, by altering the wording in the manner proposed there is the danger that psychiatrists will not be able to bring these and other conditions such as severe stress within the definition of 'mental disorder'. This led Griew to warn that replacing section 2 in the manner suggested 'might not work as well as intended; and particularly that its honesty and clarity could be a less effective device for evading the mandatory life sentence than the present provision has proved to be.'[128] In response it can of course be argued that to have a narrower and more clearly defined diminished plea would be no bad thing given that the current obscurity of section 2 has led to it being applied too widely and without consistency. A particular problem in this connection is that of the 'mercy killer' referred to above. Such cases when they come within section 2 do so by means of a benign conspiracy between psychiatrists and trial judges which involves stretching the medical evidence in order to ensure that deserving cases do not attract a murder conviction.[129]

Although this is not the place for a full rehearsal of the arguments about whether the law should be altered to permit a new offence or partial defence of 'mercy killing', it is clear that many consider that merely to allow mercy killing to be 'swept under the carpet'[130] by manipulating the plea of diminished responsibility is unacceptable. Certainly such cases are by no means rare. For example, Home Office figures reveal that between 1982 and 1991 there were twenty-two homicides described as 'mercy killings' with only a single murder verdict being returned.[131] One wonders whether *Cocker*,[132] where the accused resorted to the plea of provocation having been driven to kill his incurably ill wife, accounts for this single case of murder. In dismissing his appeal against his murder conviction the Court of Appeal made it clear that the accused's behaviour was the opposite of provocation.[133] Had there been some psychiatric evidence of depression on the part of the accused then the case might have been decided differently, which in turn supports the view that the current outcome of diminished responsibility 'mercy killing' cases is a lottery without any real legal basis. Despite this criticism the Select Committee of the House of Lords on Medical Ethics rejected any change in the law on the basis that 'mercy killing' could not be

---

[126] Criminal Law Revision Committee, n. 123 above, para. 92.   [127] Ibid.
[128] Griew, n. 83 above, 87.   [129] See Mackay, n. 2 above, 186.
[130] Ashworth, n. 51 above, 296.
[131] These figures taken from House of Lords, *Report of the Select Committee on Medical Ethics* (HL Paper 21–1 of Session 1993–4), para. 128, cited by Ashworth, n. 51 above, 295 n. 135. They do not include cases where the CPS decided not to prosecute.
[132] [1989] Crim LR 740.
[133] See P. R. Taylor, 'Provocation and Mercy Killing' [1991] Crim LR 111.

adequately defined 'since it would involve determining precisely what constituted a compassionate motive'[134] and that in any event the current law was sufficiently flexible to deal with the problem. Further, there seems little doubt that with the present Government's recent emphatic rejection of euthanasia together with its reluctance to promote a legislative framework for 'living wills'[135] there is no real prospect of any change in the law in relation to 'mercy killing'. In the light of this intransigence might it not be better then to craft a plea of diminished responsibility which can more readily accommodate such homicides? In this connection Griew's warning remains a powerful one when considering the reformulation suggested by the Criminal Law Revision Committee. Despite this one of the merits of this reformulation could be that the role of the jury would be revitalized. It will be recalled that currently most pleas under section 2 are accepted by the prosecution and do not involve any jury deliberations. However, by way of contrast it must surely be the case that psychiatric opinion would not be permitted on the issue of whether the accused's mental disorder 'was a substantial enough reason to reduce the offence to manslaughter' as this will be a matter for the Court. This then makes the reformulation very different from the current section 2, in the sense that at present psychiatrists are frequently invited to give testimony on the issue of 'substantial impairment of mental responsibility' thus encouraging 'role confusion'[136] between fact finder and expert witness. In short, the medical evidence goes to the ultimate issue to be decided—namely should 'liability be "diminished" to the level of manslaughter.'[137]—which is positively encouraged by section 2. However, this would no longer be the case under the newly proposed provision, which would only permit medical testimony to be descriptive.

With this assistance removed the jury would be required to make a finding of murder or manslaughter without the reassurance of having had experts inform them that a finding of diminished responsibility is appropriate. It is the uncertainty of how juries might respond to this new-found freedom which is perplexing enough to make some question the wisdom of the Criminal Code Bill's reformulation.[138] Again, however, it can be argued that a return to giving juries their proper role in deciding the level of the accused's responsibility for the killing is long overdue.

A much more radical approach to reform would be to abolish the plea of diminished responsibility. Indeed, this was the first-choice solution of the Butler Report but only on condition that the mandatory life sentence for murder be likewise abolished.[139] On that basis it was suggested that those currently convicted under section 2 could be subject to a 'verdict of murder

---

[134] House of Lords, n. 131 above, para. 260.
[135] See Dept. of Health, *Making Decisions* (1999) (Cm. 4655), para. 19, for the Government's proposals for making decisions on behalf of mentally incapacitated adults.
[136] Griew, n. 83 above, 85.   [137] Ibid., 86.   [138] Ibid.
[139] Butler Report, n. 35 above, paras. 19.14–16.

(or manslaughter) by reason of extenuating circumstances, the extenuation being left undefined by law.'[140] The result would be that the judge would have the same flexible sentencing powers as are presently available in cases of diminished responsibility. More recently the Select Committee of the House of Lords on Murder and Life Imprisonment[141] likewise recommended abolition of the mandatory penalty.[142] However, the Committee endorsed the view of the Criminal Law Revision Committee[143] that both diminished responsibility and provocation 'should be retained whether or not the sentence for murder were to become discretionary.'[144] This has also been the approach taken by those jurisdictions which have actually rid their law of the mandatory penalty. For example that is the current position in both New South Wales[145] and the State of Victoria.[146] Accordingly, there seems to be a reluctance to abolish these doctrines, irrespective of the mandatory penalty, as they mark out a crucial distinction between those who are 'fully' as opposed to 'partially' responsible. This in turn supports the view that it is simply wrong for the law not to take cognizance of extreme emotional and mental disturbances.[147] But if that is the case then why continue to restrict their application to the law of murder? In principle there seems no good reason for this. Indeed, the Criminal Law Revision Committee recommended that both pleas should be extended to attempted murder; the effect of which should be a conviction for attempted manslaughter.[148] It was also noted above that Scots law has already achieved a similar result in respect of attempted murder. But why stop there? This Chapter is concerned with the law of murder and a detailed analysis of this question is therefore out of place here. Suffice it to say that extending diminished responsibility to attempted murder but not to, for example, wounding with intent under section 18 of the Offences Against the Person Act 1861 is highly illogical.[149] Apart from practical considerations, particularly relating to increasing the complexity of the trial process, there seems no good reason why partial excuse pleas should not apply to all offences.[150]

[140] Ibid., para. 19.16.   [141] N. 34 above.
[142] Ibid., vol. 1, paras. 81–3. See also House of Lords, n. 131 above, para. 261, strongly endorsing this recommendation.
[143] N. 123 above, para. 76.   [144] N. 34 above, para. 83.
[145] See Crimes Act (NSW), ss. 19A, 442, which provide a life sentence as a maximum, with the judge having power to pass a lesser sentence.
[146] See Crimes Act 1958 (Vic.), as amended by Crimes (Amendment) Act 1986 (Vic.), s. 3.
[147] See J. Dressler, 'Reaffirming the Moral Legitimacy of the Doctrine of Diminished Capacity: A Brief Reply to Professor Morse' (1984) 75 J Cr L and Crim 953.
[148] N. 123 above, para. 98.
[149] But not without precedent as can be seen from the law on duress which has developed in the opposite manner. Thus the defence is not available to a charge of murder or attempted murder; see *R. v. Howe* [1987] 1 All ER 771; *R. v. Gotts* [1992] 1 All ER 832. However, the policy reasons for restricting duress in this way are surely different from those which confine provocation and diminished responsibility to murder charges.
[150] For brief discussion see Mackay, n. 2 above, 206.

Another major problem with the current scope of diminished responsibility is the way it has eclipsed the defence of insanity, as has already been referred to above. As a result there seems little doubt that potentially irresponsible defendants continue to be advised by their lawyers to plead guilty to manslaughter. Empirical support for this supposition can be found in Dell's research which found fifteen cases where, despite medical evidence of legal insanity, manslaughter convictions on the grounds of diminished responsibility were recorded.[151] An obvious way to avoid this would be to remove punitive disposals for section 2 manslaughter and to permit only those disposals which are already available for the insanity defence. However, this seems unacceptable in view of the fact that the accused has been convicted of manslaughter and will often have fully recovered by the time of the trial. In short, punitive disposals are not only commonplace in diminished responsibility but are also viewed as entirely appropriate. It is rather the fact that the boundaries between those cases where conviction and punishment are appropriate and those where it is not are obscured by the lack of a workable defence of insanity, and also by the mandatory disposal consequences which flow from it. A simple procedural solution would be to abolish the mandatory disposal which flows from an insanity finding in murder cases since, as indicated above, all this does is to discourage the use of the insanity defence in homicide cases. However, this would only be a partial solution for there is no guarantee that defendants would opt for the insanity defence even if it was made more attractive in terms of disposal flexibility.

A second procedural shift might help. If there is evidence that the accused was legally insane surely this should be considered first, whether or not it is raised by the accused[152] or the prosecution?[153] After all a finding of what would otherwise be murder is a prerequisite to a diminished responsibility verdict and such a finding cannot be made if the accused was insane at the time of the alleged offence. In short, the pleas of insanity and diminished responsibility are separate and distinct. As such juries should be told that if there is evidence that supports insanity they should consider this defence first, and only after rejecting it should they go on to consider the latter. They should be instructed to consider the application of each of the two defences sequentially and independently. In this way the jury will be given the opportunity to consider excusing the defendant first before proceeding to the issue of a partial excuse. In principle this approach must

---

[151] Dell, n. 26 above, 30.
[152] It is submitted that this is one of those 'exceptional' cases where the judge 'of his own volition' has the power to raise the issue of insanity and leave it to the jury; see *Dickie*, n. 118 above, 178.
[153] Criminal Procedure (Insanity) Act 1964, s. 6, permits the prosecution to 'adduce or elicit evidence' of insanity in reply to the accused's plea of diminished responsibility. However, the use of this section appears to be very rare (see my letter at [1992] Crim LR 751) and in any event does not answer the point raised in the text.

be right as it is surely unacceptable to allow potentially irresponsible defendants to continue to plead guilty to manslaughter.

However, the above solution is in itself inadequate while the law continues to adhere to an insanity defence which is so narrow, outmoded, and deeply stigmatic. Although this is not the place for a detailed analysis of the need for reform of the *M'Naghten* Rules or of what form this should take, nevertheless some brief comment seems justified. Clearly, if the jury is to be given the opportunity to consider completely excusing the defendant charged with murder before going on to consider diminished responsibility then any revised insanity defence must apply to other offences. Accordingly, any such reform cannot be limited to the law of homicide. An adapted radical alternative I have proposed elsewhere is as follows:

A defendant will be found not guilty on account of an aberration of normal mental functioning present at the time of the commission of the offence if, at that time, his mental functioning was so aberrant and affected his criminal behaviour to such a clear and convincing degree that he ought to be acquitted.[154]

This test would replace the *M'Naghten* Rules. However, in murder cases the plea of diminished responsibility would continue to be available but in the following form:

A defendant who would otherwise be guilty of murder is not guilty of murder if, at the time of the commission of the alleged offence, his mental functioning was so aberrant and affected his criminal behaviour to such a substantial degree that the offence ought to be reduced to one of manslaughter.

This provision would replace section 2 of the Homicide Act. Finally, in much the same way that the present defence of insanity must always come before a jury,[155] these new provisions would likewise be for a jury to decide.[156] It would no longer be possible for the prosecution to accept a guilty to manslaughter plea on the basis of 'abnormal mental functioning' thereby usurping the function of the jury and bypassing the possibility of an 'insanity' acquittal.

[154] Mackay, n. 2 above, 141.
[155] See *R. v. Maidstone Crown Court, ex p. Harrow LBC* [1999] 3 All ER 542.
[156] A possible objection to this framework is that the two provisions are so similar that juries will be unable to distinguish and apply them on a practical level. If this is considered to be so I would have no objection to adopting my alternative revised 'insanity' defence which is: 'A defendant will be found not guilty on account of an aberration of normal mental functioning present at the time of the commission of the alleged offence if, at that time, his mental functioning was so aberrant that he failed to appreciate either what he was doing or that it was wrong according to the standards of ordinary, reasonable people and as a result ought to be acquitted.' See Mackay, n. 2 above, 141.

4

Provocation: The Case for Abolition

CELIA WELLS[*]

I argue in this Chapter that, even if we could agree on the basis for a defence of provocation, and even if it were internally successful in achieving whatever its aims might be, the secondary consequences will remain unacceptable. In short, the provocation defence is bound to encourage and exaggerate a view of human behaviour which is sexist, homophobic, and racist.

The defence of provocation has an emotional, almost instinctive, appeal and fascination which calls into question many of the underlying assumptions in traditional accounts of criminal law. One of two partial defences to murder,[1] provocation is relatively well established in the common law while the second, diminished responsibility, is a much younger creature of law's imagination. In each case the effect of a successful plea is to reduce that which would otherwise be murder to manslaughter, and together they comprise the category of so-called voluntary manslaughter. Right from the start there is something a little peculiar in this. The essence of both provocation and diminished responsibility is a reduction in culpability, yet we persist in naming them 'voluntary'.[2] Murder is the only offence to which there are partial defences and the traditional explanation of their existence is as much to do with restrictions on sentencing for murder as with anything else.[3] Since the abolition of capital punishment the felt need for a symbolic

[*] I am grateful to Justine Davidge who undertook the research assistance for this Chapter, funded by the Cardiff Law School Research Committee; to Griffith, Sydney and Western Australia Universities whose libraries I raided in the summer of 1999; and to Fiona Donson and Derek Morgan for their helpful thoughts. All the errors are mine.
[1] Or three if killing in pursuance of a suicide pact is included.
[2] This appears to be a remnant from a distinction between voluntary and involuntary homicide—involuntary being 'as by mishap or misadventure (which is no felony)' (Stephen, *A History of the Criminal Law of England*, vol. III (London, 1883), ch. XXVI, 49). Commenting on Hale's later use of the terms 'voluntary' and 'involuntary', Stephen, ibid., acerbically comments: 'It is difficult to see what [he] meant by the word voluntary, which lies at the root of the whole system.'
[3] Though the Griffith Code which survives in Queensland and Western Australia includes provocation as a general defence.

condemnatory punishment and one which is largely beyond the discretion of the trial judge has taken the form of mandatory life imprisonment.

It is particularly difficult to approach provocation without running into all sorts of other questions about the structure of homicide, including the equivocal role that motive, emotion, and personal circumstances have in theories of culpability and punishment. Releasing the grip of the mandatory penalty is not by any means the whole story; provocation occupies its own iconic role in making a concession to 'human frailty', as it is traditionally termed, but is perhaps better described as 'emotional intelligence', in the doctrinal strictures of criminal law.[4] The mens rea of murder has been a major preoccupation for many commentators since the Homicide Act of 1957,[5] and although the focus of the debate inevitably ebbs and flows, two themes are constant: what does intention connote and what has to be intended? The role of provocation or any similar defence would depend on the resolution of some of those persistent questions. The narrower the reach of murder, the less the need for sweep-up defences. The ambivalence about provocation and its uncertain place in criminal doctrine is reflected in the large number of provocation appeals in England, Australia, and Canada during the last ten years.[6]

The relationship between provocation and other defences such as diminished responsibility, or the full defence of self-defence, or the presently unavailable defences of duress and necessity, raises practical as well as conceptual knots for all concerned. What we are ultimately bothered about is the extent to which individual characteristics and circumstances affect culpability. We are more concerned about this in homicide because in its worst forms it is the worst kind of offence. But the problem is that in some other forms, it is understandable and even forgivable. I argue in this Chapter that boldness is called for. We should cut our ties with a defence rooted in a criminal justice system we would hardly now recognize, in an era where punishment was (at least in its officially pronounced forms) crude and vengeful, and in a social, economic, and political world informed by entirely different values. The result is a defence that constrains and constructs homicides into distortions of people's lives, adversely affecting victims' families, defendants, and more generally lending legitimacy to superficial explanations of violence.[7]

The first section of the Chapter consists of a brief outline of provocation as currently understood, while in the second I look at the development of provocation within a broader set of ideas about violence, and our belated

---

[4] P. Rush, *Criminal Law* (Chatswood, NSW, 1997), 325.

[5] Wilson's account of the pre-1957 categories and their fate in the hands of subsequent interpretation of the Homicide Act is very useful; see W. Wilson, *Criminal Law: Doctrine and Theory* (London, 1998), 368 et seq.

[6] In most Australian states the judge retains the power (removed in England by the 1957 Act) to withdraw the issue from the jury.

[7] A similar conclusion is reached by M. Goode, 'The Abolition of Provocation' in S. Yeo, *Partial Excuses to Murder* (Melbourne, 1991), 37.

recognition of the role of gender and race in the ordering of our social institutions. I then take three recent Australian High Court cases to illustrate my argument that provocation continually confronts our anxieties and preoccupations but is never able to resolve them. In the fourth section I discuss the role of evidence in reproducing dominant notions of gender, race, and sexuality, before placing provocation in the context of criminal law generally, and homicide law in particular, in the concluding part.

A. A Brief History in Two-and-a-half Paragraphs

Although there are some differences in its formulation, throughout the common-law jurisdictions the common elements of the provocation defence are three requirements: that there was some provocative conduct; that the defendant as a result lost her self-control; and that an ordinary person (possibly with some personal characteristics of D.) might have killed in response to such conduct.[8] An excuse based on loss of self-control seems to imply an underlying aggression in all of us which is capable of release under certain circumstances. Of course, speaking of 'all of us' is inappropriate given the gendered history and present of law generally, and of criminal law and provocation especially.[9] For criminal law to flirt at the bar of determinism is uncharacteristic, which gives rise to the tension between the essentially individualized notion of loss of self-control and its mediation through the standard of the reasonable man.[10]

It seems generally accepted that provocation developed from the defence of chance-medley or sudden quarrels.[11] It rested, Stephen argued, on the fiction of implied malice. Malice was implied when a man suddenly killed another without provocation. However, the more specific origins of provocation, Horder suggests, lie in a distinct sub-branch which developed in parallel with sudden quarrels. Concepts of outrage and honour are quite distinct from the excuse of loss of self-control that dominates the modern-day provocation doctrine. At this early stage, provocation was less a generic class and more a series of recognized types of anger-based killings which attracted the excusing eye of the law. A grossly insulting assault; an attack upon a kinsman or friend; the sight of an Englishman unlawfully deprived of his liberty; and seeing a man in the act of adultery with one's wife: all came to be recognized as excused killings.[12] It does not require a rabid feminist to spot the gendered tenor of these examples.

---

[8] Ireland has abandoned the objective requirement; *People* v. *MacEoin* [1978] IR 27; *DPP* v. *Kelly* 21 July 1999. I am grateful to Tom O'Malley of the National University of Ireland, Galway, for this information.

[9] N. Lacey, *Unspeakable Subjects* (Oxford, 1998), ch. 7.

[10] Homicide Act 1957, s. 3.   [11] Stephen, n. 2 above, 59.

[12] J. Horder, *Provocation and Responsibility* (Oxford, 1992), 24.

Provocation was born out of a violent society and a criminal justice system with relatively primitive theories of individual culpability which nonetheless began to differentiate between those homicides deserving of punishment by death and those which did not. It unashamedly reflected a male view of status, property, and the place of violence. Its refinement into a broad excuse based on loss of self-control began in the eighteenth century, with the focus however firmly on the blameworthiness or illegality of the victim's provoking behaviour. The reasonable man appeared in concrete form somewhat later and by the early part of the twentieth century had developed into the man of virtue.

The modern form of the defence of provocation was partly enshrined in statutory form in 1957.

> Where on a charge of murder there is evidence on which the jury can find that the person charged was provoked (whether by things done or by things said or by both together) to lose his self-control, the question whether the provocation was enough to make a reasonable man do as he did shall be left to be determined by the jury; and in determining that question the jury shall take into account everything both done and said according to the effect which, in their opinion, it would have on a reasonable man.[13]

Common law restricted the kinds of things which could count as provocation but section 3 broadened this by explicitly stating that the provocation does not have to be an act, but could be in the form of words, and it does not need to have been done by the victim to the defendant.[14] Of the increasing number of things that perplex me about criminal law, this is one of them. Why was the provocative impact of words ever rejected?[15] The playground chant—'sticks and stones will break my bones but words will never hurt me'—is an attempt to deflect the painful truth that words can and do hurt. The need for verifiable evidence may have informed the earlier exclusion of verbal provocation, but ironically its admission has introduced a further negative aspect of the provocation defence, facilitating the defaming of the dead person's character. The main significance of section 3 was that it released provocation from the judicially developed recognized categories of behaviour capable of provoking a loss of self-control and left the determination of this question in the hands of the jury.

---

[13] Homicide Act 1957, s. 3.

[14] The provocation may be carried out by someone other than the deceased (A. tells B. of his wife C.'s affair, B. then kills D., her lover) or the defendant may not be the victim of the provoker (A. kills B. who raped C., his wife/son/daughter). The provocation should however be a human act, although it need not be intentionally provocative and may be a non-deliberate and legal action; *R*. v. *Doughty* (1986) 83 Cr App R 319. By this provocation D. must then lose his/her self-control and kill.

[15] Words are still not admitted as provocation in the Australian states of Victoria and South Australia; see *Moffa* v. *R* (1977) 138 CLR 601.

The requirement of an actual loss of self-control, the essence of provocation, is said to be there to preserve the line between revenge and provoked killing,[16] although the extent of the loss of self-control has not been much considered. From the phrases used such as 'loss of temper', 'heat of passion', or 'unable to restrain himself', it is clear that some element of control may be retained; indeed a complete lack of self-control would begin to look like automatism. While section 3 was held to have amended the common law in respect of some matters, the requirement that the loss of self-control be 'sudden and temporary' was allowed to survive, despite the absence of that phrase in the section itself. The 'classic' jury direction in *Duffy*,[17] which included this phrase, was one the courts were unwilling to abandon despite the enactment of section 3. The interpretation of this phrase as an additional requirement lay at the heart of the failure of provocation to emerge from its male honour-vindicating base to encompass cumulative provocation in the domestic setting, itself recognized as a significant social problem in the twentieth century.[18] Is it a coincidence that *Duffy*, the case which introduced 'without the support of precedent'[19] the word 'sudden', concerned a woman who killed her violent husband? In a series of 'battered wife' cases in the 1980s and 1990s, the argument was put that women who have been subjected to many years of abuse and threats do not necessarily fly off the handle at the first, second, or third provocation, but that they may eventually snap after a relatively trivial example of provocation. The requirement that the loss of self-control be 'sudden and temporary' persisted until with sleight of hand it was eventually overcome in *Thornton (No. 2)*.[20] The Court of Appeal held that sudden and temporary loss of self-control did not necessarily mean that there could be no time lag between the provocative event and the lost control. The transition from *Duffy* to *Thornton* took place against a background of major changes in social, economic, and family life, including the move from extended family dwelling to nuclear family 'private' home life.

The objective requirement, that a reasonable man would have done as the defendant did, was released from some of its common-law restrictions much earlier by the House of Lords in *Camplin* in 1978.[21] But it continues to cause conceptual difficulties and it is the main impediment to achieving any semblance of coherence in the provocation defence. For over half a century the reasonable man was the primary mechanism for containing the defence. It was one thing to say that provocation was a concession to human frailty, another to admit individual weaknesses or abnormality. The development of the defence is partly testimony to the cultural (and historical) relativity of

---

[16] Wilson, above n. 5, 380.   [17] [1949] 1 All ER 932.
[18] See M. Wasik, 'Cumulative Provocation and Domestic Killing' [1982] Crim LR 29 for examples of such cases.
[19] A. Ashworth, *Principles of Criminal Law*, 3rd edn. (Oxford, 1999), 276.
[20] [1996] 2 Cr App R 108.   [21] [1978] AC 705.

perceptions of normality. This also was a powerful reason (or motive) for law to adopt a strict approach to the reasonable man, and to refuse to endow him with characteristics of gender, age, race, impotence, mental instability, or irascibility. It wasn't that he had no identity. It was that giving him explicit identity would expose his implicit identification with a certain kind of manhood. *Camplin* was an easy case in which to challenge this. The defendant was a 15-year-old boy. The victim, and provoker, a middle-aged homosexual. And what was more he was Pakistani—a description that is gratuitously added in Lord Diplock's speech and repeated in some accounts of the case. Neither the strict, homogeneous, imperialistic version of the reasonable man, nor the personalized version, has proved manageable. In most common-law jurisdictions the defendant's characteristics clothe the reasonable man (or ordinary person) in assessing the gravity of the provocation, but the question that causes huge difficulty is how to construct the reasonable man for the purposes of assessing the standard of self-control.

A strict application of *Camplin* would leave the reasonable man intact for the purposes of establishing the standard of self-control. In Lord Diplock's words in that case:

The judge should explain to [the jury] that the reasonable man referred to . . . is a person having the power of self-control to be expected of an ordinary person of the sex and age of the accused, but in other respects sharing such of the accused's characteristics as they think would affect the gravity of the provocation to him.[22]

But courts have been torn between a narrow interpretation of *Camplin*, and one which allows the defendant's characteristics and circumstances to creep out of the gravity question and inform the self-control question as well. Of course, some of the ambivalence arises because of doubt about the true separability of the two questions anyway. The uncertainty is clearly demonstrated in the outright refusal of the Court of Appeal in *Parker*[23] and *Smith (Morgan James)*[24] to follow the Privy Council's restrictive interpretation of the relationship between diminished responsibility and provocation in *Luc Thiet Thuan*.[25] In the same period the Australian High Court has struggled with the relevance of race and sexuality. Despite a very clear endorsement of the strict *Camplin* approach in a seven-justice High Court in *Stingel* v. *R.* in 1990,[26] a quite different set of signals emerged in *Masciantonio*[27] only seven years later. McHugh J. decided that *Stingel*, to which he was a party, was wrong and argued powerfully (although mistakenly in my view, see p. 000 below) that the gender and ethnic or cultural background of the defendant should be attributed to the ordinary person as well as age.[28]

In summary, which if any personal characteristics should be considered

---

[22] [1978] AC 718.   [23] [1997] Crim LR 760.
[24] [1998] 4 All ER 387. An appeal was taken to the House of Lords in 2000.
[25] [1997] AC 131.   [26] (1990) 171 CLR 312.   [27] (1994–5) 183 CLR 58.
[28] He was the sole dissenter. The case is discussed in more detail in section 3 below.

by the jury when applying the reasonable man test, and the subjectivization of the reasonable man, are issues which continue to cause problems: *Smith*[29] and *Morhall*[30] constitute ample evidence of the continuing challenge that the provocation defence poses.

B. Lifting the Veil: Gender, Race, and Sexuality

First I should outline the argument I will be making in this section. Writing in criminal law and criminology has been dominated by men.[31] It should shock us each time we are reminded of this, but feminist or gender analysis is, even now, usually only an add-on, a chapter at the end, rather than an integral part of our understanding of crime, criminal justice, or criminal law. The emergence of gender has not infiltrated our core understanding of concepts of provocation, it has merely disrupted the surface, causing a flurry of doubt in the uneasy compromise of the post-*Camplin* interpretation of section 3. It is true that 'battered-women syndrome' (BWS) has in a very short time become part of the vocabulary with which we talk about domestic violence and women who kill as a result of it, and it has also more recently become de rigueur to note the essentializing and syndromizing effect of the admission of evidence of BWS, but I do not believe that there has been a true penetration of the implications of gender, let alone race and sexuality in the way we understand criminal law. Twitching the curtains does not shed a full light.

In both criminal law and criminology, there is still a tendency to portray the women questions as supplementary to the main agenda. Adapting Naffine's comment about criminology, 'The message to the reader is that feminism is about women, while [criminal law] is about men.'[32] Yet as Naffine herself admits, there are huge difficulties in achieving any different account when the language and concepts determine the structure in the first place.'[33] It is only by acknowledging those difficulties that we can make any sense of the question which underlies this Chapter: 'what if any role should provocation play?' As I began to think about writing this, I wondered why I might have been invited to give the paper on which this Chapter is based. I looked at my antecedents and came up with a possible explanation: I once wrote an article on *Camplin*,[34] and I am the co-author of a book (first published in 1990) which explicitly claims to bring a feminist perspective to bear on criminal law.[35] The article does not mention gender as far as I can

---

[29] N. 24 above.
[30] [1995] 3 All ER 659; the relevance of drug addiction was considered here.
[31] See, generally, N. Naffine, *Feminism and Criminology* (St Leonards, NSW, 1997).
[32] Ibid., 2.   [33] Ibid., 120.
[34] 'The Death Penalty for Provocation?' [1978] Crim LR 662.
[35] N. Lacey and C. Wells, *Reconstructing Criminal Law*, 2nd edn. (London, 1998). See also Wells, 'Battered Woman Syndrome and Defences to Homicide: Where now?' (1994) 2 LS 266.

see, nor did it draw attention other than in the usual recital of the facts to
the homosexual context. The context of the violence was not highlighted.
The book on the other hand did introduce material exploring the relevance
of context, in particular that of women killing men in response to domestic
violence. At some stage then in the ten years between those two pieces of
writing some kind of transition occurred. In 1978, when *Camplin* was
decided and BWS was not even a twinkle in the critical criminal law writer's
eye, I had hardly met any other women who taught or wrote about criminal law. I had hardly read an article or a book on criminal law written by
a woman. Should I continue to write now as though such transitions and
shifts are to be expected and not worth noting? Can we really achieve a
considered and mature appreciation of the subject without such self-reflec-
tion, by which I mean not only reflecting as an individual but as a member
of an elite group of commentators professing some knowledge of a thing
called criminal law, and in particular here, a thing called homicide law?

It is useful then to remind ourselves that the uncovering of domestic
violence and the accompanying emergence of theories of BWS are part of a
much wider developing awareness of gender. On a number of occasions in
the last ten years the House of Lords has been surprisingly open to invita-
tions to bury time-worn shibboleths in criminal law. The removal of the
marital immunity in rape in *R. v. R.*[36] and the scything of assault as the
underlying condition for some offences against the person in the 'stalking'
cases *Ireland* and *Burstow*,[37] are obvious examples. Given that it was only
in the 1980s that the Criminal Law Revision Committee was reluctant even
to recommend the abolition of the marital immunity,[38] the process by which
R. v. R. came to be considered by the House of Lords, as well as the decision itself demonstrates an extraordinary receptivity to feminist arguments.
R. v. R. was one of a number of cases brought by the Crown Prosecution
Service to test the judicial climate, but there was no conspicuous acknowledgement of the reasons for the changing perceptions about marriage, sex,
and violence. Feminist arguments are not generally acknowledged, rather
they slip in unheralded *as though we need to pretend that we always knew
their message, we just forgot to mention it before.* While the decision itself
may not be so radical, the language of *Ireland and Burstow* shows how far
we may have come, but also how far there is still to go. Lord Steyn opened
his speech with these words:

[I]t is easy to understand the terrifying effect of a campaign of telephone calls at
night by a silent caller to a woman living on her own. It would be natural for the
victim to regard the calls as menacing. What may heighten her fear is that she will
not know what the caller may do next . . . harassment of women by repeated silent
telephone calls accompanied on occasions by heavy breathing, is apparently a

---

[36] [1992] 1 AC 599.   [37] [1997] 4 All ER 225.
[38] 15th Report, *Sexual Offences* (1984) (Cmnd. 9213).

significant social problem. That the criminal law should be able to deal with this problem, and so far as practicable, afford effective protection to victims is self-evident.[39]

Welcome as it is—we would surely rather have a judiciary that is perceptive and sensitive than one that is not—this kind of judicial statement describes in isolation an example of the phenomenon of male sexual power. It does not acknowledge the wider structural picture. Sexual violence is strongly implicated in many crimes involving women. In the case of partner-killings there has nearly always been a history of marital discord and violence, particularly male violence. However, this does not mean that the killings represent an incident of 'normal' violence gone wrong.[40] Overall, in nine homicide cases out of ten, the killer is male.[41] Women comprise just under one-third of all homicide victims but there are more than twice as many female victims of *partner*-homicide as male. One characteristic of the male killers in partner-homicide is that they are often separated from their (former) partner and the killings arise from disputes about sexual exclusivity and child custody. The violence is about possession and pride, about coercion and control.[42] Women, on the other hand, do not usually kill from jealousy or following the termination of a relationship. When they kill, there has usually been a high degree of violence within an ongoing relationship, and they are responding to precipitating masculine violence.[43] The 1996 British Crime Survey was supplemented with a self-completion questionnaire which revealed higher levels of domestic violence than the more conventional interview method. Nearly one-quarter of women had experienced assaults by their partner at some time in their lives, and one in eight on a repeated basis.[44] This accords closely with research in Australia, Canada, and the US which discloses similar levels of violence,[45] and all studies suggest that victimization varies according to age, educational attainment, and social class.

This raises questions for the operation of the provocation defence as it

[39] N. 37 above, 227–8.
[40] M. Levi, 'Violent Crime' in Maguire et al., *Oxford Handbook of Criminology* (Oxford, 1997), 841, 851.   [41] Ibid., 865.
[42] M. Mahoney, 'Legal Images of Battered Women: Redefining the Issue of Separation' (1991) 90 Mich LR 1, 65–6.
[43] A. Wallace, *Homicide: The Social Reality* (Research Study No. 5) (NSW Attorney-General's Department, 1986); K. Polk and D. Ranson, 'Patterns of Homicide in Victoria' in D. Chappell, P. Grabosky, and H. Strang, *Australian Violence: Contemporary Perspectives* (Canberra, 1991), 53
[44] Home Office, *Domestic Violence: Findings from a British Crime Survey Self-Completion Questionnaire* (1999) (Home Office Research Study no. 191).
[45] Ibid., app. C. See also C. Coumarelos and J. Allen, 'Predicting Violence against Women: the 1996 Women's Safety Survey' (1998) 42 CICJ 1 and J. Mouzos, *Femicide: An Overview of Major Findings, Trends and Issues in Crime and Criminal Justice* (Australian Institute of Criminology, August 1999).

applies to men who kill their partners, and as it applies to women who kill their partners before they are further abused (or killed) by them. Contemporary understanding of the phenomenon of domestic violence has been influenced by the emergence of BWS.[46] The syndrome maps the stages through which a woman subjected to long-term physical abuse within a relationship might pass, postulating that after repeated violence a woman is likely to become immobilized, passive, and unable to act to escape the oppression of her situation. It is often remarked that women should leave a violent relationship rather than endure it. BWS offers one explanation as to why she might not. Through a series of high-profile cases in the 1980s, appellate courts struggled to accommodate the newly discovered social reality of domestic violence, including the fact that women sometimes kill their abusive partners, and the gendered basis of legal constructions of provocation as a partial defence. The advantage of BWS is that it is a medicalized specialist term and as such might be admitted as expert evidence. It is difficult otherwise to bring before a court generalized evidence about domestic violence or social and economic disadvantage—courts are assumed to need no help in understanding the 'normal' world. Yet the acceptance of evidence of BWS carries with it all sorts of problems, including these: by rendering matters into the rarefied sphere of the expert, domestic violence is seen as unusual; the woman's own experiences are taken over by the expectations of others; the issue is driven towards the 'psychological/iatric' and thus more suitable for diminished responsibility with all the unfortunate associations of 'only women who are mad commit offences'; it is internally inconsistent because BWS at once speaks of the woman's helplessness while explaining the fact that she has killed; and it distracts attention from all sorts of other valid reasons why a woman might stay in a violent relationship, or ignores the fact that she might well have made many attempts to leave.[47]

Evidence of a woman's mental state, including that she was suffering from BWS, is admissible in order to assess both the 'subjective' and 'objective' aspects of the provocation defence. In other words, the evidence can be used to help support the claim that she lost her self-control and that a reasonable woman would have also lost hers in the circumstances.[48] This should not delude us. The recognition of gender, race, and sexuality as potentially relevant contextual features in provocation cases may have exposed the incoherence and flaws in provocation as a partial defence, but at the same time it has had a legitimizing effect which we should both acknowledge and seek to avert. This is seen most

---

[46] BWS was included in the standard British classification of mental diseases in 1994. See the discussion in *Hobson* [1998] 1 Cr App R 31.

[47] S. Sheehy, J. Stubbs, and J. Tolmie, 'Defending Battered Women on Trial: The Battered Woman Syndrome and its Limitations' (1992) 56 J Cr L 369.

[48] *Ahluwalia* [1992] 4 All ER 889.

clearly in relation to the so-called 'homosexual advance defence' (HAD) and its close cousin the 'homosexual panic defence' (HPD),[49] which has evident appeal in some jurisdictions. Homosexual panic has been used in the United States to back up defendants' claims that their violence was triggered by an acute panic brought on by the fear that they were being molested sexually.[50] 'Acute homosexual panic' was first described by a clinical psychiatrist in the 1920s and was used at that time to support insanity or a diminished capacity defence. Homosexuality was of course itself a classifiable psychiatric disorder at that time. The modern successor to these defences is the 'homosexual advance defence' in which juries are asked to acquit on the grounds of such an advance, or where sentences are reduced in mitigation, rather than construct the problem into a psychologically based defence. Exactly the same process, or ambivalence, is seen in the reception of BWS.[51] It is important that this argument is not misconstrued. It is not being argued that women who kill their violent partners after enduring years of abuse and fear are comparable with those who seek to justify violence against homosexual men on the grounds that they were in fear, or suffered a 'normal' reaction to the advance. The argument is that the provocation defence cannot discriminate between excusable violence and blind prejudice. The development of BWS, and its deployment on behalf of battered women is cruelly mirrored in the ready reception of HPD and HAD. This goes beyond the now almost standard arguments summarized above that we should take care with BWS evidence because it may stereotype and categorize women. Those arguments presuppose that there is scope within the paradigm provocation defence to accommodate specific contextual nuances, such as gender and race. This however, constitutes women as the 'other', non-white as the 'other', and homosexual as 'other', and thus retains the hegemony of male, white, and heterosexual norms.

To illustrate this argument I will examine three recent Australian High Court cases. They are emblematic of the inherent instability of the provocation defence, with the defendant's individual characteristics and the reasonable man or ordinary person locked in combat in most common-law jurisdictions.

---

[49] See generally A. Howe, 'More Folk Provoke their own Demise (Homophobic Violence and Sexed Excuses: Rejoining the Provocation Law Debate, Courtesy of the Homosexual Advance Defence)' (1997) 19 Syd LR 336 and N. K. Banks, 'The "Homosexual Panic" Defence in Canadian Criminal Law' (1997) 1 Criminal Reports (5th) 371.

[50] Howe, ibid., cites R. Bagnall et al., 'Burdens on Gay Litigants and Bias in the Court System: Homosexual Panic, Child Custody and Anonymous Parties' (1984) 19 Harv Civil LR 499.

[51] Howe, ibid., cites Editors of the *Harvard Law Review*, *Sexual Orientation and the Law* (London, 1990).

C. LOOKING BEHIND THE CASES

1. *OSLAND*[52]

Osland was the first case in which the High Court in Australia considered the relevance of BWS. Osland was charged with the murder of her husband. She and her son had dug a hole the previous day. Osland crushed some tranquillizers into her husband's food and then watched her son kill his stepfather with an iron pipe. Together they buried him and then fabricated his disappearance. They were jointly tried. They did not dispute that they had dug the hole, nor that she had drugged his food, nor that the stepson had struck the fatal blows. Both argued provocation and self-defence. The prosecution accepted that the deceased had been violent and abusive in the past, and that the killing took place against a background of 'tyrannical and violent behaviour . . . over many years.'[53] The jury convicted her of murder but were undecided about the stepson. He was acquitted at a retrial. The main points at her unsuccessful appeal in the High Court were whether she could be tried as principal and whether the verdicts were inconsistent. There was a strong dissenting judgment on the inconsistency argument. The dissenters argued that any prior agreement between Osland and her son regarding the homicide must have terminated if he was later found to have acted in self-defence or under provocation. But the majority rejected the argument that

A person cannot act pursuant to an understanding or arrangement with another that, together, they will kill a third person and, at the same time, act under provocation.[54]

In the discussion on BWS the court first pointed to the possibility that the context in which women come to kill their partners does not necessarily have to emerge through expert evidence, with Callinan J. commenting that these are now becoming matters on which there is a 'growing community awareness', in which case they are for a jury to decide with proper assistance from the trial judge.[55] This leaves real difficulties in knowing where BWS sits between scientific discourse and common sense. Secondly, Kirby J. took the opportunity to make some general comments about BWS—or 'battered woman reality'—speaking specifically of the need to avoid stereotyping. Lastly, and more controversially, he counselled the avoidance of sex-specific terms, pointing to the possibility that partner-violence in a gay relationship may give rise to similar responses.

In these comments, members of the court show a high degree of awareness

---

[52] (1998) 73 ALJR 173.   [53] Ibid., Gaudron and Gummow JJ. 177.
[54] Ibid., 178.   [55] Per Callinan J., ibid., 227.

of the contemporary legal literature on BWS. The point I want to make about *Osland* is that despite this apparent understanding, the case nonetheless fails to lift the fog with which provocation has tended to envelop 'domestic' homicide cases. There was plenty in the evidence as told by the court to indicate that the defendant had spoken, rather as Sara Thornton had, of the need to be rid of her abusive husband.[56] There was plenty in the case that would enable a jury to read into her actions evidence of premeditation and calculation. But at the same time the story that emerged was of a woman who was unable to articulate her predicament of living with an abusive husband. Her evidence in chief, which Callinan J. quoted extensively, included the following:

What did you do when you dug the hole?
We had no plan to do him any harm. We just waited for him to come home.
Before he came home did you do anything else?
We waited at the front windows to see him get out of the car, like we usually did, to see what mood he was going to be in.
. . . Why were you doing that?
We always stood there watching. We did that for . . . for months; used to watch him when he got out of the car just to see what mood he was in. If he was laughing more jovially with his mates, then we knew we were in trouble when we [sic] got inside. If he was more solemn when he got out of the car, he wouldn't be so bad when he got inside.
On the Tuesday night, what was he like when he got out of the car? . . .
He was laughing. He was as happy as anything.
How did that make you feel? . . .
We knew. We listened for him to walk down the driveway and we knew we were in trouble.
What happened when he came inside? . . .
He verbally abused me over having me hair cut . . .
How long was he verbally abusive after he got home? . . .
I reckon a good hour, hour and a half.
What were you doing during that time? . . .
Just listening.
How did you feel during that time? . . .
I knew I was in trouble. I was full of fear.
What were you fearful of? . . .
My life, I knew that if David went that day I knew I was . . .
Were you fearful that David would leave that day? . . .
Yes, I thought he'd chuck him out the door like he did E. [her daughter]

This does not sound like a woman who had thought through and carried out a cold-blooded revenge murder. That she played a role in what her son did was not doubted. Two juries failed to convict him. One of those juries convicted her of murder. How have appellate courts responded to appeals

---

[56] *Thornton (No. 2)*, n. 20 above.

from the verdicts of juries in other provocation cases? The second
Australian case raises an additional factor, that of race or ethnicity.

2. MASCIANTONIO[57]

The accused killed his son-in-law. There was evidence that he believed the
son-in-law had been violent towards his daughter and had caused financial
difficulties through excessive gambling. When he challenged him to do
better the son-in-law responded by telling him to 'piss off', and by pushing
or shoving him. The defendant then grabbed a knife from his car and
stabbed the son-in-law, who staggered away but was pursued by the defendant who stabbed him again while he lay collapsed, surrounded by passers-
by, on a footpath. It was unclear whether the fatal wound was caused by
the first or second stabbing. The appeal was centred on whether the judge
was right to withdraw provocation in relation to the second stabbing. The
Court of Criminal Appeal dismissed the appeal, with one judge holding that
provocation should not have been out to the jury at all, let alone in relation
to the second stabbing. The High Court allowed the appeal.[58]
Masciantonio had migrated to Australia from Italy when he was nineteen.
The majority held that there was clear evidence of provocation:

> . . . the deceased told the appellant to 'piss off' and attempted to kick him [and] also
> pushed the appellant to the ground so that he injured his elbow. The gravity of this
> provocation must be seen against the appellant's longstanding concern over the
> deceased's treatment of his daughter and his emotional response to the situation . . .
> Whether an ordinary person could have reacted in the way in which the appellant
> did would pose a more difficult question for a jury. However, if a jury were to
> conclude, as it might, that the provocation offered by the deceased was, in the
> circumstances in which the appellant found himself, of a high degree (and there was
> some evidence to support such a conclusion) then it is possible that a reasonable jury
> might conclude that an ordinary person could, out of fear and anger as a result of
> that provocation, form an intention to inflict at least grievous bodily harm and act
> accordingly.[59]

Although it is instructive to compare the tenor of the court's attitude to
Masciantonio with that of the portrayal of Mrs Osland as a premeditated
murderer, the most significant point to arise from this case is contained in
McHugh J.'s dissent. In a disquisition on the characteristics of the ordinary
person he argued that the ordinary person would retain some meaning if it
were to incorporate the general characteristics of an ordinary person of *the
same age, race, culture, and background as the accused on the self-control
issue*:

---

[57] N. 27 above.

[58] The defendant was convicted of manslaughter on retrial and sentenced to $5\frac{1}{2}$ years in
prison; L. Waller and C. R. Williams, *Brett, Waller and Williams: Criminal Law Text and
Cases*, 8th edn. (London, 1997), 239.   [59] N. 27 above, 69.

Without incorporating those characteristics, the law of provocation is likely to result in discrimination and injustice. In a multicultural society such as Australia, the notion of an ordinary person is pure fiction. Worse still, its invocation in cases heard by juries of predominantly Anglo-Saxon-Celtic origin almost certainly results in the accused being judged by the standard of self-control attributed to a middle-class Australian of Anglo-Saxon-Celtic heritage, that being the stereotype of the ordinary person with which such jurors are most familiar.[60]

McHugh J. is striking at the very heart and soul of provocation here.[61] Some would argue that the lack of fit between jurors' experiences and those of defendants suggests not so much an adjustment of the ordinary man test as a good reason to abandon it.[62] Provocation's concession to human frailty sits uncomfortably in a criminal law which is premised on the denial of explanations based on individual circumstances. Provocation therefore never knows quite where to place itself in the turmoil of competing realities and tensions. It tends to function as a distorting echo of contemporary fears and concerns. This is further illustrated by the third case I want to discuss.

3. GREEN[63]

Green killed a friend who made homosexual advances to him after a night's drinking. Green argued that because of his family history (his father had abused his sisters) he was peculiarly sensitive to matters of sexual abuse. By a three-to-two majority, the High Court ordered a retrial on the ground that the judge should not have directed that this history was not relevant on the issue of provocation.

McHugh J., who was in the majority, reiterated in his account of the law of provocation that ethnic or cultural background was relevant to the objective standard of self-control. The issue in Green's case, however, was the relevance of his family history, whether it bore any connection with the provocation he experienced. The Court rejected the Crown's argument that this was a non-violent homosexual advance which could not be said to connect with Green's family history.

The sexual, rather than homosexual, nature of the assault filtered through the memory of what the accused believed his father had done to his sisters, was the trigger that provoked the accused's violent response.[64]

---

[60] Ibid., 73.

[61] He explicitly adopted the arguments of S. Yeo, 'Power and Self-Control in Provocation and Automatism' (1992) 14 Syd LR 3.

[62] K. J. Heller, 'Beyond the Reasonable Man? A Sympathetic but Critical Assessment of the Use of Subjective Standards of Reasonableness in Self-Defense and Provocation' (1998) 26 Am J Cr L 1.   [63] (1997) ALJR 19.

[64] McHugh J., ibid., 38.

What do these three cases show us?[65] That the High Court can empathize with men who protect their daughter's honour, and whose concern about their father's treatment of their sister and mother, makes them peculiarly susceptible to a sexual advance, but not with a woman whose stepson is acquitted as principal in the joint enterprise of murdering her abusive husband? This is not intended as a comment on the legal points raised in these appeals, particularly as *Osland* raised an issue about consistency in joint enterprise which clearly has wider application. But there was sufficient opportunity, had the court been willing to take it, to reconsider the justice of her conviction for murder against the background of her son's subsequent acquittal.[66]

In relation to *Masciantonio*, the court's account of the background to the defendant's loss of self-control and the actual provocation painted him in an extremely favourable light. There was no indication that there might be something patriarchal in his attitude to his daughter's marriage, or that he might have felt differently had it concerned a son whose wife had left him. The majority regarded as grave, provocation which consisted of telling his father-in-law to 'piss off', and possibly shoving him, when to many it sounds, in all the circumstances, an entirely predictable and mild reaction on the son-in-law's part.

When it comes to *Green*, the court again presents a favourable account of the provocation. Toohey J. suggested that the provocation was 'very grave', and that it must have been 'a terrifying experience' for the appellant: 'The grabbing and the persistence are critical.'[67] What in Green's case was depicted as clearly capable of being provocation to me sounds like the kind of sexual advance most women, unless they have never shared accommodation (or a taxi) with a man, would recognize as hardly unusual. McHugh J.'s effort to downplay the homosexual nature of the encounter was disingenuous for the obvious reason that men do not routinely have to fend off violent advances of a sexual nature from women. It is therefore difficult to imagine a court considering that a woman who made unwanted sexual advances to a man would be considered to have provoked him, whether he had a family history of sexual abuse or not. Nor is it very easy to imagine a court taking much notice of a woman who claimed sensitivity to a male sexual advance on the ground that her father had sexually abused her brothers.

---

[65] It should be noted that *Osland* and *Masciantonio* were appeals from the Supreme Court of Victoria. Unlike NSW, Queensland, the Northern Territory, and ACT, Victoria has no defence of diminished responsibility. Green was appealed from the Supreme Court of New South Wales.

[66] The Court was unanimous in holding that the acquittal at retrial was not inconsistent. The question was whether the jury's failure to agree on a verdict in relation to the stepson at their joint trial was consistent with their verdict in relation to her.

[67] N. 63 above, 24.

The High Court's empathy with Masciantonio and Green compares oddly with their attitude to Stingel, who had killed his former girlfriend's new lover after being told by the deceased 'piss off you cunt'. The trial judge was held to have been correct in refusing to allow provocation to go to the jury at all. There were distinguishing features such as the transience of the relationship and the clear evidence that he had followed and sought her out following the breakdown of their relationship. What marks out *Masciantonio* and *Green* is that the defendants were upholding, in their reactions, an ideal of family life, patriarchal in the one case, and heterosexual in the other.

D. Distorting Tragedies: Real People, Real Lives

Many writers have observed the capacity for law to generate stories, and that cases are highly constructed versions of events. Criminal law lends itself to this 'novelization' more than many areas of law and the classic features of drama are inevitably present in provocation cases. Storytelling and fictional writing both reflect and create dominant cultural ideas, and this provides a helpful perspective in an examination of the development of the provocation defence.[68] A related strand of contemporary legal literature recognizes the role played by the law of evidence in the creation of these stories, and in the reinforcement of attitudes and assumptions about different social groups, whether these are dissected by age, gender, ethnicity, class, or sexuality. A familiar example is the reception of evidence in relation to sexual offences including the relevance of a woman's sexual history in rape cases.[69] In this section I look at the ways in which these theories might assist us in thinking about provocation cases.

Neither dead men nor women tell tales. Provocation invites the defamation of the dead person. Men who invoke HAD are given free rein to describe their victims as sexual predators. Men who kill their partners can invoke their victims' infidelity, nagging, or other undesirable characteristics. Of course, women who kill their partners can do the same. There is a general point here. As Mason J. once noted, 'a case of provocation by words may be more easily invented than a case of provocation by conduct', although he added mysteriously 'particularly when the victim was the wife

---

[68] See D. Nicolson, 'Telling Tales: Gender Discrimination, Gender Construction and Battered Women Who Kill' (1995) 3 FLS 185; A. Young, 'Femininity as Marginalia: Conjugal Homicide and the Conjugation of Sexual Difference' in P. Rush, S. McVeigh, and A. Young, *Criminal Legal Doctrine* (Aldershot, 1997), 227; J. Morgan, 'Provocation Law and Facts: Dead Women Tell No Tales, Tales are Told About Them' (1997) 21 Melb ULR 237.

[69] See now the Youth Justice and Criminal Evidence Act 1999, s. 41, which restricts the adduction of evidence of a complainant's sexual history and cross-examination in relation to it.

of the accused.'[70] The way that provocation stories are told in legal judgments profoundly affects our interpretation of the parties' behaviour.

But the problem goes far beyond the fact that provocation acts as an
open invitation to make up unappealing stories that might vindicate the
defendant's behaviour but at the same time leave an even sourer taste in
the mouths of the deceased's relatives. We have already seen that women
are most vulnerable to partner killings so, as a group of victims, are more
prone to having their marital history retold than are male victims of
homicide. What is told as a discovery of infidelity could sometimes be
retold as a story of male possessiveness. As Morgan puts it, ' "[F]acts" are
not just sitting out there with only one story to tell.'[71] Stories create
stereotypes and stereotypes create stories. Those very same stereotypes of
nagging, emotional women, serve to undermine women's stories when
they need to recount their marital history with the men they eventually
kill. Similarly, if we are receptive to negative stereotypes about the sexual
predatoriness of homosexual males, we are more likely to believe the
excuse that the defendant thought he was being subjected to a sexual
assault if his victim is gay.[72] Sometimes the reverse takes place and the
stereotype actually robs the victim of any personality. Rather than the
victim being constructed into someone else, she may scarcely get a look in
as a once-real person.[73]

Although she is sensitive to the need to avoid essentialized theories about
women, Rosemary Hunter notes that 'women who survive violence . . . are
feminized by the very harms they have suffered.'[74] They appear before the
court as wives, mothers and/or sexually invaded bodies.[75] Rules of
evidence, based on an enlightenment epistemology, often decontextualize
events and in so doing ignore behaviour patterns or the social worlds in
which they take place.[76] Laws of evidence also assume universal cognitive
competence, the assumption that normal unbiased people are able to assess
the information presented and reach the same conclusion.

The underlying theory is that common experience gives rise to universally accepted
generalisations about human behaviour that are available to all triers of fact.[77]

[70] Mason J. in *Moffa* n. 15 above, 620, quoted in Morgan, n. 68 above.
[71] N. 68 above, 247. And consider more generally the *Rashomon* factor—events seen from
different perspectives—named after the Japanese film, *Daiei* (1951) (Halliwell's synopsis: 'In
Medieval Japan, four people have different versions of a violent incident when a bandit attacks
a nobleman in a forest' *Film Guide* (London, 1993)).
[72] Or if the defendant says he was; see the discussion of *Murley* (Supreme Court of Victoria,
28 May 1992) in Howe, n. 51 above, 353.   [73] Ibid.
[74] R. C. Hunter, 'Gender in Evidence: Masculine norms vs. Feminist Reforms' (1996) Harv
Women's LJ 127.
[75] Ibid., 130. See also C. Smart, *Law, Crime and Sexuality* (London, 1995), ch. 5.
[76] Norrie of course argues that criminal law itself decontextualizes criminal behaviour; see
A. Norrie, *Crime, Reason and History* (London, 1993), 196. Hunter is making a related point
about evidence.   [77] Hunter, n. 74 above, 131.

Taking the admission of evidence about BWS as her example, Hunter shows how difficult any exercise of educating jurors about women's lives can be.[78]

Whatever the creators and proponents of the concept of BWS may have intended, the rules of evidence and the preconceptions of judges have filtered the concept into a narrow, stereotypical portrait of the essential battered woman, and only those women who fit the profile are able to take advantage of it.[79]

This is a problem that goes deeper than gendered reception of defendants' evidence. Whether the defendant is male or female, and whether the deceased is male or female, the provocation defence itself invites and legitimizes stories about the deceased. Legal stories work both ways, they can undermine as well as boost the defendant's case. As Callinan J. commented in *Osland*, 'The jury would have been conscious of the fact that, as in all cases of homicide, the deceased was not able to give his version of events which might have been markedly different from the two accused.'[80] But why did he feel the need to say this when the prosecution had accepted the abusive nature of the marriage? It is difficult to believe that she could have completely fabricated a story which spanned a relationship of twenty years and which contained an all-too-familiar mixture of possessiveness, violence, and reconciliations. Studies in the US of the way women's evidence is received in court indicate that women litigants and witnesses are frequently subjected to inappropriate and demeaning conduct that affects their credibility, including 'informal modes of address, the use of endearments, comments on appearance, sexual innuendo, sexist remarks or jokes, patronising behaviour, physical and verbal bullying.'[81] A woman's credibility is often intertwined with the substance of her evidence. These tactics undermine women's testimony or lead to its being trivialized.[82]

The fact that a witness is a woman does appear to trigger a set of moral judgments for determining credibility that is not applied to men. In other words, fact finders tie the worth of a woman's testimony to her moral worth.[83]

A further twist is the debate about the relevance of race in assessing the reactions of 'the ordinary person'. Yeo has persuaded at least one member of the High Court in Australia that ethnicity (or perhaps migrancy) should be taken into account in the same way as age both in assessing the loss of self-control and the gravity of the provocation:

---

[78] There is some research suggesting that the evidence has some, though not a great educative effect on juries; ibid., 146.   [79] Ibid., 151.

[80] Callinan J., n. 52 above, 227.   [81] Hunter, n. 74 above, 162.

[82] Ibid.

[83] Ibid., 165. Support for this is found in a random sample McColgan took of provocation cases showing that male defendants pleading provocation seem to be more successful than female defendants; see A. McColgan, 'General Defences' in Bibbings and Nicolson (eds.), *Feminist Perspectives on Criminal Law* (forthcoming).

As regards provocation based on compassion to human infirmity ... it could be argued that the law should take account of the comparative lack of exposure on the part of the migrant to the various socialising institutions of the host country, such as the family and school, when compared to one who has been raised since early childhood in that country.[84]

If there is to be an ordinary person, there is some argument for taking account of age. We expect to make allowances for the level of toleration of a 13-year-old compared with that of a 17-year-old, and possibly that of a 20-year-old compared with someone who is 30. But we should not make allowances on grounds of gender or race. We should ask a jury to imagine an ordinary person of the same sort of age as the defendant. This of course is an entirely different question from taking into account 'characteristics' which affect the gravity of the provocation—being called a stupid woman is a different insult if you are a woman, being called a 'stupid nigger' is a different insult if you are black, and so on. Otherwise we are in danger of adopting an 'essentialised view of race and ethnicity, that is, the notion that there is one authentic experience of an ethnic identity for each ethnic group.'[85] Such an approach could actually endorse racism.

The debates about the characteristics of the ordinary person lead to the inexorable conclusion that it is the nature of the provocation defence which needs questioning, not its finer contours. It is precisely because assessments of provocativeness are culturally relative,[86] and the need to have regard for 'equality' for the victim as well as equity for the accused,[87] that we need to move beyond provocation as an organizing concept in excusing or mitigating homicide.

E. Provocation does not Fit

Possibly one of the most remarkable features of modern criminal law has been its resistance to notions of excuse based on individual characteristics or circumstances.[88] 'Liability for theft is not compromised by poverty ... liability for murder is not compromised by good motive, let alone bad.'[89] A number of reasons can be advanced for this, some of which relate to the particular characteristics of legal decisions themselves. As David Nelken points out, legal decisions have many intended audiences.[90] Unlike scientific

[84] Yeo, n. 61 above, accepted by McHugh J. in *Masciantonio*, n. 27 above. Yeo has since revised his views; see id., 'Sex, Ethnicity, Power of Self-Control and Provocation Revisited' (1996) 18 Syd LR 304. [85] Morgan, n. 68 above, 259.
[86] On the cultural relativity of emotions, see R. Harre (ed.), *The Social Construction of Emotions* (London, 1986), esp. C. Armon-Jones, 'The Social Functions of Emotion', 57–83.
[87] Horder, n. 12 above, 272.
[88] This section draws on C. Wells, ' "I blame the parents": Fitting New Genes in Old Criminal Laws' (1998) 61 Mod LR 724, 736–7. [89] Wilson, n. 5 above, 375.
[90] D. Nelken, 'A Just Measure of Science' in M. Freeman and H. Reece (eds.), *Science at Court* (Aldershot, 1998).

disciplines which are typically addressed mainly to academic peers, legal decisions are directed at other judges, lawyers, the jury, and, at least indirectly, the general public. Lawyers and judges are involved in processing already categorized data, events which have been generated by non-academic actors, judges, litigants etc. Legal practice cannot therefore aspire to develop the sort of cumulative knowledge characteristic of certain scientific disciplines.'[91] This has profound implications for any descriptive analysis of principles of responsibility.

For most contemporary criminal law scholars, individual responsibility rests on the principle of capacity and a fair opportunity to act otherwise developed by Hart.[92] Any argument that the fair opportunity was compromised by social deprivation or from genetic predisposition runs up against the difficulty that not everyone succumbs to criminal behaviour.

As much as we may suspect that individuals' life choices are overwhelmingly determined by social constraints, such as class and gender, the criminal justice system requires individuals to be regarded as the architects of their destiny in order to found a basis for holding them accountable at law.[93]

Much has been written about the mixed message which provocation seeks to carry. On the one hand it is a concession to human frailty, on the other it is based on wrongdoing by the victim, or someone other than the defendant. The moral equation that the circumstances arose from another's wrongdoing is attractive at an intuitive level.[94] But beyond the superficial the cracks appear. Excuses such as provocation can be accommodated at a general level because they respond to particularized events rather than general conditions, such that the empirical question of whether others would succumb can be incorporated in the defence itself, into a prescriptive inquiry as to whether a person of reasonable firmness would have acted similarly.

It is full of internal contradiction—the loss of self-control posited against the reasonable man, ordinary person test. There are three broad options: clarify the objective standard, abandon the objective standard, or abolish the defence altogether. Attempts to take account of specific characteristics which might affect either the provocation itself or the reaction to it has proved problematic, as has the accommodation of hitherto ignored differences, such as gender, race, and sexuality. The question posed by Heller has not been resolved:

Is the reasonable person simply Everyman, an individual without race, class, gender, or any other non universal characteristics? Or is the reasonable person someone

---

[91] See further Morgan, n. 68 above.

[92] H. L. A. Hart, *Punishment and Responsibility* (Oxford, 1968).

[93] G. Hubble, 'Feminism and the Battered Woman: The Limits of Self-Defence in the Context of Domestic Violence' (1997) 9 CICJ 113, 121.

[94] Ashworth, n. 19 above, 245, suggests this is a coherent justification.

who resembles the defendant herself, possessing some or all of the defendant's characteristics?[95]

Or would it be enough to abandon the objective requirement as some have proposed. Particularly in its strongest form,[96] the objective standard presupposes that individuals possess free will, which is consistent with criminal law's 'most basic political axioms'.[97] As Packer puts it, '[T]he law treats man's conduct as autonomous and willed, not because it is but because it is desirable to proceed as if it were.'[98] While he does not doubt the force of this argument may be desirable, Heller argues that it is unachievable.[99] Or has the weakness in the structure as a whole finally been exposed?[100]

The obvious question remains. How do we reflect the different circumstances in which people kill in our homicide laws? The role of any excuse will be determined by fixed points in the structure as a whole such as the culpability elements for murder and the extent of justificatory defences. Both murder and manslaughter in their current forms are crude and over inclusive. It is unacceptable that, forty years after its abolition, vestiges of the felony-murder rule remain in the implied malice rule for murder, and that the unlawful act rule still has full rein in manslaughter. If murder were tightened by the removal of intention to cause grievous bodily harm, and involuntary manslaughter were based on recklessness or negligence as to serious injury or death, the terrain of homicide would already look significantly different. Self-defence would acquire an enhanced role whether or not provocation were retained in some form. Some, but not all, of the problems that I have identified with the operation of the provocation defence would also hold true for self-defence. The dangers of fabrication, of character assassination, and cultural prejudice in the assessment of evidence would not be removed. But they would not be deployed in the service of a defence which contains an unappealing message condoning anger over restraint, and whose very essence is not only contradictory but deeply unsound.

---

[95] Heller n. 62 above, 4. Proposals to modify the objective test include: Criminal Law Revision Committee, 14th Report, *Offences Against the Person* (1980) (Cmnd. 7844), para 81; Law Commission, *A Criminal Code for England and Wales* (Law Com. no. 177) (1989), Draft Criminal Code Bill 1989, cl. 58. The Model Penal Code abandons the notion of provocation, replacing it with '*extreme mental or emotional disturbance for which there is reasonable explanation or excuse. The reasonableness of such explanation or excuse shall be determined from the viewpoint of a person in the actor's situation under the circumstances as he believes them to be.*' (American Law Institute, 1985, s. 210.3).

[96] J. Horder, 'Between Provocation and Diminished Responsibility' (1999) King's College LJ 143.   [97] Heller, n. 62 above, 105.

[98] H. Packer, *Limits of the Criminal Sanction* (Stanford, 1969), 74–5.

[99] Heller, n. 62 above, 108.

[100] See the New South Wales Law Commission, *Partial Defences to Murder: Provocation and Infanticide* (Report no. 83) (1997), para. 2.81. The Commission proposes the following reformulation: 'That the jury be satisfied that the accused should be excused for having so far lost control as to have formed an intention to kill or inflict grievous bodily harm or to have acted with reckless indifference to human life as to warrant the reduction from murder to manslaughter.' (Ibid., para. 2.129).

5

Partial Defences to Homicide: Questions of Power and Principle in Imperfect and Less Imperfect Worlds . . .

NICOLA LACEY[*]

Partial defences to crime occupy an uncomfortable position in the architecture of contemporary English criminal law. They sit at a badly lit boundary between what Paul Robinson[1] has distinguished as 'criminal law standards' and 'liability rules' on the one hand and 'grading issues' on the other, with issues of 'labelling' arguably impinging from yet another direction. The dingy lighting in the area makes it difficult to decide whether their position is dictated by the pragmatic need to respond to local and temporary peculiarities, or whether some unlit infrastructure would reveal deeper foundations—foundations which, once perceived, might dictate the construction of further such defences.

In this Chapter, I shall try to effect a modest increase in the wattage directed at the partial defences, using, of course, the context of homicide as my main focus. Firstly, I shall consider the relationship between the articulation of standards, the delineation of conditions for liability, labelling, and grading in substantive criminal law, teasing out the current division of labour in English homicide law and illustrating its contingency (indeed its peculiarity) by reference to the broad division of labour effected by some other European systems. Secondly, I shall relate these criminal law functions to accounts of the proper role (and rationale) of defences, considering in particular recent contributions to criminal law theory which argue that defences (as opposed to exemptions) are inextricably bound up with an evaluation of the defendant's character and/or reasons (as opposed to an assessment of his or

[*] Professor of Criminal Law, London School of Economics. My warm thanks are due to participants at the Conference 'Rethinking English Homicide Law', and in particular to my commentator Ian Dennis, for lively discussion of its contents; and to the Wissenschaftskolleg zu Berlin, which has provided the ideal environment in which to work on it.
[1] P. Robinson, *Structure and Function in Criminal Law* (Oxford, 1997), Pt. III, esp. ch. 6.

her capacities or opportunities).[2] Thirdly, I shall move to a critical analysis of the current operation of partial defences in the imperfect world of English homicide, and to a consideration of what this analysis implies for any possible reform of the range of partial defences. Through a discussion of some possible 'new' partial defences, I shall raise questions about forensic and other practical limitations on the capacity of courts to apply defences on the character/reasons model. In particular, I shall be concerned with the nature of the substantive judgments which criminal courts could properly be expected to make even if the context in which partial defences to homicide operate were to be rationalized by the abolition of the mandatory sentence for murder—hence becoming the 'less imperfect world' of my title.

A. REGULATING, LABELLING, AND GRADING

According to Robinson,[3] we should make a distinction between issues concerning criminal law's substantive standards of conduct or its conditions for liability on the one hand and issues relating to the grading of the seriousness of offences on the other. While the first two operate in terms of necessary minimum conditions for a defendant's liability, the third essentially concerns a spectrum of seriousness. To Robinson's distinction it is useful, for my current purposes, to add a further function of criminal law, that is the articulation of labels which are thought to identify distinctive wrongs.[4] This classification is, I would argue, suggestive, not least because it helps to rationalize the widespread tendency in English criminal law to allocate grading issues to the sentencing stage of the criminal process, where judgments can be fine-tuned to accord with social and moral, as well as legal, standards. It also raises the question of whether defences are concerned with setting standards of conduct or conditions of liability, with grading, with labelling, or with some combination of these.

Yet to articulate the distinction between liability rules, standard-setting, grading, and labelling is immediately to suggest its limits. For, implicitly, many liability and standard-setting rules may themselves be seen as being engaged in grading judgments and in the constitution of significant labels. Even leaving aside the provisions for statutory maximum penalties attaching to these rules, it would not take a legal expert to tell, for example, that the

---

[2] These contributions take different forms which, for the purposes of this Chapter, I shall synthesize. Important recent contributions include J. Gardner, 'The Gist of Excuses' (1998) 1 Buffalo Crim LR 575; J. Horder, 'Between Provocation and Diminished Responsibility' (1999) 9 King's College LJ 143; K. Huigens, 'Virtue and Incapacitation' (1995) 108 Harv LR 1423; D. M. Kahan and M. C. Nussbaum, 'Two Conceptions of Emotion in Criminal Law' (1996) 96 Col LR 269.   [3] N. 1 above.
[4] On labelling, see A. Ashworth, *Principles of Criminal Law*, 3rd edn. (Oxford, 1999), 77, 90–3; J. Horder, 'Two Histories and Four Hidden Principles of Mens Rea' (1997) 113 LQR 95 and 'Rethinking Non-fatal Offences against the Person' (1994) 14 OJLS 335.

offence of intentionally causing grievous bodily harm is a more serious offence than that of assault occasioning actual bodily harm. There is, in other words, a division of labour here, with grading issues being distributed across different institutional locations and moments within the criminal process.

Problematically, however, this division of labour is not effected—at least in English criminal law—in a consistent way. Two different kinds of inconsistency or, perhaps, variety are of interest. Firstly, and most obviously, the substantive law's engagement in grading is spectacularly uneven. The offence of theft for example covers everything from the impulsive stealing of an item of negligible value to the meticulously planned appropriation of property worth millions of pounds within one compound label, with judgments of grading left almost entirely[5] to the sentencing stage within very wide parameters.[6] By contrast, the law of non-fatal offences against the person makes a wide variety of distinctions between different forms and contexts of personal violation—distinctions which arguably imply at least some messages about grading.[7] Of course, it can be argued with some plausibility that the Offences Against the Person Act 1861 is concerned here not so much with grading—that is with offence distinctions based in straightforward judgments of seriousness—as with labelling—with fine-tuned judgments about the distinctiveness of particular wrongs. I shall return to this point in due course, but for the moment we can observe that the grading/labelling distinction is itself not evenly observed in criminal law. A more straightforward example of 'legislative grading' without significant labelling is provided by the Misuse of Drugs Act 1971, which is structured in part in relation to distinctions between drugs categorized simply in terms of their perceived harmfulness.

A final example of legal grading is, of course, the law of homicide, in which the offence (and highly distinctive label) of murder encapsulates what might be seen as a relatively narrow grading-band, while that of manslaughter encompasses everything from a highly reckless killing through to a killing resulting from a much lower degree of recklessness or negligence in the context of the commission of another offence; and in

---

[5] Note that the prosecution may also have a role, e.g. where there is a lesser offence, such as 'taking a conveyance without authority' which can be charged. This example illustrates nicely the interaction between legislative specifications of offences and the distribution of power across the criminal process. While in this Chapter most of my examples of such distribution bear on the relationship between the conviction and sentencing stages, I would also maintain that the stages of prosecution decision-making, plea-bargaining, and execution of sentence are of great significance in understanding the actual and potential operation of partial defences. This is why I generally prefer to work within the analytic framework of 'criminalization' rather than adopting the conventional distinction between criminal law, sentencing, and other aspects of the criminal process; see N. Lacey, 'Contingency and Criminalisation' in I. Loveland (ed.), *Frontiers of Criminality* (London, 1995).

[6] For a classic exposition of the interaction between the form of criminal law and the regulation of sentencing, see D. A. Thomas, 'Form and Function in Criminal Law', in P. R. Glazebrook (ed.), *Reshaping the Criminal Law* (London, 1978), 21.

[7] Offences Against the Person Act 1861; see Horder (1994), n. 4 above.

which special offences such as causing death by dangerous driving and infanticide engage in a distinctive but patchy process of labelling. Yet even the assessment of murder as a relatively narrow-band offence can be questioned: limits on the doctrinal consideration of motive and the circumscribed scope of defences mean that some killings—those motivated by mercy, for example—may count as murders from a legal point of view, while they would generally be seen as less serious than many manslaughters from a moral point of view.

The second kind of inconsistency—here the more neutral word 'variety' is certainly appropriate—in substantive criminal law's enactment of grading judgments can also be illustrated by the example of homicide. This is the variety of ways in which the grading distinction is made.[8] In drawing the distinction between murder and manslaughter, criminal law—unusually— relies exclusively on the mens rea requirement to mark the grading. In relation to infanticide and causing death by dangerous driving, the distinction relates to the context in which the killing takes place. Of course, it could be argued that these offences simply imply that killing on the roads or within a certain period of childbirth are *different from* rather than *less serious than*—respectively—manslaughter and murder. But I would argue that these offences—like all criminal laws—must be read in the light of their maximum penalties, and that therefore we should indeed see them as making grading judgments as well as expressing labels.

Another means of enacting grading judgments *in the substantive law* is that of distinguishing offences simply on the basis of the degree of harm which they cause. An example would be the Law Commission's proposals for the reform of offences against the person,[9] which, in the case of less serious harm, distinguish the main offences merely in terms of the harm level and not in terms of the mens rea requirement. And a final means of grading is the provision of partial defences, reducing liability from a more to a less serious offence. Indeed, we could argue that the very existence of partial defences is testimony to the fact that *substantive criminal law itself* is indeed making grading judgments: otherwise, how could the relevant 'lesser' offence be identified? But in a criminal law in which the grading function is exercised as unevenly as it is in England and Wales, the opportunities—and arguably the need—for grading via partial defences are themselves very uneven. This is just one feature of the imperfect world in which we have to think through the question of partial defences.

We should note, finally, a further complexity about the issue. This is the fact that the effect of—and perhaps the rationales underlying—partial defences are themselves ambiguous. For example, the 'partial defence' of

---

[8] This in itself is a good example of the difficulty of drawing a clear distinction between issues of 'wrongdoing' and those of 'attribution of responsibility'; see p. 115–116 below.

[9] Law Commission, *Legislating the Criminal Code: Offences against the Person and General Principles* (Law Com. no. 218) (1993) (Cm. 2370).

provocation certainly engages in a grading judgment in so far as it reduces what would otherwise be murder to manslaughter. But one could also argue—as some commentators have—that provocation is primarily about labelling; it works in much the same way as infanticide, and the grading judgment of mitigation from murder to manslaughter is both pragmatic and parasitic on the idea that provoked killing is a qualitatively different activity from other killing. Alternatively, we could see partial defences as qualifications to the liability rules for murder. Moreover, if the 'partial defence' of diminished responsibility is regarded as in the nature of a partial exemption from liability, it is not clear that it implies anything direct about seriousness at all, since its impact is to suspend the normal processes of criminal law judgment.[10]

B. PARTIAL DEFENCES TO MURDER: LOCAL KNOWLEDGE IN A COMPARATIVE CONTEXT

Before turning to the rationale for defences and to actual and potential partial defences to murder, I want to try to convey both the contingency and the peculiarity of the current situation in England and Wales. The most obvious peculiarity is, of course, the existence of the mandatory sentence for murder. Many commentators would argue that the partial defences of provocation, diminished responsibility, and suicide pacts (as well as the offence of infanticide) are primarily motivated today by the need to protect certain categories of less blameworthy defendant from the full rigour of the mandatory sentence. On this view, the partial defences are in principle concerned not with exculpation but with mitigation: with a judgment about the grading of the seriousness of conduct which is properly decided through the exercise of sentencing discretion. This well-established practice of mitigation being blocked by the mandatory sentence (and by the inadequate structuring of the discretion which governs its execution), the institution of partial defences provides a pragmatic solution to cases where the injustice entailed by the mandatory sentence is most egregious.

This question of what 'in principle' ought to be a question going to conviction via the specification of offence elements or defences and what ought rather to be left to sentencing discretion indeed raises, as I shall argue, important questions about what it is proper and realistic to expect of criminal law. But a quick comparative survey unsettles the idea that there

---

[10] See Gardner, n. 2 above; Horder, n. 2 above; J. Horder, 'Pleading Involuntary Lack of Capacity' (1993) 52 CLJ 298; see also A. Duff, 'Mental Disorder and Criminal Responsibility' in Duff and N. Simmonds (eds.), *Philosophy and the Criminal Law* (Wiesbaden, 1984), 31; and, more generally, Duff's *Trials and Punishments* (Cambridge, 1986). As I shall suggest below, there is a tension between the view of diminished responsibility as an exemption and as a *partial* excuse. This tension is what leads Horder to float the idea of a 'third verdict' in this context.

is any hard and fast logical rule about which factors should count as mitigation, about which factors should rather structure substantive rules of
offence and defence, or—these things being held constant—about how decision-making power should be distributed across prosecution, defence,
judge, and jury. The legal systems of the Council of Europe states show
wide variation in the substantive defences, labelling principles, and mitigating factors they recognize: many systems, for example, accord special status
to homicides committed by householders during the burglary of their home,
or single out homicides of certain categories of victim as especially serious.
But, more significantly for my purposes, the systems also vary according to
whether they recognize each substantive issue as a matter of offence definition, defence, or mitigation. Moreover, and even more importantly, the
very distinction between issues going to conviction (via offence or defence)
and those going to sentence is far less significant in the majority of Western
European and Scandinavian systems than it is in England and Wales.

Let me give a brief illustration—or perhaps a cautionary tale—drawn from
my work on this Chapter. Taking up the editors' invitation to think comparatively about the topic, I read the fifth Appendix to the House of Lords' Select
Committee report on the mandatory life sentence.[11] Given that this was
already an instructive lesson in the difficulty of preparing comparable
summaries of differently structured systems, I decided to make a chart, locat-
ing the different systems in relation to the two variables which seemed important to my question in the English context—that is, did they have mandatory
sentences and/or partial defences to homicide? Since I already knew that
sentencing discretion is far more structured in most other countries than it is
in Britain, and since I am well aware that reading one system through the
lenses of another is one of the most dangerous pitfalls of comparative
research,[12] this was an unforgivable mistake. But it was also an instructive
one, because it became clear to me after analysing only two or three 'other'
systems that the 'partial defence' and 'mandatory sentence' categories simply
did not make sense in relation to systems like those of, for example, Germany,
Spain, or Sweden. Certainly, many systems provide for what looks at first
sight like a mandatory penalty, particularly for the most serious forms of
homicide. But this is almost invariably defeasible on the basis of mitigating
factors—factors which, crucially, *are specified in the Criminal Code itself*
rather than being left to unstructured sentencing discretion.

In this context, the distinction between sentencing issues, matters of formal
mitigation, and partial defences becomes difficult to draw. Or, to put it more
neutrally, the distinction becomes relatively unimportant, especially if one

---

[11] *Report of the Select Committee on Murder and Life Imprisonment* (HL Paper 78–1 of
Session 1988–9). Appendix 5 summarizes the law of, and sentencing provisions in relation to,
murder in the Council of Europe states.
[12] See L. Zedner, 'In Pursuit of the Vernacular: Comparing Law and Order Discourse in
Britain and Germany' (1995) 4 SLS 517.

assumes that the evidential burden in either case would be with the defendant.[13] In systems in which sentencing discretion is structured either by sentencing guidelines or by legal mitigating factors which displace presumptions in favour of particular penalties, formal partial defences simply lose their significance. Moreover, although at a formal, legal level, most of the countries discussed in the Appendix only grade or label two or three general forms of homicide, the closer integration of substantive and adjectival (sentencing) law entails that criminal law is more centrally and unambiguously concerned with grading—and criminal courts more publicly and legally accountable for grading decisions—than is the case in England and Wales.

C. Assessing the Partial Defences in English Criminal Law: the Rationale of Defences

The idiosyncrasy of English criminal law's partial defences to murder is striking. Formally, the existing partial defences are of course provocation, diminished responsibility, and killing in pursuit of a suicide pact.[14] For a start, these existing defences form a group which achieves the peculiar distinction of being tiny yet motley in both philosophical and historical terms. Furthermore, the group excludes a number of possible defences— duress and disproportionate self-defence, for example—which appear as compelling as the current defences on almost any conceivable conceptual, moral, or practical basis. In this context, it is tempting to rush headlong into a critique without pausing to consider the general rationale for exculpatory or mitigating factors. This, however, would be a mistake, because such a rationale is of central importance if we are to determine more clearly both the proper contours of the existing defences and the possible case for additional defences. In this section, therefore, I turn to the general arguments precluding, expunging, or mitigating a defendant's liability for a crime, before returning later in the Chapter to the question of how the allocation of decision-making about such factors should be determined across the various stages and personnel of the criminal process.

[13] But see, in the English context, M. Wasik, 'Partial Excuses in the Criminal Law' (1982) 45 MLR 516 and 'Excuses at the Sentencing Stage' [1983] Crim LR 450. Wasik notes among other things the evidentiary implications of defining a certain issue as pertaining to defence or to sentencing mitigation. See also Wasik's contribution to this collection, Chapter 7 below.

[14] We might include infanticide, for though this is formally an offence, it operates in a similar way to the other principles of formal mitigation to manslaughter. We could also argue that, although it is formally merely evidence of lack of mens rea (*Kingston* [1994] 3 All ER 353), the *Majewski* ([1977] AC 443) rule that intoxication may remove capacity to form a specific intent effectively converts extreme intoxication into a relatively discrete ground of formal mitigation. Given the crucial interaction between stages of the criminal process, I cannot resist the temptation to point out that, were we thinking about 'criminalization' rather than 'criminal law', we would be justified in listing, at the prosecution stage, 'killing while driving a car', some forms of 'mercy killing' and—at least until recently—'killing in a domestic context'.

1. THE 'CAPACITY VIEW'

We can usefully distinguish two main traditions in theorizing about defences. The first[15] draws a line between justifying and excusing defences: while justifying defences mark out conduct which criminal law does not regard as wrongful, excuses rather mark out situations in which the internal or external conditions under which a defendant acts are such as to displace—partly or completely—the attribution of responsibility for an admittedly wrongful act.[16] In this tradition, the main questions arising about justificatory defences relate to their implications for third-party liability: if an act is genuinely justified, can it be lawfully assisted by third parties, and is it necessarily unlawful to resist it, for example by self-defending conduct which might itself be justified? From a policy point of view, debate abounds about the implications of expanding justificatory defences given that they (on some interpretations) give priority to the defendant's view of the wrongfulness of the conduct over the criminal law's.[17]

In relation to excuses, the main questions arise in relation to the sorts of conditions which block an attribution of liability: which sorts of mental disorders or handicaps should prevent us from holding a person genuinely responsible in the sense of having had adequate cognitive and volitional capacities to have had a fair opportunity to do otherwise than she did; under what sorts of external conditions is it incumbent on the law to find that the conduct was not voluntary in the necessary sense? Excuses, on this

[15] In sketching the 'capacity view' I am synthesizing arguments from a number of authors who would not necessarily agree on all points of detail yet whose positions are founded on key shared assumptions.

[16] The literature on justification and excuse is enormous: see e.g. J. C. Smith, *Justification and Excuse in Criminal Law* (London, 1989); G. Fletcher, *Rethinking Criminal Law* (Boston, Mass., 1978), ch. 10. See also G. Fletcher, 'The Nature of Justification' in S. Shute, J. Gardner, and J. Horder (eds.), *Action and Value in Criminal Law* (Oxford, 1993), 175, suggesting that justifications, as opposed to excuses, flow from an ideal theory which overlays defence elements, and which appeals to broad notions of good and wrongfulness which do not have to be encapsulated in criminal legislation; on this point, see further p. 118 below.

[17] There are at least two ways in which this concern has arisen. The first arises out of a fully subjective conception of justification, according to which a person who e.g. acts on the mistaken assumption that she needs to defend herself behaves in a way which is not merely excusable but actually not wrongful in the first place. On this view, the defendant's own perception rather than a legal standard provides the criterion for wrongfulness. The second arises most vividly in relation to claims of necessity in which the defendant argues that her conduct amounted, notwithstanding its prima facie breach of criminal law norms, to the least of available evils. On one view, this sets the defendant's judgment of the balance of reasons over the judgment encapsulated in criminal law. In either case, the judgment of justification modifies the substantive standard to be applied. See A. Norrie, *Crime, Reason and History* (London, 1993), ch. 8; N. Lacey and C. Wells, *Reconstructing Criminal Law*, 2nd edn. (London, 1998), ch. 3.II.f. For a fascinating account of how concern about criminal law's authority vis-à-vis other normative systems such as 'the customs of the sea' influenced the (non-)development of the necessity defence, see A. W. B. Simpson, *Cannibalism and the Common Law* (Chicago, 1984).

view, are based in internal or external circumstances which significantly affected the scope or the 'fairness' of the opportunities available to the defendant to choose or control her conduct such that it is appropriate for criminal law to make concessions to human frailty or bad luck.[18] Hence discussion ranges over issues such as the balance to be struck between medical and legal criteria; the adequacy of conceptions of 'moral' or 'physical' voluntariness; and the implications of determinism for the relevant ideas of capacity and free, responsible agency.

On this framework, we can easily see that—particularly within the category of excuses—one can mount a strong argument for an expansion of partial defences to murder in the context of the present sentencing structure. Leaving aside the (persuasive) argument that provocation finds at least its history in ideas of partial justification,[19] most commentators would agree that the partial defences tend more to the nature of excuse than of justification: they are instances in which either internal incapacities or external circumstances are such as to convince us that some—if not a total—recognition of incapacity, empathy for extreme distress, or concession to normal human frailty should be made by criminal law. The partial defences affect, in other words, either the scope or the 'fairness' of the defendant's opportunity to conform her conduct to legal standards. Hence many commentators have argued that factors such as 'battered-women's syndrome', 'post-traumatic stress disorder' or even 'pre-menstrual tension' should be either accepted as evidence relevant to the defence of diminished responsibility or provided for specifically. Externally, the extremity of the different sorts of pressure experienced by those who kill under duress of threats or circumstances (including in the latter category certain varieties of mercy killing) or who use what is regarded as disproportionate force in self-defence also call, on the capacity view, for acknowledgement by way of a reduction in liability.

This capacity-based, subjective view of responsibility along with its concomitant approach to defences has been highly influential in Britain over the last thirty years. It has generally provided the framework within which debate about partial defences to murder has gone forward. In recent criminal law theory, however, some important criticisms have been made both of the framework of justification and excuse and of the capacity-based judgments of voluntariness which have structured debate about excuses. Let me mention just three relevant difficulties. Firstly, it can be argued that the rigid distinctions between judgments of wrongdoing and attributions of responsibility, between acts and actors implied by the distinction between

---

[18] The classic statement of this subjectivist, capacity-based view of criminal responsibility is to be found in H. L. A. Hart's *Punishment and Responsibility* (Oxford, 1968). Not all subjectivists rely explicitly on the justification/excuse distinction; see e.g. Ashworth, n. 4 above, though his framework is consistent with the distinction.

[19] See J. Horder, *Provocation and Responsibility* (Oxford, 1992), chs. 3, 4, 6 and 7.

justification and excuse is conceptually and practically fragile.[20] This is primarily because many of the judgments made in the application of both offence definitions and defences are what might be called contextual judgments. In other words, they assess, label, and grade the relevant conduct in an integrated way such that the wrongfulness of the conduct cannot be understood independently of the attitude of the actor. In this sense, though criminal law's judgments are sometimes focused more clearly on conduct than on agent and vice versa, they are typically engaged in assessing conduct in an 'agent-relative' way.[21]

Secondly, questions have been raised about this framework's location of excuses within a generally capacity-based approach to criminal responsibility: the essence of an excuse, for example, is that it in some sense affects the genuine capacities of the agent to conform her conduct to legal proscriptions. This appears to raise the spectre of determinism. If it can be argued that our actions are either generally causally determined or, more modestly, significantly influenced by environmental factors in a much wider range of cases than is generally acknowledged by the defences—in cases of extreme social deprivation, for example—then the normative basis for criminal law's judgments and distinctions seems to be precarious.[22]

Thirdly, the capacity-based approach arguably asks criminal courts to make assessments which pose serious practical difficulties: assessments of the genuine capacities, choices, and opportunities of the defendant. The difficulty inherent in such assessments is illustrated by the unevenness with which expert testimony is used in cases, for example, of diminished responsibility and provocation, and by the difficulty which courts find in assessing such evidence.[23] Furthermore, it may be argued that this practically

---

[20] See e.g. Lacey and Wells, n. 17 above, ch. 1.II a–d; for approaches which reinterpret the significance of the justification/excuse, wrongdoing/attribution distinctions, see J. Gardner, 'Justifications and Reasons' in A. P. Simester and A. T. H. Smith (eds.), *Harm and Culpability* (Oxford, 1996), 103; and which question its utility, Kahan and Nussbaum, n. 2 above. On the utility of the actus reus/mens rea distinction more generally, see A. T. H. Smith, 'On *Actus Reus* and *Mens Rea*' in Glazebrook, n. 6 above, 108; and P. H. Robinson, 'Should the Criminal Law Abandon the Actus Reus–Mens Rea Distinction?' in Shute et al., n. 16 above, 187.

[21] On the notion of agent-relative judgments, see D. Husak, 'Justifications and the Criminal Liability of Accessories' (1989) 80 J Cr L and Crim 491; B. Fisse, 'Partial Excuses and Critical Assumptions' in S. M. H. Yeo (ed.), *Partial Excuses to Murder* (Melbourne, 1991), 258.

[22] The literature on the relationship between freedom and responsibility is, of course, vast. See e.g. the essays in G. Watson (ed.), *Free Will* (Oxford, 1982), which includes Peter Strawson's famous defence of the independence of judgments of responsibility from the truth of determinism ('Freedom and Resentment' in ibid., 59, originally published in *Proceedings of the British Academy* xlviii (1962), 1–25). For other positions which argue that freedom is oblique or even irrelevant to responsibility, see J. L. Austin, 'A Plea for Excuses' and W. I. Matson, 'On the Irrelevance of Free-will to Moral Responsibility and the Vacuity of the Latter' at, respectively, pp. 39 and 94, in P. French (ed.), *The Spectrum of Responsibility* (London, 1991).

[23] This is particularly so where courts are confronted with conflicting accounts. A spectacular instance is the case of Peter Sutcliffe, the so-called 'Yorkshire Ripper', whose entire trial turned on the production and evaluation of competing psychiatric testimony; see Lacey and Wells, n. 17 above, 585–6.

problematic focus on issues of subjective capacity lends to criminal legal judgment a false air of empiricism, directing attention away from the substantive evaluation of 'fairness' which is being made (notably in the application of 'reasonableness' criteria) and failing to provide any analysis or rationalization of that evaluation.

2. The 'Reasons View'

Emerging from these criticisms of the first approach, several writers have been developing a different approach which responds persuasively to some of these difficulties and which turns out to be particularly suggestive for the analysis of the partial defences to murder.[24] Writers within this second tradition typically either reject the justification/excuse distinction altogether or regard it as of secondary importance in criminal law. For on this second, 'reasons-based' view, the rationale of defences, whether focused on act, actor, or agent-relative conduct, is to provide for a more sensitive evaluation of the defendant's conduct than is generally captured in offence definitions alone. Hence motive—generally argued to be irrelevant to the definition of offence elements on the capacity view, and acknowledged only as relevant to the specification of certain defences—becomes a central focus on the reasons view.

Another relatively frequent feature of this strand of thinking—which finds its deepest roots in Aristotelian philosophy but which may also be traced to the ideas of philosophers as different as Spinoza and Hume[25]—is its drawing of a distinction between 'exemptions' and 'exculpatory defences'. Exemptions such as insanity and diminished responsibility mark out subjects who are beyond the purview of criminal law's proscriptions and other communications. In contrast, defences such as duress, self-defence, or (perhaps) provocation mark out subjects who have—according to different versions of the theory—acted on reasons which are approved as within the range which would be expected of a normal, socially responsible

---

[24] A full discussion of the variety of contributions to this interesting development in criminal law theory lies outside the scope of this Chapter. What I shall therefore attempt is a synthesis which captures the main elements of various developments without purporting to represent the views of any particular writer. Important contributions include the articles already cited in n. 2 above. These articles have something in common with approaches to criminal responsibility which emphasize character rather than capacity (see e.g. M. Bayles, 'Character, Purpose and Criminal Responsiblity' 1 L & Phil (1982) 5; N. Lacey, *State Punishment* (London, 1988), ch. 3) but take the character view in a somewhat different—and, in my view, promising—direction. See also G. R. Sullivan, 'Making Excuses' in Simester and Smith, n. 20 above, 131. See more generally F. Schoeman (ed.), *Responsibility, Character and the Emotions* (Cambridge, 1987); J. G. Murphy and J. Hampton, *Forgiveness and Mercy* (Cambridge, 1988); C. Taylor, 'Responsibility for Self' in French, n. 22 above, 214.

[25] On Spinoza, see M. Gatens and G. Lloyd, *Collective Imaginings* (London, 1999), chs. 3 and 6; for Aristotle, see extracts from the *Nichomachean Ethics*, Books III and IV and for Hume, 'Of Liberty and Necessity' in French, n. 22 above at, respectively, 24–38, 78–93.

person, or acted in a way which manifests no disposition to resist or violate the norms or values protected by criminal law.[26]

The evaluation of the defendant's reasons includes, crucially, an evaluation of the emotions which motivated his or her conduct: these emotions are seen not merely as psychological facts but as things about which human beings can be expected to reason. Our emotions, and the ways in which we act upon them, are seen as basic constituents of our character, and this character, *as manifested in our conduct*,[27] is seen—in stark contrast to the capacity approach—as being a proper object of the judgment of a criminal court. Indeed, the defences are seen as importantly concerned with the specification of positively and negatively evaluated emotions, and this in turn opens up an important space for what we might call an immanent critique of the defences: do they, for example, respond even-handedly to the mitigating influence of outrage, fear, self-preservation, panic, despair, and so on? This feature of its argument means that the reasons view provides an illuminating perspective on recent debates about the delineation of defences such as provocation, duress, and self-defence.[28]

The reasons view of exculpatory defences seems to promise particular illumination in the context of partial defences. This is because, in at least some of its forms, it emphasizes the idea that the substantive judgments being made in criminal courts are relative to a mean of normal, law-abiding or practically reasonable behaviour. While offence definitions provide minimum socially approved standards of behaviour, defences respond to circumstances in which the defendant appears to have acted on the basis of reasons which do not depart—or, crucially for partial defences, which depart to only a limited degree—from what is normally expected. Hence partial defences can easily be accommodated as cases where there has been some departure from socially approved reasons but where this departure is not so great as to justify conviction of as serious an offence as that charged. We could draw an analogy here with the sorts of relative, contextual judgment being made in the law of involuntary manslaughter when it is insisted that negligence be 'gross' in order to justify liability.

One controversial feature of this view of defences is that it implies—indeed, not infrequently, it claims explicitly—that courts are essentially engaged in making evaluative judgments which relate to assessments not so much of the defendant's capacities but of her character. It is important, however, to be clear about the very specific sense in which the reasons

---

[26] This distinction is similar to that drawn by Strawson, n. 22 above, between cases calling forth 'objective' (practical) as opposed to 'reactive' (judgmental) attitudes.

[27] The italicized phrase marks an important qualification; see the discussion of *Kingston*, n. 31 below.

[28] See e.g. A. McColgan, 'In Defence of Battered Women who Kill' (1993) 13 OJLS 508. The argument about evaluative emotions which I have sketched is most fully explored in Kahan and Nussbaum, n. 2 above.

approach relates to character. The focus, crucially, is upon the quality of the attitude manifested *in the defendant's conduct, evaluated in the light of (a generous interpretation of) the context in which it occurred.* It is not, therefore, a globalized evaluation of the person's character; rather, it is an evaluative judgment which is *analogous* to the contextualized evaluations of character found in moral discourse. A defendant whose conduct is based on reasons which are thought to be consistent with the attitudes required of good citizens will be exonerated, while one who departs from those standards is seen as justifiably condemned notwithstanding any inquiry into whether she had the capacity to behave in—for example—a less hot-blooded or cowardly way. At an explanatory level, the reasons approach offers one way of rationalizing the widespread application of 'reasonableness' standards in the specification of defences.

It therefore seems to be worth exploring the implications of this emerging 'reasons-based' view of defences for partial defences to murder in England and Wales. However, as I shall suggest, a consideration of these implications begins to raise some difficult questions about the practicality of the reasons-based approach—questions which will be highlighted in the more concrete discussion of the next section.

D. A Framework for Assessing Partial Defences to Murder in the Imperfect World

I now want to sketch a framework within which a reasons approach might contribute to an assessment of the range of actual and potential partial defences to murder in English law. For these purposes, two discrete forms of defence can be distinguished. The first are the 'exemptions' which recognize features of the defendant which mark her out as beyond the purview of criminal law's evaluative judgments. Defendants pleading defences such as insanity are not so much pleading excuses which remove responsibility as arguing that they were not capable of acting responsibly in the given sense. Hence exemptions are in a deep sense capacity-based.[29] On the reasons-based approach to defences, those pleading exemptions are simply those who are incapable of normal modes of practical reasoning. It appears to follow that exemptions should operate as total rather than partial defences, and that decisions about the appropriate social response to someone who engages in harmful or dangerous conduct but who qualifies for an exemption from criminal responsibility should be made outside the purview of the criminal process. In current English law, of course, diminished responsibility occupies the peculiar position of a 'partial exemption'—a

---

[29] On this point, see H. Fingarette, 'Criminal Insanity', in French (ed.), n. 22 above, 242–50.

position which is closely related to the specific context of the mandatory life sentence for murder. Arguably, however, on the basis of a more adequate elaboration of partial defences, some cases currently treated as cases of diminished responsibility might be assimilated with other partial defences, leaving genuine cases of exemption to be dealt with in something like the way that insanity cases are dealt with today.

The second group of defences would be those based on the evaluation that the defendant has acted on the basis of socially approved reasons, or has departed from the norm of what can reasonably be expected of someone in the defendant's social position and circumstances only to an understandable or partially forgivable degree. Here we can include the majority of existing defences such as duress, self-defence, provocation, mistake and so on. In principle, there seems to be no reason why any of these should operate exclusively as total or as partial defences. On the reasons-based approach, since criminal law is inevitably involved in moral grading, the main imperative would seem to be to achieve, through a combination of offence definitions, defences, and sentencing principles, a reasonably even-handed and finely tuned practice of evaluation, at least within categories of offence of particular levels of seriousness. Hence any of the defences might operate as partial defences—*if* there were a suitable lesser offence on offer. This, of course, brings us back to the imperfect world in which the existence of such offences is uneven. I shall return to the implications of this imperfection below. A priori, it would seem that this approach would militate in favour of an expansion of partial defences across criminal law, because such an expansion would promote publicity and accountability in evaluative reasoning. An important question arises, however, as to how the relevant decision-making functions should be divided between judge and jury. This, again, is an issue to which I shall return.

The two categories of exemption and exculpatory reasons undoubtedly accommodate the vast majority of defences currently known to English criminal law. There is, however, a troubling third category of situations which pose real normative difficulties for criminal liability yet which do not fit neatly into the first two categories of defences. These are what we might call 'situations of blocked evaluation'. Take, for example, a case such as *Kingston*:[30] a defendant who, through a high level of involuntary intoxication, behaved in a way in which—it can plausibly be argued—he would never have behaved had he not been intoxicated.[31] Like the person claiming

---

[30] N. 14 above.

[31] A complication of Kingston's case was the fact that there was evidence that he had an underlying sexual preference for the kind of (illegal) behaviour in which he engaged while intoxicated. This allowed the Court to infer that the intoxication merely loosened his inhibitions, and that he had indeed acted with the requisite mens rea. The legal effect of the decision is to confirm that intoxication, whether voluntary or involuntary, is never a genuine defence, but merely evidence of the lack of mens rea. However, if we are considering the proper place of intoxication among defences, the case is highly instructive, not least in demonstrating the

an exemption, such a person is arguing that her situation was such that she was incapable of reasoning in a normal way and hence of responding to the criminal law framework. But unlike the person claiming an exemption, the circumstances are such that we are not inclined to make any more general judgment about her capacity to participate in criminal law's reasoning system. This is not least because the circumstances in which the incapacity arose are not ones which would be regarded as unreasonable. Hence prior fault would exclude such defences. These people might be regarded, as Sullivan has argued, as suffering a temporary lapse of character.[32] I suggest that it might be better to think of these cases in terms of temporary lapses of normal conditions of agency, given that the lapse is of the kind which removes or seriously undermines the normal reasoning process. Whatever label is chosen, the point is that it is difficult to evaluate such defendants' conduct on the basis of the reasons-based approach of the second group of defences—or, to put it in a different way, the usual inferences about character or attitude to criminal law proscriptions are blocked. The seriously involuntarily intoxicated defendant is simply not engaged in the usual process of practical reasoning, and it seems obtuse to insist on either judging her as if she is or consigning her to the category of exemptions.

Even without the addition of this third, troubling category, the classification which I have sketched cuts to some degree across the distinction between character- and capacity-based approaches. Certainly, it differs from the familiar model of incapacity-based excuse. Let me pause for a moment to consider what, if anything, is lost by this. Are there plausible defences which are excluded from this framework? The main candidate here is the excuse of the person who has made an honest but unreasonable mistake. This will doubtless discomfit commentators of a strongly subjectivist persuasion. I will simply confess that I do not find it seriously troubling, for three reasons. The first reason is that, wherever the mistake is not grossly unreasonable, it might well be that a more general instantiation of partial excuses on the reasons-based approach would accommodate the

---

pitfalls implicit in an incautious interpretation of the idea that issues of 'character' are relevant to the defences. For this reason, though I am persuaded by Sullivan's argument about involuntary intoxication (see immediately below), I prefer to think of such cases as instances of 'blocked evaluation' or, perhaps, 'temporary lapse of the normal conditions of agency' rather than, as he puts it, as instances of 'lapse of character'. This is not to say, however, that a subtle interpretation of the role of character in evaluative judgments is incompatible with a critique of the decision. One could argue, e.g., that the relevant question of evaluation was not Kingston's character in the sense of his sexual preferences but rather his character, manifested in his previous life, as someone who did not act on those preferences when they were proscribed. Hence the sort of 'character evidence' relevant to the exculpatory reasons defences may also be relevant to defences of blocked evaluation: the fact that Kingston had apparently not acted on his paedophile preferences before was indirect proof of the fact that, at the time, his normal powers of practical reasoning were temporarily suspended.

[32] N. 24 above; see also W. Wilson, 'Involuntary Intoxication: Excusing the Inexcusable?' (1995) 1 RP 25.

defendant. Hence the person who kills in self-defence and who is mistaken either in the sense that she misjudges the existence of the threat or in the sense that she misjudges the degree of force needed to avert it may plead her case within the reasons-based framework, and may argue that her departure from the mean of reasoned assessment is not so great as to justify total liability. The second reason is that those in what is probably the most troubling group—that is, defendants of whom we have reason to doubt, in the circumstances, their ability to conform to a reasonable standard—are likely to fall within either the group of exemptions or the group of blocked evaluation due to a temporary lapse of normal conditions of agency. The third (and least telling) reason is the familiar argument that, notwithstanding its primacy in doctrinal debate, the subjective/objective distinction is of relatively low practical significance given that unreasonable mistakes will often be disbelieved by the trier of fact. Hence even if they afford a defence (or exculpating argument) as a matter of law, as a matter of practice, defendants like those in *DPP* v. *Morgan*[33] will often find themselves convicted. Without the first two reasons, however, the third would be inconclusive, not least because the existence of a purely subjective test may be relevant to decisions about prosecution.

On the basis of the three-fold classification, let me set out a possible scheme for analysing partial defences to murder.

Defences	*exemptions*	*blocked evaluation (falling short of exemption)*	*exculpatory reasons*
	insanity diminished responsibility[34]	involuntary intoxication [situations of extreme duress, fear, distress, despair] involuntary automatism (without prior fault)	self-defence ? provocation [mercy killing] [necessity] reasonable mistake
Evidential base	specialist evidence about capacity	specialist evidence about capacity plus evaluative argument about inference	general evidence plus evaluative argument
Consequences	acquittal; further decision-making outside criminal process	acquittal; reduction to lesser offence; sentencing mitigation	acquittal; reduction to lesser offence; sentence mitigation

---

[33] [1976] AC 182.
[34] See p. 116 above, on whether the conceptualization of diminished responsibility as an exemption is consistent with its being only a partial defence.

E. IMPLICATIONS FOR THE EXPANSION OF PARTIAL DEFENCES

Let me now consider what implications such a framework might have for some of the circumstances which have given rise to difficulty in the current framework, prompting calls for an expansion of the defences to homicide. I shall take just a few examples which raise very different sorts of difficulty, and which therefore give us a reasonable idea of how the proposed framework might affect current debates.

The first example is that of so-called mercy killing. As it stands, English law recognizes no defence, partial or total, to murder which could accommodate mercy killing, and cases which attract sufficient sympathy or moral ambivalence are filtered out of the penal system by the exercise of prosecution discretion, by 'perverse' jury verdicts, or by manipulation of the evidence into the conceptual straitjacket of diminished responsibility. By contrast, on the suggested approach, certain kinds of mercy killing might fall into the category of exculpatory reasons (or, though more tenuously, into that of blocked evaluation—see further, p. 124 below). It is interesting to note in this context that the 'reasons' category implies a more fluid structure for defences than is currently the case, suggesting a number of broad headings which function as signals for criminal law's subjects rather than as exclusive, legal-precedent driven categories. Hence we could imagine a partial defence of either necessity or duress of circumstances finding a foothold in the reasons-based approach: a person who, for example, kills a close relative who is in unbearable agony which medical intervention is powerless to alleviate might well be judged to have acted out of sufficiently socially approved emotions, reasons, or motives as to merit evaluation as guilty of a lesser form of homicide. In principle, then, the reasons approach would militate in favour of such a defence. However, as I shall discuss below, both legal-institutional practicalities and political constraints—not least the ambivalence or opposition of relevant interest groups such as religious institutions—directly affect the feasibility of translating this normative argument into legal practice.

A second example would be that of involuntary intoxication and, perhaps, other forms of involuntary automatism. Let us consider a subset of such cases, characterized in the following way. Firstly, let us assume an absence of prior fault—supposing, for example, that a third party has laced a defendant's drink or that involuntary exhaustion has caused her to be in a state of somnambulism. Secondly, let us assume that the circumstances are such as to raise no expectation that the situation will reoccur. Thirdly, let us make the closely related assumption that the circumstances generate no reason to make any more general inference about reasoning capacity such as would be appropriate to an exemption. As I have already argued, Sullivan has provided a convincing account of why such cases should attract a defence. But should they attract total or partial defences? In principle, they appear to militate in favour of complete defences: the normal process of evaluation, which could generate a finding of partial defence, is blocked. It might be argued that in cases where there is some degree of prior fault in the creation of the state of intoxication or automatism, a partial defence might be appropriate. Such a legal position is, very unevenly, realized in the current legal rules on voluntary intoxication and so-called 'self-induced automatism'.[35] But, on the face of it, it would seem more consistent simply to provide for a specific offence of committing an offence while intoxicated, specifying aggravating and mitigating factors which should determine the grading of such an offence.

Is the category of blocked evaluation exhausted by the *sui generis* cases of involuntary intoxication and involuntary automatism? It must be admitted that the boundaries of the category are extremely difficult to draw. To explore this problem, let us return to the example of mercy killing. Yet more controversial than the reasons analysis explored above is a somewhat different and very acute kind of case where someone commits a 'mercy killing' in a moment of extreme distress or despair. It might be argued that this person merits formal mitigation on the basis that the exigency of their situation edges out the normal processes of reasoning while also blocking the inferences which would normally be drawn from their behaviour. This might be a more appropriate way of thinking, for example, about someone who in a crisis of despair impulsively switches off a life-support machine because they simply cannot bear the sight of another person's agony. The line between this and the reasons analysis is, admittedly, fine, but I raise it because I entertain some doubts about the suitability of the reasons analysis in the context of such extreme circumstances. It is a difficult judgment, however, whether this situation is sufficiently analogous to the instance of involuntary intoxication or temporary automatism which fit most neatly into the blocked evaluation category.

Let us take, finally, the case of someone who uses what would generally be regarded as disproportionate force in legitimate self-defence. Here again, both the blocked evaluation and the reasons categories would suggest that a partial defence can be accommodated. In cases of extreme urgency and immediacy, we might be inclined to argue that a full inference of culpability is blocked by the stringency of the situation; particularly in the context of, for example, a victim of long-term domestic abuse, there may be good reason to think that evaluation on the basis of the normal conditions for practical reasoning is simply excluded, and here evidence of the psychological effects of long-term violence may be relevant even beyond what I have called the exemptions. More usually, however, the argument will be framed within the category of exculpatory reasons: though someone who reacts

---

[35] See Ashworth, n. 4 above, 217–26.

excessively in self-defence may depart from the normal standards of practical reasonableness, this departure is morally distinguishable from that of the person who knows no such pressure. Moreover, this could be fine-tuned according to what is expected of people occupying different social roles—the trained soldier, the civilian, the victim of long-term violence (though, as Gardner recognizes, the specification of the roles which should be objects of criminal law's cognizance is a matter of some difficulty).[36] Obviously, a similar argument can be made about duress by threats: on a reasons view, the law's current distinction between defendants who kill under provocation and those who kill under duress looks both bizarre and unjust. In each of these cases, there would be little justification, on a reasons approach, for limiting relevant evidence too closely to the narrow time frame of the killing: since the evaluative judgment at stake is inevitably contextual, any features of history or social context bearing on the evaluation ought in principle to be admissible.

F. PRACTICAL ISSUES ARISING FROM A REASONS-BASED APPROACH

Let me now consider some of the difficult practical questions arising from the claim that many defences operate by evaluating the defendant's reasons for action. As will be apparent, I am in principle sympathetic to the approach. I find it both morally plausible and persuasive in its full acknowledgement of the degree to which criminal courts are engaged in making evaluative judgments, and therefore need to draw on a legal framework which speaks directly to evaluative concerns. However, as may also be apparent from the foregoing discussion, I perceive a number of difficulties arising out of the approach.

The reasons approach proceeds from a view of legal judgment as strongly continuous with moral judgment. Criminal law decision-making is, however, a judgment which takes place in a very distinctive institutional context, and which has equally distinctive practical effects in terms of

---

[36] Gardner, n. 2 above, 592 et seq. He argues, e.g., that the role of 'victim of long term violence' cannot legitimately be recognized by criminal law since it is defined in terms of conduct which criminal law itself proscribes. I am not convinced that this conclusion follows: given that the role would be constructed for purposes consistent with criminal law's rationale, it is not clear that the case is substantially different from that of, say, duress by threats, where criminal law recognizes a victimized-subject position in order to provide for adequate exculpation. Be that as it may, this is certainly not a straightforward issue for contemporary criminal law, as the inconclusive debates about the 'subjectification' and gender of the viewpoint of the 'reasonable' person demonstrate; see e.g. H. Allen, 'One Law for All Reasonable Persons' (1988) 16 IJSL 419. One important reason, Gardner argues, is that the law's categories are no longer role-based. Yet the so-called regulatory offences appear to be a rather broad exception here, and one merit of the reasons approach is its potential to rationalize defences in the regulatory area more satisfactorily than does the capacity approach.

conviction and punishment. This institutional particularity has both moral
and practical implications. One of the most insistent moral implications is
a set of arguments associated with the rule of law: that is that criminal law
must be framed in a reasonably clear, accessible and intelligible way, such
that criminal law's subjects are able to adjust their behaviour according to
its dictates. Whatever the plausibility of a rational-choice conception of
criminal conduct, it seems clear that there are, in any democratic society,
strong reasons to respect values of publicity and accountability in the articulation and operation of the defences. From one point of view, the reasons
approach responds to precisely this concern through its articulation with
'socially approved' motivations of emotional and instrumental reason. But,
in the late twentieth or early twenty-first century, can these socially
approved motivations or standards of practical reasonableness be assumed
to be sufficiently clear, sufficiently widely agreed upon, to generate a
predictable structure for the operation of defences? Can the point of view
of the 'practically reasonable citizen' be identified with any less difficulty
than that of the 'reasonable person'?[37]

Of course, it could be (and often is) argued that the rule of law argument
is less pressing in relation to defences than to offence definitions: defendants
have a pressing need to be informed of conduct which is proscribed,
whereas defences are merely privileges, concessions to human frailty, on the
basis of which we would not expect people to adjust their conduct.[38] This
argument, which is comforting to the capacity approach, cannot, however,
entirely satisfy the reasons theorist. For, just as the reasons framework tends
to loosen the justification/excuse divide, it is less obviously premised on a
very clear offence/defence distinction. Even on the capacity view, the implications of the offence/defence distinction for the rule of law are uncertain:
justificatory defences such as self-defence, for example, may be relied upon
with some confidence as rules of conduct.

On the reasons view, the distinction is yet more fragile. For, on a broad
interpretation of the approach, the structure of the argument seems to be
that a defendant's satisfying an offence definition merely puts in place a
presumption of blameworthiness—a presumption which must then be
examined in relation to a range of possible 'defences' which might question whether the presumptive evaluation can really be justified according
to prevailing social standards. Indeed, one might argue on the reasons
approach that defendants should not even have to plead a specific defence:
rather, they should be invited to lead evidence which might persuade a
judge (or jury; see p. 128 below) that their conduct did not in fact fall (or

---

[37] On the feminist issues arising from the 'reasonable person' debate, see Allen, n. 36 above,
and Celia Wells's contribution to this collection, Chapter 4 above.

[38] See Fletcher (1993), n. 16 above. He argues e.g. that excuses are not things which we
should be able to rely on in deciding our actions, while justifications should be accessible *ex
ante* (cf. the contrary view of the editors in Shute et al., n. 16 above, 12).

sufficiently far) short of prevailing standards of practical reasonableness. Yet even in the context of homicide—a generous case study for the reasons approach given its evident resonance with widely shared moral values—such prevailing standards are notoriously contentious, as is illustrated by cases such as provoked and mercy killing. This prompts the question whether the reasons approach is feasible, or really captures the nature of the distinctively legal mode of judgment.[39] In short, have the social conditions which made a reasons approach feasible as a *social* framework in, for example, Ancient Greece, long since been displaced: can criminal law today solve its various problems of coordination and legitimation through the recognition of the role of courts in general evaluation of motive, character, and conduct?

In assessing the case for institutionalizing the reasons view, one therefore has to take account of both the increasing scope of criminal law and the increasing value-pluralism which is recognized as not only legitimate but also healthy in a democratic society. These historical conditions, it might be argued, are precisely what underpins the appeal of the alternative, strongly subjective, capacity-based approach, which founds excuses (as well as mens rea) primarily in terms of morally neutral, factual criteria like voluntariness, choice, and capacity.[40] This would explain the discomfiture among subjectivists about the pervasive 'reasonableness' standards which structure both mens rea and defences. It would also suggest a basis for the fact that justifications, which overtly evaluate the substantive recommendations of the defendant's conduct, are generally seen as more problematic within the capacity tradition than are the excuses, whose purchase is argued to be confined merely to the conditions for attribution.

My argument here is not the familiar objection that the reasons approach is unduly perfectionist. Indeed, I would accept the idea that criminal law is inevitably in the business of what might be called 'negative perfectionism': that is, of enforcing some conception of what is beyond the purview of a good life. Rather, my argument questions how detailed, how 'thick' that conception can practicably be. This is a particularly pressing concern in the area of so-called regulatory offences—and perhaps corporate manslaughter—where the standards of reasonableness are obviously role-based and highly contentious. On the one hand, the reasons-based approach holds out the hope that criminal law might reflect—or construct?—shared judgments about reasons relevant and appropriate to

---

[39] One could draw an analogy here with the difficulties arising out of the recent development of the law of theft, in which sharply delineated definitional elements have progressively been loosened by both legislation and case-law, inviting less legally structured judgments of guilt and, arguably, much greater inequality in the substantive standards being applied; see Lacey and Wells, n. 17 above, ch. 3.II.a.

[40] For an elaboration of the argument, see Norrie, n. 17 above; for an examination of the 'subjectification' of standards of fault in homicide and its broader implications for criminal law, see L. Farmer, *Criminal Law, Tradition and Legal Order* (Cambridge, 1997), ch. 5.

the differentiated social roles which modern criminal law underpins. In the area of corporate wrongdoing, for example, it seems less intractable a model for working out appropriate defences than the subjective, capacity-based approach. On the other hand, the reasons approach begs the yawning question of how this mode of argumentation can be mobilized within a relatively rigid institutional framework—criminal law—operating in a morally pluralistic social order.

The foregoing argument demonstrates that moral and practical implications are impossible fully to separate. However, it is worth noting a specific practical question which also arises from the reasons approach. Who should set the terms of the evaluation: legislature, judge, or jury? If at least part of the role of criminal law is to reinforce shared social evaluations, it would seem that the legislature should delineate at least the main headings under which prima facie culpability is displaced. But beyond this, an implication of some reasons theorists' argument would seem to be that the main decision-making power should rest, in serious cases, with the jury, who can be expected to reflect social assumptions about deviations from the practically reasonable norm. Yet, as we know very well from many current areas—the operation of the dishonesty test in theft, the interpretation of the reasonableness requirement in defences such as provocation and duress—this leads to inequalities in the treatment accorded to different defendants and moreover to an unevenness which, because of the secrecy of jury determinations, it is impossible even to identify, debate, or rationalize. Furthermore, questions can be raised about the capacity of juries to become involved in the more differentiated decision-making that a more finely graded criminal law or a wider array of partial defences would imply. If, as many reasons theorists seem to assume, the criminal trial is in some sense a space for dialogue and debate about the content and application of key social norms, this would suggest a predominant role for judges. Furthermore, on this view of the criminal trial, grading is integral to the practice of judgment; hence defendants should presumably be allowed to lead and dispute evidence relevant to the evaluation of their conduct in just the same way irrespective of whether it happens to be defined as an issue going to offence element, defence, or sentencing mitigation.[41]

This argument in turn raises interesting issues about the nature of criminal law judgments in contemporary England and Wales. Let us assume for a moment that we could come up with a framework for defences which struck an appropriate balance between articulating and leaving open for contextual evaluation the scope of defences, and that we could find a means of specifying clearly, on the basis of a convincing rationale, the proper division of labour between judge and jury. Even if these conditions were met, it might be argued that a full instantiation of the reasons approach would

---

[41] See Wasik, n. 13 above.

somewhat unsettle the idea that criminal law is in the business of making dispositive decisions—or, as the systems theorists would have it,[42] engaging in binary coding: convict or acquit, guilty or not guilty, murder or manslaughter. As I have already argued, the reasons framework appears to militate in favour of a general instantiation of partial defences: it envisages courts as being inevitably involved in grading, and in a more finely-tuned grading than is usually the case in England and Wales. It seems to be an implication of this approach that decisions about sentence are intimately related to the core role of the court, and this in turn implies the far closer articulation of sentencing, evidential, and substantive law than is currently the case.

The reasons approach also implies a more evenly graded substantive criminal law. This is arguably particularly urgent in the case of offences such as homicide, for at least two reasons. Firstly, the gravity of homicide places a special burden on criminal law to attempt systematic fine-tuning of judgments of relative seriousness; secondly, the emotive nature of public reactions to certain kinds of homicide—one has only to think of the recent debates about Robert Venables, John Thompson, and Mary Bell[43]—gives good reason not to leave the final grading to unstructured sentencing (let alone executive) discretion. The reasons approach implies, in short, a system significantly different from that which currently pertains: a world not just less imperfect in the sense of the abolition of the mandatory sentence for murder, but also in which so-called 'broad band' offences are refined and restructured, at least where the seriousness of the offence is such as to call forth widely shared judgments of evaluative distinction.

G. Imperfect Worlds, Less Imperfect Worlds, and Utopias . . .

Let me conclude by summarizing the implications of this discussion for law reform in imperfect and less imperfect worlds. In the radically imperfect world in which we are faced with the incoherent architecture of a mandatory life sentence for murder, a broad band offence of manslaughter and a wide degree of relatively unstructured sentencing discretion, there is a strong case not only for maintaining the existing partial defences to murder but for expanding them to include duress of circumstances or threats, the use of excessive force in self-defence, and for introducing a properly specified defence of mercy killing. The rationale in each case is the judgment that the defendant's behaviour resonates with what are generally regarded as

---

[42] See e.g. G. Teubner, *Law as an Autopoietic System* (Oxford, 1993).
[43] See A. Norrie, 'The Limits of Justice: Finding Fault in Criminal Law' (1996) 59 MLR 540.

appropriate social reasons and motivations to a sufficient degree that the attribution of the murder label—let alone the imposition of a mandatory life sentence—is inappropriate. Furthermore, there is a case for clarifying the relevance of evidence about social and emotional context and for ensuring that behaviour prompted by reasonable levels of emotions such as fear, despair, and distress are mitigated at least as generously as behaviour prompted by emotions such as anger, jealousy, and self-preservation.

A less imperfect world, however, would be one in which the coherence of the infrastructure would be improved by the removal of the mandatory sentence. At that stage, one would have to ask hard questions about the real importance of labelling homicides as 'murder' and 'manslaughter', and about the relationship between labelling and grading. Would it make sense to have two separate homicide offences with the same sentencing provisions? Does the increased legal technicality which is often argued to be a consequence of more finely graded offences pose a serious objection to their development? If labelling is really important, one might argue that we should then reconstruct voluntary manslaughter in relation to a discrete set of labels: provoked killing; killing under duress; killing in panic; mercy killing and so on. Grading might then still be left to sentencing discretion. But if we think that the labels themselves have grading implications, and/or if we think that the jury or indeed prosecution should have a further say in grading, the clear implication is that we need further sentencing guidelines.[44] In the English system, the likeliest sources of such guidelines are the Sentencing Advisory Panel and the Court of Appeal. A gradual elaboration of criteria in these fora would fit well with the idea of the criminal process as a forum for the elaboration of and debate about shared evaluative standards, while avoiding the rigidity of legislative sentencing frameworks. But, given the huge practical importance of legal grading, the evenness and systematicity of such guidelines will have to be much improved if they are to deal justly with defendants. In a system of moral judgment, it may well be the label which counts. In a system of legal judgment, the grading has the most vivid effect on defendants.

Finally, should we hope ultimately to move from the less imperfect world of no mandatory sentence, expanded partial defences, and elaborated sentencing criteria to the utopia of at-large moral evaluation by criminal courts which seems to be implied by some of the more expansive interpretations of the reasons-based approach? The answer is a simple and resounding 'no'. Even in the quintessentially 'moral' area of homicide, criminal law is not, at root, a system of moral judgment. It is a system of social judgment which we require to depart as little as possible from shared moral ideas. But it is a system which also faces its most intractable coordination and legitimation

---

[44] We also need a more systematic approach to the admissibility and testing of evidence relevant to sentence; again, see Wasik, n. 13 above.

problems precisely because few moral ideas are unambiguously shared in pluralist societies. Even in the field of homicide, cases such as abortion and mercy killing show that deep moral divisions exist. Furthermore, these divisions tend to surface with particular clarity in the context of defences— claims which, as the reasons theorists show so well, inevitably raise questions of motivation. In this context, the criminal law's job is to fix with reasonable specificity a standard which it applies as even-handedly as possible. Hence though Lord Hoffmann may have been right to argue that the decision about the ending of Anthony Bland's life was ultimately a moral one,[45] this was in part because of a failure in existing legal provisions. In a democracy, the most we can ask of our system of criminal law is that it apply articulated standards in a consistent, open way and according to distributions of power which maximize effectiveness and accountability. It is rather the political system which we should be able to call upon to provide an adequate forum for the constant renegotiation of contentious issues provisionally crystallized in criminal laws.

[45] *Airedale NHS Trust v. Bland* [1993] AC 89.

6

Context and Culpability in Involuntary Manslaughter: Principle or Instinct?

C. M. V. CLARKSON[*]

A. Introduction

When a person has been unlawfully killed, the law's response (in terms of investigation, prosecution, and offence categories) is strongly influenced by the context in which the killing took place. Most killings occur as a result of unlawful[1] risk-creating activity such as careless or dangerous driving, breaches of the Health and Safety at Work etc. Act 1974, or criminal attacks such as assault. With respect to the first of these two categories, the most common response is for a prosecution to be brought in relation to the underlying dangerous activity. Thus defendants will simply be charged with careless or dangerous driving or with breaches of the Health and Safety at Work etc. Act 1974 and the fact that death has resulted will only be considered, if at all, at the sentencing stage. In driving cases there is a further option: causing death by dangerous driving[2] or causing death by careless driving when under the influence of drink or drugs.[3] However, in all these cases there is a further possibility: manslaughter. While this is a statistical rarity in cases of deaths on the road or at work, this charge is commonly employed where a death results from a violent attack (assuming a murder charge is inappropriate) and, further, a manslaughter charge is often the only option where a death results from a prima facie lawful activity such as caring for frail persons or performing surgical operations.

The offence of manslaughter is exceedingly broad and there has been much clamour for its reform. This pressure has come from two opposing extremes. On the one hand, there are those who assert it is too broad and that the minimum fault threshold needs raising. On the other hand, there are those who argue that its reach needs broadening (either in substantive

---

[*] Professor of Law, University of Leicester.
[1] Not necessarily unlawful for purposes of constructive manslaughter.
[2] Road Traffic Act 1988, s. 1.   [3] Ibid., s. 3A.

or enforcement terms) so that it can be more effectively utilized in cases where deaths have been caused at work or in 'disasters', such as train crashes, or on the road. The Law Commission has addressed some of these concerns and has proposed a fundamental restructuring of the law of involuntary manslaughter. In doing this it stated: 'We believe that the law should be founded on principle rather than instinct.'[4] Naturally enough, the Law Commission believes that its proposals for reform are indeed founded on principle and that counter-proposals are based purely on instinct. In this Chapter it will argued that a rethinking of the law of involuntary manslaughter could involve some principles different to those underlying the Law Commission's proposals.

I shall first briefly outline the present law and then consider the Law Commission's proposals for reform. In doing this, the relationship between involuntary manslaughter and its close cousin, vehicular homicide, will be sketched.[5] Following this, a rethinking of the law will be suggested. This will involve a consideration of whether involuntary manslaughter should exist as a single broad offence or be subdivided into more specific offences. Next there will be a discussion of the criteria upon which such specific offences should be based. As part of this enquiry it will be necessary to consider, in particular, the role of such offences in cases of deaths at work, in 'disasters', and on the road. In suggesting new specific offences there will be a consideration of the minimum fault requirements, nomenclature, and the level of seriousness of each offence.

B. PRESENT LAW

The crime of manslaughter is a single offence encompassing all unlawful killings, other than murder and certain other homicides specifically catered for by statute.[6] Certain cases of manslaughter are commonly termed 'voluntary manslaughter'.[7] The remainder are labelled 'involuntary manslaughter'. This is not a discrete crime in the sense that one is charged with or convicted of the offence. It is simply a convenient label to describe those residual unlawful killings not otherwise specifically catered for by the law.

Involuntary manslaughter covers killings just short of murder all the way

[4] Law Commission, *Legislating the Criminal Code: Involuntary Manslaughter* (Law Com. no. 237) (1996), para. 5.15.
[5] Detail relating to the fault requirements for the vehicular homicide offences is beyond the scope of this Chapter.
[6] Infanticide (Infanticide Act 1938, s. 1); causing death by dangerous driving (Road Traffic Act 1988, s. 1); causing death by careless driving when under the influence of drink or drugs (Road Traffic Act 1988, s. 3A).
[7] These are cases where the defendant has the mens rea of murder but is afforded a partial excuse because of the existence of a mitigating factor: provocation, diminished responsibility, or suicide pact (Homicide Act 1957, ss. 2–4).

down to killings little more than accidents.[8] The culpability necessary for manslaughter can be established in one of three ways:

1. SUBJECTIVE-RECKLESS MANSLAUGHTER

Where the defendant subjectively foresees a risk of death or serious injury (but the degree of foresight fails to come within the *Woollin*[9] test of intention required for murder), there will be liability for manslaughter.[10] As the law of murder has been progressively narrowed with tighter tests of intention, so this category of manslaughter has been correspondingly broadened to occupy the 'area vacated by murder'.[11] There is little specific authority about this species of manslaughter because in practice such cases are usually dealt with as unlawful-act manslaughter.[12] This category also covers cases where the defendant is charged with murder but the jury convict of manslaughter[13] or the appellate courts substitute a verdict of manslaughter[14] or where the defendant pleads guilty to manslaughter having a plea of not guilty to murder accepted.[15]

2. CONSTRUCTIVE MANSLAUGHTER

Where the defendant commits a dangerous and unlawful act which results in death there will be liability for manslaughter. The unlawful act must constitute a crime and be criminal for some reason other than that it has been negligently performed.[16] It must also be a positive act as it is doubtful whether an omission will suffice as the requisite unlawful act.[17] Most significantly, the unlawful act must be dangerous in the sense that it must expose the victim to the risk of some bodily harm resulting therefrom.[18]

3. GROSS-NEGLIGENCE MANSLAUGHTER

Where the defendant owes a duty of care to the victim[19] and breaches that duty in a grossly negligent manner causing death, there can be liability for

---

[8] *Walker* (1992) 13 Cr App R(S) 474, 476.   [9] [1999] 1 Cr App R 8.

[10] Law Commission, n. 4 above, paras. 2.26, 2.27.

[11] J. C. Smith, Commentary to *Adomako* [1994] Crim LR 758, 759.

[12] Law Commission, n. 4 above, para. 2.27.

[13] e.g. *Kime* [1999] 2 Cr App R(S) 3; *Pigott* [1999] 1 Cr App R(S) 392.

[14] e.g. *Woollin*, n. 9 above; *Nedrick* [1986] 1 WLR 1025.

[15] e.g. *Jackson* [1999] 2 Cr App R(S) 77.   [16] *Andrews* v. *DPP* [1937] AC 576.

[17] *Lowe* [1973] QB 702.

[18] *Church* [1966] 1 QB 59. Exposure to a risk of shock or fright will not suffice unless it was foreseeable that the shock would lead to a physical injury such as a heart attack; see *Dawson* (1985) 81 Cr App R 23.

[19] Whether a duty of care exists is of particular importance in cases of omissions. See e.g. *Singh* [1999] Crim LR 582; *Khan* [1998] Crim LR 830. In relation to positive acts presumably all persons owe duties to others not to expose them to serious risks of death.

manslaughter. Whether there has been gross negligence is 'supremely a jury question';[20] the essence of the matter is whether 'having regard to the risk of death involved, the conduct of the defendant was so bad in all the circumstances as to amount in their judgment to a criminal act or omission'.[21] Thus, while constructive manslaughter only requires that a risk of some physical harm be foreseeable, gross-negligence manslaughter requires that a risk of death[22] be foreseeable.

Gross-negligence manslaughter is available in cases of 'motor manslaughter' despite the existence of the separate offences of causing death by dangerous driving and causing death by careless driving when under the influence of drink or drugs. It is also the species applicable in cases of 'corporate manslaughter'. However, as shall be seen, manslaughter convictions in such cases are something of a rarity.

It is difficult, in the absence of any research findings specifically on the point, to know the extent to which prosecutors rely on each of these categories especially as in many cases a plea of guilty to manslaughter is accepted on an indictment charging murder. However, a survey of the fifty-six involuntary manslaughter cases[23] reported between 1994 and mid-1999 in the Criminal Appeal Reports (Sentencing) reveals that there were arguably[24] only five cases in which there had been no unlawful act that could have sufficed for constructive manslaughter.[25] Of the fifty-one cases where an unlawful act had been committed, the facts are consistent with a finding of reckless manslaughter in thirty-one instances and in five cases there would

---

[20] *Adomako* [1995] 1 AC 171.   [21] Ibid., 187.

[22] This point is not uncontroversial. In *Adomako*, n. 20 above, 183, Lord Mackay appears to agree with the Court of Appeal (*Prentice* [1994] QB 302) that 'indifference to an obvious risk of injury to health' will suffice. Further, his approval of other authorities such as *Bateman* (1925) 19 Cr App R 8 ('disregard for life and safety'), *Stone* [1977] QB 354 ('disregard of danger to the health and welfare of the infirm person') and *R. v. West London Coroner, ex p. Gray* [1988] QB 467 ('obvious and serious risk to the health and welfare') suggests that a risk of something less than death will suffice. However, he twice emphasized that the risk must be one of death (187). This latter view has now been supported in *Singh*, n. 19 above.

[23] There were 2 convictions for 'motor manslaughter' where a vehicle was used, with hostility, as a weapon (*Gault* (1995) 16 Cr App R(S) 1013; *Ripley* [1997] 1 Cr App R(S) 19).

[24] The Court of Appeal, in sentencing appeals, does not often articulate which category of manslaughter it is dealing with, e.g. in *Cawthorne* [1996] 2 Cr App R(S) 445 the court considered that the jury verdict could have been returned on the basis of constructive manslaughter, provocation, or gross negligence. For the purposes of this survey I exercised my own judgment, not as to the actual basis of the trial prosecution and/or verdict, but as to which categories the case *could* have fallen into. Any findings from this survey must thus be treated with caution. Further, it is obvious that findings from appeal cases need not correlate with the general practice in the Crown Courts.

[25] Two of these cases involved asphyxiation during consensual sexual activity (*Billia* [1996] 1 Cr App R(S) 39; *Williamson* (1994) 15 Cr App R(S) 364); one involved a doctor prescribing drugs (*Saha* (1994) 15 Cr App R(S) 342); one involved the organization of leisure activities (*Kite* [1996] 2 Cr App R(S) 295) and one concerned the firing of a rocket at a football ground with the defendants believing it was only a flare (*A.-G.'s Refs. Nos. 27, 26 of 1994 (McAllister and Still)* (1995) 16 Cr App R(S) 675).

have been little problem establishing gross negligence.[26] Of some importance to the analysis later in this Chapter is the fact that in fourteen cases constructive manslaughter was the only possible route to a conviction.

C. Law Commission's Proposals

The Law Commission is highly critical of the present law seeing it largely as incoherent and devoid of principle. In essence, its main objections are three-fold:

1. Constructive Manslaughter

This offence is seen as 'unjustifiable in principle'[27] in that there need be no correspondence between the defendant's culpability and the resultant death which might be entirely fortuitous.

2. Gross-negligence Manslaughter

Apart from there being some uncertainty surrounding the present law (for example, the meaning of 'duty of care' under the *Adomako* test[28] and the extent of liability for omissions[29]) the main objection is that the *Adomako* test is circular in that the jury should convict of a crime if they think the defendant's conduct was criminal. This leads to problems with prosecutors being uncertain whether to prosecute and there being a danger of inconsistent verdicts. It also amounts to the jury deciding questions of law as it is for them to decide whether conduct amounts to a crime.[30]

3. Corporate Manslaughter

The Law Commission roundly condemns the identification doctrine and the difficulties it poses for manslaughter convictions. It also stresses the inadequacy of reliance upon the regulatory offences in the Health and Safety at Work etc. Act 1974.

Accordingly, the Law Commission has proposed abolishing the present law of involuntary manslaughter and replacing it with three new offences:

---

[26] Two other cases concerned intoxication where the defendant was too drunk to form the mens rea of murder.   [27] Law Commission, n. 4 above, para. 5.15.
[28] Ibid., paras. 3.10–3.13.   [29] Ibid., paras. 3.14–3.16.
[30] Ibid., para. 3.9. Prof. Sir John Smith has also argued that the *Adomako* test is defective in that the jury merely have to determine that the conduct is bad enough to be a crime whereas they should be asked whether it is bad enough to be 'condemned as the very grave crime of manslaughter' (Commentary to *Litchfield* [1998] Crim LR 507). However, this point loses some force when it is recalled that the decision to regard the conduct as criminal must be made with reference to the risk of death involved.

1. Reckless Killing

A person whose conduct causes the death of another will be guilty of this offence (punishable by a maximum of life imprisonment) if:

(a) he is aware of a risk that his conduct will cause death or serious injury; and
(b) it is unreasonable for him to take that risk having regard to the circumstances as he knows or believes them to be.[31]

This proposal is the least controversial and would cover the vast majority of cases currently dealt with as involuntary manslaughter.[32] Two points can, however, be made. The inclusion of awareness of a risk of serious injury in this category of manslaughter has been criticized[33] but is defended by the Law Commission 'as a matter of principle'[34] and 'in order to create parity with the law of murder'.[35] Given the ferociousness of recent attacks on the GBH rule in murder[36] one must question the wisdom of pursuing parity on this point. Secondly, this proposal has been criticized on the basis that there is no reference to the probability of the risk materializing. There is a risk that something will happen if there is any risk at all that it will happen, even if that risk is one in a thousand.[37] However, it is possible to support the Law Commission here. As they state, 'this type of conscious risk-taking . . . [is] the most reprehensible form of unintentional homicide, on the very borders of murder'.[38] Those who deliberately and knowingly take risks with the lives of others rightly deserve conviction for the proposed offence if the risks materialize and death results.

2. Killing by Gross Carelessness

A person whose conduct causes the death of another will be guilty of this offence (with a maximum sentence unspecified by the Law Commission) if:

(a) a risk that his conduct will cause death or serious injury would be obvious to a reasonable person in his position;
(b) he is capable of appreciating that risk at the material time; and
(c) either—
    (i) his conduct falls far below what can reasonably be expected of him in the circumstances; or
    (ii) he intends by his conduct to cause some injury or is aware of, and unreasonably takes, the risk that it may do so.[39]

---

[31] N. 4 above, Involuntary Homicide Bill, cl. 1(1).   [32] See p. 136 above.
[33] S. Yeo, *Fault in Homicide* (Sydney, 1997), 161–2.
[34] N. 4 above, para. 5.10. It is difficult to discern what this principle might be. The Report states that there is a very thin line between conduct that risks serious injury and conduct that risks death and that 'much time could be spent arguing' about it in court (ibid., para. 5.26). This smacks of pragmatism rather than principle.   [35] Ibid., para. 5.10.
[36] e.g. Lord Mustill in *A.-G.'s Ref. No. 3 of 1994* [1997] 3 All ER 936, 938, 946.
[37] Yeo, n. 33 above, 162.   [38] N. 4 above, para. 4.10.
[39] Ibid., Involuntary Homicide Bill, cl. 2(1).

This last subsection only applies if 'the conduct causing, or intended to cause, the injury constitutes an offence'.[40]

This new offence is modelled on the test of dangerousness in road traffic offences.[41] Despite a history of being deeply committed to subjectivism in criminal law, the Law Commission concedes that inadvertence may be culpable where the harm risked is great and the defendant is capable of perceiving the risk. Whether such an approach is justifiable is discussed later in this Chapter.

An undoubtedly controversial issue is the proposal to abolish the offence of constructive manslaughter in its present form. The Law Commission in its Consultation Paper[42] was of the view that constructive manslaughter should be completely abolished without any form of replacement. However, it recognized that there was 'a strong feeling in certain sections of the general public' that in such cases the law ought to mark the fact that death has been caused.[43] While clearly feeling that such views were irrational and ought not to influence the criminal law, the Commission nevertheless suggested that if it were felt, after consultation, that the 'emotional argument'[44] should prevail, then a separate lesser offence of 'causing death' could be created to cover cases where the defendant caused death while intending to cause injury to another or being reckless as to whether injury is caused. A maximum penalty of three years' imprisonment was suggested.[45]

Perhaps startled by the strength of the response from respondents favouring retention, in some form, of constructive manslaughter, the Law Commission in its Report chose for the first time to consider some of the philosophical '"moral luck" arguments'.[46] While ultimately still being unpersuaded, such views undoubtedly paved the way for the Commission to be able to 'sympathise with . . [such] instinct[s]'[47] and include a modified form of unlawful act manslaughter in its proposals. As an alternative to the requirement that the defendant's conduct fall far below reasonable expectations, under clause 2(1)(c)(ii) it is sufficient if the defendant intends to cause some injury or is aware of the risk of such injury and unreasonably takes the risk—provided this conduct constitutes an offence. It must be stressed that

---

[40] Ibid., cl. 2(4).

[41] N. 4 above, para. 5.25. It has been argued that 'there is something remiss in using a test devised to establish a situation (in this case, driving dangerously) for the purpose of describing the risk of a result occurring (in this case the risk of causing death or serious injury)' (Yeo, n. 33 above, 181). However, this criticism seems misplaced as under the provision the defendant's conduct must *both* fall far below what can reasonably be expected in the circumstances (describing the circumstances of the conduct) *and in so acting* expose the victim to an obvious risk of death or serious injury.

[42] Law Commission, *Involuntary Manslaughter* (Law Com. Consultation Paper no. 135) (1994).

[43] Ibid., para. 5.8.

[44] Ibid., para. 5.13.

[45] Ibid., paras. 5.12, 5.15.

[46] N. 4 above, paras. 4.30-4.42.

[47] Ibid., para. 5.15.

this is not merely a narrowing of constructive manslaughter to unlawful acts of violence where there is intention or recklessness as to injury. In addition to committing such an act of violence, it must be obvious from the defendant's conduct that there is a risk that death or serious injury will be caused. As the Commission state: '[this] alternative adds little or nothing to the reach of the offence'.[48] Virtually all such cases would satisfy the requirement of conduct falling far below the required standard. The alternative is added ostensibly to simplify the task of the jury and covertly as a 'sop' to the instinctive irrationalists who were opposed to the abolition of constructive manslaughter. Fuller argument in favour of a retention of some form of constructive manslaughter is reserved until later in this Chapter.

3. CORPORATE KILLING

A company commits this offence if:

(a) a management failure by the corporation is the cause or one of the causes of a person's death; and
(b) that failure constitutes conduct falling far below what can reasonably be expected of the corporation in the circumstances.[49]

Clause 4(2) explains that 'there is a management failure by the corporation if the way in which its activities are managed or organized fails to ensure the health and safety of persons employed in or affected by those activities'.

The important innovation in this provision is that it abandons the identification doctrine, under which it is necessary to identify a senior controlling officer of the company who committed the crime, and instead provides that the requisite culpability can be found in the company's policies and organizational practices if these fail to ensure the health and safety of other persons. While this offence is defined as being committed by management (human people) as opposed to the company itself because of the Commission's view that companies are only metaphysical entities and that it is people within companies that commit crimes,[50] it is nevertheless clear that the emphasis is on the *company's* management and organizational activities and failures. This is a virtual acceptance of the notion that a company itself can be at fault or possess mens rea (without any individual or even group of individuals being culpable), with the requisite fault being found in its defective (or, perhaps, non-existent) and dangerous policies and practices. This notion of direct corporate liability (as opposed to attribution doctrines) has been introduced in Australia[51] and strongly advocated in

---

[48] N. 4 above, para. 5.33.   [49] Ibid., Involuntary Homicide Bill, cl. 4(1).
[50] Ibid., para. 8.3. For a similar view, see G. R. Sullivan, 'Expressing Corporate Guilt' (1995) 15 OJLS 281.
[51] Criminal Code Act 1995. See Rose, '1995 Criminal Code Act: Corporate Criminal Provisions' (1995) 6 CLF 129.

both the United States[52] and the United Kingdom.[53] It should be noted that the new proposed offence of corporate killing would not preclude the possibility of a company being convicted of the Law Commission's offence of killing by gross carelessness in exceptional cases where the identification doctrine was satisfied.[54]

Finally, the Law Commission would retain the present offences of causing death by dangerous driving and causing death by careless driving when under the influence of drink or drugs but would allow the prosecution to charge either of the two new offences in exceptional cases, for example, if there were uncertainty as to whether the defendant was driving on a public road.[55]

D. The Way Forward

In rethinking the present law and assessing reform proposals, the first issue is whether there should be a single broad offence of involuntary manslaughter[56] or whether, as proposed by the Law Commission, there should be separate offences covering the same, or similar, territory. A separate offence is one bearing its own label and sentencing maximum. Secondly, if there is to be some degree of specificity in offence classifications, on what basis is this to be done? Should a new hierarchy be based on different degrees of culpability or on other criteria such as the context of the killing, the method of killing or the identity of the victim or killer? Finally, having established the basic structure, the issue of determining the minimum fault requirements for each offence must be assessed.

1. Separate Offences

The principle of fair labelling is widely accepted as one of the guiding principles that should underpin the criminal law.[57] Criminal offences should be categorized and labelled for symbolic reasons to capture the essence of the

---

[52] E. Ragozino, 'Replacing the Collective Knowledge Doctrine with a Better Theory for Establishing Corporate Mens Rea: The Duty Stratification Approach' (1995) 24 Southwestern LR 423, 424, 441–3; Laufer, 'Corporate Bodies and Guilty Minds' (1994) 43 Emory LJ 647, 666 et seq.

[53] C. Wells, *Corporations and Criminal Responsibility* (1993); C. M. V. Clarkson, 'Kicking Corporate Bodies and Damning their Souls' (1996) 59 MLR 557; id., 'Corporate Culpability' [1998] 2 Web J.

[54] N. 4 above, paras. 8.1, n. 1, 8.20, n. 28. This would apply particularly in cases where a 'one-man company' is involved as was the case in *Kite*, n. 25 above.

[55] N. 4 above, para. 5.69.

[56] This Chapter assumes the continued existence of the crime of murder and that calls for the merger of murder and manslaughter into a single broad offence of unlawful homicide will be resisted.

[57] See e.g. A. Ashworth, *Principles of Criminal Law*, 3rd edn. (Oxford, 1999), 90–3.

wrongdoing involved and to convey the level of rejection of the activity involved. Different levels of punishment should usually be imposed to reinforce this degree of rejection.[58] To take a simple example: the wrongdoing in robbery is qualitatively different from that in theft (involving an attack upon a person which can induce fear, risk of injury, further violence and so on). This difference is marked by the existence of a separate offence and, to emphasize that it is a more serious offence, robbery carries a much higher maximum penalty.[59]

From this, two things flow. Offences must be defined with sufficient specificity to capture what is morally significant about them and, secondly, they should be structured to reflect a hierarchy of seriousness. The present offence of manslaughter fails both tests. As seen, it is such a broad offence ranging from killings just short of murder to those little short of being accidents that the crime label has become morally uninformative. Secondly, the relative seriousness of various killings within this broad category remains unmarked and runs the risk of allowing too much discretionary power to sentencers—and to the police in the enforcement of the law. This problem is exacerbated by the fact that the offence can be committed in three different ways and the sentencer does not necessarily know the factual basis of the conviction when the defendant has pleaded guilty or even when there has been a jury conviction.[60] In *Cawthorne*[61] it was stated that while the trial judge had a discretion to ask the jury how it had reached a particular verdict, this would be inappropriate in cases of involuntary manslaughter as not all jurors might have arrived at the verdict by the same route. In *Jones*[62] it was stated that judges could ask jurors to explain the basis upon which the verdict had been reached (for instance, by handing written questions to the jury during the summing up indicating the different possible verdicts and the reasons for reaching the verdict). The fact still remains that there could be a wide diversity of responses by the jury leaving the judge with little guidance as to the overall basis of the verdict. These same problems reverberate through the system: appellate courts have similar difficulties when reviewing sentences and it poses problems in the evaluation of previous convictions and classification in prison.[63]

---

[58] As the criminal law should reflect common values and understandings such labelling must also be consistent with societal views of different forms of wrongdoing. A recent survey by Mitchell confirmed that public opinion endorses the principle of fair labelling and that, in relation to homicide, there should be distinct offence categories (B. Mitchell, 'Public Perceptions of Homicide and Criminal Justice' (1998) 38 Br J Crim 453, 468).

[59] Of course, not all crimes must carry different maximum penalties, e.g. one could conclude that two offences such as theft and obtaining property by deception involve such different wrongs that they need to be demarcated as separate offences, but that they are of comparable seriousness justifying the same maximum penalties (as was originally the case under the Theft Act 1968).

[60] M. Wasik, 'Form and Function in the Law of Involuntary Manslaughter' [1994] Crim LR 883.   [61] N. 24 above.
[62] (1999) 149 NLJ 249.   [63] Ashworth, n. 57 above, 91.

Acceptance of the above argument still leaves open the issue of how much specificity is required in order to mark relevant moral distinctions and levels of seriousness—and, critically, the problem of determining the bases upon which such distinctions are to be made.

In addressing these concerns three important issues need to be raised. Firstly, one must be cautious that moral specificity does not lead to moral (or, at any rate, public) confusion: the vice of 'particularism'.[64] Gardner, for instance, has argued in relation to non-fatal offences against the person that, in order to capture interesting moral differences between offences, one needs to retain much of the present plethora of offences contained in the Offences Against the Person Act 1861 such as choking, suffocating, or strangling (section 21), using stupefacients and overpowering substances (section 22), poisoning (sections 23 and 24), starving and exposing to the elements (section 26), burning, maiming, disfiguring, and disabling by the use of explosives (sections 28 to 30) and so on. To him, such offences are 'notable for the moral clarity with which they are differentiated'.[65] One can concede that there are indeed some moral differences between these offences but the issue is whether these differences are significant enough to warrant reflection by the substantive law. Given that the criminal law is a communicative enterprise, the labelling and structuring of offences must be done in such a manner that assists, rather than obscures, communication. In the United States when various states were trying to reduce and control judicial discretion in sentencing, several efforts were made to introduce greater specificity into offence categories so that narrower bands of punishment could be applied to each offence. The Twentieth-Century Fund Task Force examined the crime of armed robbery and concluded it would be necessary to divide the crime into six degrees, each with its own penalty.[66] As has been pointed out:

if the legislature actually *tried* to anticipate every conceivable offence and offender variation, the result would be a penal law of enormous length and complexity, replete with hair-splitting distinctions. We doubt whether any legislature would be willing or able to spend all its time hammering out a definition of Robbery in the 68th Degree; but even if it were, it is doubtful whether all offence variations could really be anticipated.[67]

Some homicide statutes in the United States have developed such a number of specific homicide offences (which can each be committed in several quite

[64] J. Horder, 'Rethinking Non-fatal Offences against the Person' (1994) 14 OJLS 335, 340.
[65] J. Gardner, 'Rationality and the Rule of Law in Offences against the Person' [1994] CLJ 502, 515. See also, Horder, n. 64 above.
[66] Report of the Twentieth-Century Fund Task Force on Criminal Sentencing, *Fair and Certain Punishment* (New York, NY, 1976), 18.
[67] Executive Advisory Committee on Sentencing in New York, *Crime and Punishment in New York: An Inquiry into Sentencing and the Criminal Justice System* (report to Governor Hugh L. Carey) (1979), 220.

distinct specified ways) that the result can only be described as morally bewildering.[68] Fair labelling is not an endorsement of the Trade Descriptions Act philosophy under which every detailed difference must be marked. Fair labelling inevitably involves something of a broad-brush approach and calls for questions of judgment as to when moral differences need to be marked by the criminal law. There must be sound reasons, say in terms of different levels of culpability or different contexts in which the offence is committed, justifying the existence of separate offences. In exercising this judgment common understandings of crimes can also be important and can endow the prohibited actions with social meaning.[69] Everyone understands the broad differences between, and different wrongs involved in offences of theft, deception,[70] burglary, handling stolen goods, and blackmail.[71] The same is simply not true with some of the arcane offences in the Offences Against the Person Act 1861 where one needs crime theorists to articulate the moral differences.

The second introductory caveat is that the degree of specificity in offences depends in part on, or is influenced by, one's sentencing system. Over the past few decades there has been an increasing recognition in the United States, Australia, and the United Kingdom (to name but a few) that some control over judicial discretion in sentencing is necessary.[72] One way of controlling this discretion is to subdivide substantive offences with some precision so that each offence has a narrow sentencing range. For reasons suggested above, this approach has been largely rejected although specific instances of this approach do occasionally occur.[73] For indictable offences in England and Wales (which all homicide offences are) the basic sentencing control device is the guideline judgment. The importance of such judgments has recently been strengthened by the creation of the Sentencing Advisory Panel whose function is to assist and advise the Court of Appeal in the development of sentencing guidelines. The creation of this Panel will, it is hoped, lead to a more systematic coverage of areas of law subjected to guideline judgments. At present no guideline judgment exists for involuntary manslaughter but one can perhaps predict the development of such

[68] See e.g. Ariz.Rev.Stat.Ann., ss. 13-1102–05; Colo.Rev.Stat.Ann., ss. 18-3-101–6; Ky.Rev.Stat., ss. 507-010–50.
[69] J. Gardner and S. Shute, 'The Wrongness of Rape' in J. Horder (ed.), *Oxford Essays in Jurisprudence*, 4th Series (Oxford, 2000).
[70] Of course, it is well known that *Gomez* [1993] AC 442 blurred the distinction between theft and obtaining property by deception; see generally S. Shute and J. Horder, 'Thieving and Deceiving: What is the Difference?' (1993) 56 MLR 548.
[71] An attempt to highlight some of the different wrongs involved in these offences can be seen in C. M. V. Clarkson, *Understanding Criminal Law*, 2nd edn. (London, 1995), 194–200.
[72] C. M. V. Clarkson and R. Morgan (eds.), *The Politics of Sentencing Reform* (Oxford, 1995).
[73] e.g. the Criminal Justice Act 1991 drew a distinction between burglaries of dwellings (maximum 14 years' imprisonment) and burglaries of non-dwellings (maximum 10 years' imprisonment).

guidelines in the foreseeable future. However, this would not remove the need, in fair labelling terms, for some division of the present broad offence. It simply means that over-specificity is not necessary as each new specific offence can be scrutinized by the Panel and its recommendations incorporated in a guideline judgment. In essence, the question would simply change to: what moral differences are so significant that they need to be reflected at the substantive offence level bearing in mind that lesser moral distinctions can be dealt with at the sentencing stage?

A final introductory point cannot be ignored—and this relates to the role of pragmatism. The criminal law, however reformulated, has to be operated by the mechanisms and personnel of the criminal justice system, particularly the police, the CPS, judges and (for homicide offences) juries. Pragmatism (in securing convictions for offences widely thought to deserve conviction) cannot be ignored here. Let us assume, for example, that a view is reached that causing death by dangerous driving is in every sense as morally reprehensible and serious as causing death by other dangerous activities (say, an attack with a knife).[74] This would not *necessarily* mean that the offence of causing death by dangerous driving should be abolished. *If* it were strongly and rationally believed (say, on the basis of empirical research) that juries would simply not convict of the offence of manslaughter in such cases,[75] there would be a strong case for retaining the present separate offence—and reflecting the lack of significant moral difference at the sentencing stage. There must, however, be strong reasons before pragmatism be allowed to prevail over principle.

2. BASES OF SEPARATE OFFENCES AND THEIR FAULT REQUIREMENTS

How then, bearing these issues in mind, should involuntary manslaughter and related offences involving unlawful killings be restructured? The problem is particularly acute here as, unlike non-fatal offences against the person where there is a variable resulting harm, the harm in homicide is prima facie[76] constant: the victim is dead. The prime candidates for capturing the essence of the wrongdoing are the culpability of the defendant (mens rea and/or negligence), the method of killing (for example, killing with a dangerous weapon, by torture[77] or poison[78]) or the context of the killing

---

[74] See, for instance, the views of some respondents to Law Commission, n. 4 above, para. 5.66.

[75] This was part of the reason for the introduction of the original offence of causing death by reckless driving; see B. MacKenna, 'Causing Death by Reckless or Dangerous Driving: A Suggestion' [1970] Crim LR 67.

[76] It is possible to argue that there could be further harm in some cases such as where the victim was made to suffer excessively prior to death; see C. M. V. Clarkson and H. Keating, *Criminal Law: Text and Materials*, 3rd edn. (London, 1994), 811.

[77] Idaho Code, s. 18-4003(a).   [78] Cal. Penal Code, s. 189.

(for example, through a business operation, while driving on a road, during the commission of an unlawful act, contract killings[79] or during an act of terrorism). Drawing on the experience of various states in the United States, other possible criteria could relate to the identity of the victim (killing a child[80] or a police officer engaged in the performance of duty[81]) or the identity of the killer (for example, a murderer confined in prison[82]).[83]

It is the argument of this Chapter that it is only the culpability of the defendant and certain contexts in which the killing occurs that should be relevant in structuring offences in the territory presently occupied by involuntary manslaughter and vehicular killings. The other potential factors listed above are not of sufficient moral significance and taking account of them at the substantive stage would raise the spectre of over-specificity warned against above.

There are two main reasons for ignoring the method of killing. In *Powell; English*[84] the House of Lords allowed knowledge of the method of killing (a knife or a wooden post) to be determinative of an accessory's liability. The argument is that a knife or a gun is intrinsically more dangerous than a wooden post. Engaging in an attack knowing that the more dangerous weapon could be used aggravates the offence. However, as has been argued elsewhere,[85] in all homicide cases the danger has materialized: the victim is dead. What should matter for murder is the state of mind of the defendant engaging in the attack. There can be little moral difference between an attack with a wooden post *realizing that death will result* and a similar attack involving a gun and having the same foresight. The same is logically true of reckless manslaughter (where what should matter in either case is the foresight of the possibility of death) and gross negligence: if the risk of *death* is obvious and death indeed results, the manner of causing death seems irrelevant. The argument is more difficult with constructive manslaughter as, if any form of this offence were to be retained, it could be limited to dangerous attacks and the use of a gun or knife could be regarded as indicative of such a level of danger. However, leaving aside the problem of which weapons or methods of killing would qualify for this limited category, it is surely the broader circumstances of the killing that determine the dangerousness of an attack. Fairly typical of constructive manslaughter cases is the fight scenario outside a pub or club where the victim is kicked to death. Repeatedly kicking someone, particularly in the region of the head or neck, is surely more dangerous than the

---

[79] La.Rev.Stat., s. 14.30(4).
[80] Ariz.Rev.Stat.Ann., s. 13-604.01(A).
[81] La.Rev.Stat., s. 14.30(2).
[82] NY Penal Law, s.125.27(1)(a)(iv).
[83] For a fuller list of the various factors taken into account in the United States in distinguishing homicide offences, see C. M. V. Clarkson and H. Keating, *Criminal Law: Text and Materials*, 4th edn. (London, 1998), 721–2. Current parole policy in England and Wales also distinguishes between different categories of murder; ibid., 722.
[84] [1998] 1 Cr App R 261.
[85] C. M. V. Clarkson, 'Complicity, *Powell* and Manslaughter' [1998] Crim LR 556.

actions of the defendant in *Larkin*[86] who caused death with a knife—but one that he only waved about as a threat with no intention of using it at all.

The second reason for ignoring the method of killing is that most of the methodological distinctions employed to subdivide homicide offences in the United States relate to intentional killings where the method of killing tells us *something else* about the blameworthiness of the defendant which can be important in jurisdictions where the death penalty is employed for certain categories of murder. For instance, poisoning a victim is the clearest possible evidence of premeditation, widely regarded in the United States as the 'worst' form of murder.[87] The same is true of some of the instances referred to above where the context of the killing could potentially be relevant: in particular, contract killings and deaths caused during acts of terrorism. However, cases of manslaughter (unintentional killing) by poison, torture, contract killing etc. are a statistical rarity. Such persons will generally intend to kill, so removing themselves from the realms of manslaughter. Nevertheless, there will be the occasional case where the torturer or poisoner does not have the mens rea of murder. (This would be more likely if the GBH rule were abolished and 'intention' restricted to direct intention.) There could well be something morally interesting about such actions. For example, the torturer is deliberately inflicting pain and suffering and will often be asserting power and causing degradation to the victim. However, it is questionable whether such a wrong is sufficiently distinctive and different from the typical manslaughter case (for example, repeatedly kicking someone on the head which also causes pain and suffering) to warrant separate classification. Bearing in mind the dangers of a proliferation of homicide offences and the rarity of such cases, factors such as prolonged pain and degradation are better regarded as aggravating factors at the sentencing stage.

The identity of the victim and the killer is also an inappropriate basis for distinguishing between homicide offences. This *might* be a legitimate criterion for the aggravation of non-fatal offences against the person such as assaulting a police officer in the execution of his or her duties or racially aggravated assault where the unaggravated offence carries a very low maximum penalty. However, the maximum sentences for homicide offences will almost inevitably be sufficiently high for such aggravating features (if that were deemed appropriate) to be incorporated into a guideline judgment and reflected at the sentencing level. While there might be deterrent and other reasons justifying an increased penalty for an assault upon a police officer, for example, it would be inappropriate to use such a criterion at the substantive level where the victim has been killed. Quite simply, all human life is equally valuable and the law should reflect this. For much the same

---

[86] (1942) 29 Cr App R 18.   [87] Clarkson and Keating, n. 83 above, 717–20.

reasons, the identity of the killer should be discounted.[88] In the United States there are deterrent rationales in relation to the death penalty for aggravating homicides by prisoners; these have no application in the United Kingdom.

What of the context of the killing in cases other than those considered above? Could that context be sufficiently material to justify the existence of a separate aggravated or mitigated homicide offence—or sufficiently morally distinctive to warrant a separate offence, albeit one not necessarily more or less serious?

The context in which the killing occurs should have no relevance in the case of reckless killings. Subject to the minor reservation noted above concerning foresight of serious harm, there can be little objection to the Law Commission's proposed offence of reckless killing.[89] It is simply a clearer articulation of the one species of involuntary manslaughter that presently exists uncontroversially. Respondents to the Law Commission's Consultation Paper overwhelmingly endorsed such an offence.[90] If a person is knowingly and unjustifiably prepared to risk another's life it is difficult to see how any context could mitigate the seriousness of the offence. Such killings are the near-neighbours of murder and should be treated and punished as such—as recommended by the Law Commission.[91]

However, once one has moved down the crime-seriousness ladder to rungs below reckless killings, the context in which the killing took place can be sufficiently morally significant to justify the existence of a separate offence. Persons can be killed as a result of lawful[92] activities such as driving, corporate operations, execution of a job (doctors, train drivers, plumbers etc.), caring for the young or elderly and so on. And, of course, persons can be killed as a result of unlawful actions, most especially violent attacks. It is submitted that from these different contexts in which killings can occur, four further separate offences, in addition to reckless manslaughter, should be created and/or retained, albeit in a modified form: (i) vehicular homicide; (ii) corporate killings; (iii) grossly careless killings by individuals in circumstances not covered by (i); and (iv) killings resulting from attacks.

---

[88] It will be argued later that different rules should apply where the killer is a company. This argument is based largely on the context in which the killing takes place. However, the identity of the killer is material because of the different *nature* of a company (compared to a human being). The situation of a person, such as the mother in an infanticide case or a 'battered wife' pleading provocation might of course be relevant in relation to the raising of excuses.

[89] Whether this is the appropriate nomenclature with which to describe the offence is discussed later (see below).

[90] Law Commission, n. 4 above, paras. 5.7–5.9.

[91] For a view that advertent risk-taking is not necessarily more blameworthy than inadvertent risk-taking, see H. Keating, 'The Law Commission Report on Involuntary Manslaughter: The Restoration of a Serious Crime' [1996] Crim LR 535.

[92] This is used in the same sense as currently employed by constructive manslaughter. Dangerous driving is of course an unlawful act but only because of the manner in which the lawful activity of driving is carried out.

(i) Causing death by driving

The issue here is whether the context in which the killings take place is of sufficient moral significance to justify the existence of the present separate offences or whether such killings should be brought back within the general homicide offences. There has undoubtedly been some shift in public attitudes towards road deaths with calls for the abolition of the separate offences.[93] A hardening of public opinion against dangerous motorists is also evidenced by the increase in the maximum penalty for the separate offences from a maximum of five to ten years' imprisonment.[94] A survey of 91 cases reported in the Criminal Appeal Reports (Sentencing) between 1994 and mid-1999 on these offences reveals that the increase in maximum penalties has resulted in an increase in the severity of sentences imposed as all sentences 'must take their colour' from what the maximum sentence is.[95]

However, there are several reasons for resisting such calls. Firstly, there are fair-labelling and 'cultural reasons'[96] for condemning such deaths differently. The use of motor-vehicles, despite their inherent dangers, is so widespread and accepted that we assign responsibility to (even bad) drivers differently to those who cause deaths in different contexts. Their wrong is 'situationally relevant'[97] to ourselves. We can identify with the actions more than in cases of violent attacks or expert surgeons displaying gross negligence. Gardner describes the causing of such deaths as belonging to a different family of offence from murder and manslaughter.[98] A (narrow) majority of respondents to the Law Commission favoured retention of the special offences and felt that such killings should not fall within the general law of homicide.[99] Further, there is the danger that if these offences were abolished, juries might still be unwilling to convict of a general homicide offence, especially the 'ugly'[100] crime of manslaughter. Indeed, at the moment the separate offences are not extensively used. In 1995 there were 3,621 persons killed on the road and only 240 people charged with causing

---

[93] Law Commission, n. 4 above, para. 5.66.

[94] Introduced by the Criminal Justice Act 1993, s. 67(1).

[95] *A.-G.'s Ref. No. 1 of 1994 (Day)* (1995) 16 Cr App R(S) 193, 195. e.g. in *Severn* (1995) 16 Cr App R(S) 989 it was stated that the sentence in the particular case would probably not have exceeded 12 months' imprisonment before the increase in maximum penalty but should now be increased to 18 months' imprisonment.

[96] Law Commission, n. 4 above, para. 5.66.

[97] S. Lloyd-Bostock, 'The Ordinary man and the Psychology of Attributing Causes and Responsibility' (1979) 42 MLR 143, 156.

[98] J. Gardner, 'On the General Part of Criminal Law' in R. A. Duff (ed.), *Philosophy and the Criminal Law* (Cambridge, 1998), 247–8. See also, Gardner, n. 65 above.

[99] N. 4 above, para. 5.65. The CPS is cited as favouring this view as it was not clear when manslaughter should be charged rather than the statutory offence. However, to try to improve consistency in this regard, 'Charging Standards' were introduced in 1996; see [1996] Crim LR 458.   [100] MacKenna, n. 75 above.

death by dangerous driving.[101] Forcing prosecutors to have resort to the general homicide offences could simply result in even more persons being merely charged with dangerous or careless driving, which could have the unfortunate result of further undermining the seriousness of causing death by motor-vehicles. Finally, there can be no sentencing reasons for abolition so that the higher range of sentences for manslaughter (under the present law) can be utilized. My survey revealed that despite general sentence inflation since the increase in the maximum penalty and despite the driving in several cases being described as 'a shocking piece of driving',[102] 'a very bad case'[103] and 'a dreadful piece of driving',[104] a sentence in excess of five years' imprisonment was only confirmed or imposed in five cases, the highest being seven years' imprisonment.[105]

Accordingly, there is a strong case for agreeing with the Law Commission that the separate vehicular offences should be retained. However, the Law Commission's view that a charge of grossly careless killing should remain an option has little to commend it other than in cases where the vehicular offences do not apply (for example, driving on private property). Allowing alternative convictions dependent on the standard of driving[106] would simply confuse the law's communicative endeavours. Further, little is to be gained in terms of the higher sentencing range as a conviction for manslaughter is unlikely to generate a sentence in excess of ten years' imprisonment. In *Sherwood and Button* seven years' detention was imposed in 'almost as bad a case of motor manslaughter as can be envisaged'[107] and even this was imposed as a longer than normal sentence under section 2(2)(b) of the Criminal Justice Act 1991. However, it is suggested that it ought to be possible to bring charges of reckless manslaughter or constructive manslaughter where death has been caused by driving. In the former case the defendant would foresee death as a possibility and in the latter case would be using a vehicle as a dangerous 'weapon' to attack the victim.[108] Such a high degree of culpability and the changed context of an attack, respectively, trump all arguments concerning the cultural context in which driving offences take place. There can be no moral distinction between using a gun or a car if foreseeing the possibility of death or attacking one's victim.[109]

---

[101] Dept. of Transport, *Road Accidents Great Britain, 1995: The Casualty Report* (London, 1995); Home Office, *Criminal Statistics, England and Wales 1995* (1996), supplementary tables, vol. 2.   [102] *Shaw* (1995) 16 Cr App R(S) 960, 963.
[103] *A.-G.'s Ref. No. 22 of 1994 (Nevison)* (1995) 16 Cr App R(S) 670, 674.
[104] *Robbins* [1996] 1 Cr App R(S) 312, 314.
[105] *A.-G.'s Ref. No. 67 of 1995 (Lloyd)* [1996] 2 Cr App R(S) 373.
[106] For killing by gross carelessness there would need to be an obvious risk of death (or serious injury), whereas for causing death by dangerous driving there need only be a risk of injury or serious damage to property (Road Traffic Act 1988, s. 2A(3); see Law Commission, n. 4 above, para. 2.21).   [107] (1995) 16 Cr App R(S) 513, 517.
[108] e.g. *Gault*, n. 23 above; *Ripley*, n. 23 above.
[109] J. R. Spencer, 'Motor Vehicles as Weapons of Offence' [1985] Crim LR 29.

(ii) Corporate killings

When a death results in the workplace as a consequence of unsafe corporate practices, the charge most commonly brought is under the Health and Safety legislation. While fines for these offences have been increasing[110] and in isolated instances relatively large fines have been imposed,[111] the media and various pressure groups (such as the Centre for Corporate Accountability) have emphasized the perception that these are mere 'regulatory offences'. The focus is on risk-creation: the failure to ensure reasonable safety. In contrast to traditional criminal offences it is irrelevant whether anyone is killed.[112] The fact that these offences are so differently structured from traditional crimes, and are the creation of statutes whose main focus is on regulation by the Health and Safety Executive,[113] contributes to the feeling that they are not 'real crime'. Conviction for such offences does not express, in fair labelling terms, the extent of the wrongdoing involved. As a result of intense publicity surrounding some of the major disasters over the past decade there have been increasing efforts to bring corporate killings within the mainstream of criminal offences in order to emphasize the culpability of such corporate actors and as a greater deterrent. Pressure has mounted on the CPS to bring manslaughter charges against companies in cases where large numbers of persons have been killed.[114]

There are two ways of ensuring the seriousness of these crimes are recognized. The first method is to leave these cases to be covered by the general law of manslaughter or the Law Commission's proposed offence of grossly careless killing. The alternative approach, advocated by the Law Commission and discussed above, is that there should be a separate offence of 'corporate killing'.

The objection to the creation of such a special offence is that by having a separate crime with its own special rules, there is a danger of marginalization in that the crime would not be regarded as being as serious as the normal homicide offences. Without the fair labelling stigma and censure of

---

[110] Health and Safety Commission, *Annual Report and Accounts 1997/98* (London, 1998). See also *R. & F. Howe* [1999] 2 All ER 249, 253.

[111] In 1999 Balfour Beatty Civil Engineering was fined £1.2m after the collapse of the Heathrow Express Tunnel and Great Western Trains was fined £1.5m as a result of the Southall train crash.

[112] See further, C. M. V. Clarkson, 'Corporate Risk-Taking and Killing' (2000) 2 RM J 7.

[113] The HSE operates a compliance strategy and only brings a prosecution in 35% of cases where a death has been caused. Further, unlike homicide offences, most of those prosecutions are brought in the Magistrates' Court—again underwriting the perception that these are not serious offences. See, further, Clarkson, ibid.

[114] e.g. manslaughter prosecutions were (unsuccessfully) brought after 192 people were killed by the capsize of the *Herald of Free Enterprise* and after 37 people were killed in the Southall train crash. In the aftermath of the Paddington train crash there were immediate calls in many sections of the press for such charges to be brought.

a manslaughter (or equivalent) conviction, it could become regarded as little more than a regulatory offence. This in turn could impact on the enforcement procedures adopted with the new offence being no more rigorously enforced than present incidents under the Health and Safety at Work legislation. Indeed, the present author has entered this caution elsewhere.[115] However, there are several reasons for endorsing the creation of a new special offence of corporate killing. Firstly, in fair labelling terms there is something distinctive about the context in which such killings occur. Corporate defendants are engaged in lawful activities that would generally be regarded as socially beneficial were they safely performed. A primary lawful motivation drives the actions. While it has become fashionable to talk of 'corporate violence', in reality, like causing death by dangerous driving, such killings belong to a different family of offence. Unlike acts of violence, running a train company, for example, does not have harm of any degree to the victim as part of its rationale in acting. This is not to minimize the reprehensibility of the conduct of those who disregard the safety of others or to suggest that significant punishments should not be imposed. It is simply to argue that the context in which the deaths have occurred is sufficiently different from the paradigmatic homicide to warrant separate appellation and treatment. Secondly, this fear of marginalization could be misplaced. Having separate vehicular homicide offences has not resulted in trivialization of their seriousness as can be seen by the sentences imposed in such cases.[116] Further, concerns about the perceived lack of seriousness of the special offence are largely premised on the assumption that it will be introduced alongside the present (unreformed) offence of manslaughter,[117] and thus would seem a 'poor relative'. However, if the present or even the Law Commission's proposals were accepted in toto, there would be several new offences each bearing different appellations and thus the risk of marginalization would be reduced. However, I have to confess that ultimately it is pragmatism that, added to the above arguments, has brought about a change of mind in this respect. The short point much expounded elsewhere[118] is that it is seemingly impossible to obtain a conviction for corporate manslaughter other than against a 'one-person company'. Because of immense difficulties involved with the identification doctrine

---

[115] Clarkson (1996), n. 53 above.

[116] Vehicular killings are investigated by the police within the mainstream of the criminal justice system. There is no separate body, as there is under the Health and Safety legislation, whose operational and prosecutorial practices can obscure the gravity of corporate killings. However, all deaths at work are now reported to the police. The probability of easier convictions under a separate offence could have an important impact on the manner in which the HSE and the police investigate such cases.

[117] Given the recent publication of the Home Office Consultation Paper, *Reforming the Law on Involuntary Manslaughter: The Government's Proposals* (London, 2000), this premise seems misplaced. The Consultation Paper proposes a complete overhaul of the law on involuntary manslaughter, largely accepting the Law Commission's recommendations.

[118] Wells, n. 53 above; Clarkson [1998], n. 53 above.

only six prosecutions for corporate manslaughter have ever been brought[119] and only two convictions have been secured.[120] The existence of a separate offence with a changed emphasis on there being a *management* failure (as opposed to an individual senior manager's failure) could open the door to successful prosecutions in appropriate cases. If such an offence were to be introduced, the Law Commission's proposal of permitting a prosecution for killing by gross carelessness in exceptional cases should be rejected. Such a possibility would blunt the attempt to sharpen the law's message. Allowing one company to be convicted of corporate killing and another of killing by gross carelessness (say, on the basis that the former was a large company and the latter a small one) would simply cause confusion in public understanding of offence categories.

(iii) Grossly careless killings

These killings, which under the present law and practice normally involve the defendant acting lawfully, can occur in a variety of contexts. Very often, however, they will occur when a person is performing a job (for example, a doctor, electrician, train driver, nanny, or baby-sitter). It is tempting to classify such killings as analogous to corporate killings in that the doctor, for example, has a primarily lawful motivation in acting. Harm of any degree to the victim is not part of his/her rationale in acting. Clearly such cases could not be incorporated into the offence of corporate killing as the essence of that offence is that it is the company (and not individuals), through a joint management failure, that is punished. It would be possible to argue for the introduction of a separate homicide offence encompassing those who kill in the course of their employment. However, in fair-labelling terms, and bearing in mind the dangers of over-specificity, there seems no reason for distinguishing individuals carrying out their job from others who are also acting lawfully, for example an unpaid carer. Of course, it is possible to link those doing a task of social utility (irrespective of whether it is their job) and argue that killings in the course of such socially approved activities are morally different from other killings such as where the death results from the playing of consensual sexual 'games' or from the actions of the excited football fan who thinks he is lighting a flare.[121] However, apart from the difficulty of assessing social utility, the essential point is that all these persons have other explanations for their actions quite unrelated to harming their victims. None of them has been involved in an attack on the victim. This has more relevance to a homicide offence than whether there was social utility underlying the activity. With such diverse killings what is

---

[119] G. Slapper and S. Tombs, *Corporate Crime* (1999), 34. Since the five prosecutions cited there, manslaughter charges were brought in 1999 against Great Western Trains following the Southall train crash.

[120] *Kite*, n. 25 above; *Jackson Transport (Ossett) Ltd., Health and Safety at Work*, Nov. 1996, 4.   [121] See n. 25 above.

needed is a general culpability standard applicable to all cases where the actions causing death are lawful.[122] What should this minimum fault requirement be?

The Law Commission has long been committed to subjectivism in the criminal law on the basis that criminal liability and punishment should be linked to moral guilt which involves blaming only those who have chosen to cause harm in the sense of intending or knowing that harm could occur.[123] However, while such cognition clearly does involve moral guilt,[124] it is not obvious that moral guilt *must* be linked to cognition. We can blame people for making choices even when the possibility of harm is not in the forefront of their minds. As Duff has argued: a failure to consider obvious risks to others demonstrates an attitude of indifference.[125] Assuming the person is capable of foresight, failing to recognize obvious risks when choosing to act demonstrates that s/he regards them as unimportant or 'couldn't care less'. Students almost never forget a final exam; some students forget tutorials. Exams are of critical importance and care is taken not to oversleep etc; attendance at tutorials, to some students, is not important and careful precautions (setting the alarm clock etc.) are not taken.

Such uncaring indifference could be condemned even more strongly than the choices of the classically subjective risk-taker who recognizes a small chance of a risk occurring, hopes it will not materialize, but nevertheless goes ahead and acts.[126] This indifference is a state of mind, albeit an affective one rather than a cognitive one.[127]

In many situations Duff's account is 'easy'. For example, the boorish man who assumes that all women would consent to intercourse with him clearly demonstrates indifference when having intercourse without consent. But some cases are 'harder'. Horder has argued that there are two forms of gross negligence: indifference and a great departure from expected standards.[128] However, assuming a capacity to choose otherwise had all the relevant facts been brought to the actor's attention, the latter is better regarded as evidence of the former. For example, doctors because of their

---

[122] If my argument below concerning killing by attack is accepted, this category would need to embrace the causing of death by unlawful acts not amounting to attacks.

[123] For a variant on this theme, see A. Brudner, 'Agency and Welfare in the Penal Law' in S. Shute, J. Gardner, and J. Horder (eds.), *Action and Value in the Criminal Law* (Oxford, 1993) who argues that criminal punishment is only justifiable where there has been an 'intentional or (advertently) reckless disdain for the autonomy of another' (35) and that 'an unwitting imposition of excessive risk . . . implies no denial of an obligation to respect liberty and hence no licence for the disrespect of one's own' (ibid., 34).

[124] Assuming the absence of excuse or justification.

[125] R. A. Duff, *Intention, Agency and Criminal Liability* (Oxford, 1990), 163.

[126] This was the view of Lord Goff in *Reid* (1992) 95 Cr App R 393, 406.

[127] S. Shute, 'The Second Law Commission Consultation Paper on Consent: Something Old, Something New, Something Borrowed: Three Aspects of a Project' [1996] Crim LR 684, 686–7.

[128] J. Horder, 'Gross Negligence and Criminal Culpability' (1997) 47 UTLJ 495.

training and rules of conduct regarding their profession are expected to act in the best interests of their patients and achieve a basic level of competence. If, through inattentiveness or tiredness, they make a slight error (not a *great* departure from expected standards) we would probably not conclude that their actions demonstrated uncaring indifference sufficient for criminal liability. But where there is a gross or substantial departure from *expected* standards (bearing in mind that what is expected could vary depending on working conditions) indifference (given the doctor's situation) can more easily be inferred. The fact that s/he is overworked by a stretched NHS will not serve to exculpate. Unless so tired as to be an effective automaton the doctor chose to act knowing of the fatigue. While the primary motivation in acting might be concern for the care of the patient, ultimately other secondary concerns (career prospects, willingness to obey superior's orders etc.) prevailed thereby demonstrating an attitude of indifference to the patient's interests. For instance, the conduct and attitude of the anaesthetist in *Adomako* was described by an expert witness as 'a gross dereliction of care'.[129] Such a choice can be condemned (although we might also wish to blame others for putting the doctor in such a situation).

Other 'hard' cases will be where the circumstances of acting could, prima facie, serve to rebut a presumption of indifference: for example, the untrained passer-by who comes across an accident victim and, motivated out of concern, makes every effort to save them but bungles the job. By such actions, it looks as though care and concern and not indifference is manifest. However, again, it must be emphasized that an inference of indifference should only permissible where there has been a *great* departure from *expected* standards. What is expected of persons is relative to their training, age, experience and so on. In short, the rescuer would need to botch the job fairly spectacularly before we would conclude that an inference of indifference was possible. But if their conduct did plunge to such depths (assuming always that they were capable of appreciating the risks) we could conclude that there was indifference. Like the overworked doctor, other subsidiary concerns, such as desire for favourable publicity, must also have been driving them.

The Law Commission, while touching on some of the arguments justifying the imposition of liability based on inadvertence in all cases, preferred to rely on Professor Leigh,[130] and only accept these arguments where the harm risked is very serious: 'We may plead that we trod on the snail inadvertently: but not on the baby—you ought to look where you are putting your great feet.'[131] What is interesting, if not ironic, is that despite this

---

[129] N. 20 above, 182.

[130] 'Liability for Inadvertence: A Lordly Legacy?' (1995) 58 MLR 457, 467.

[131] N. 4 above, para. 4.23, citing J. L. Austin, 'A Plea for Excuses' in *Proceedings of the Aristotelian Society*, New Series, vol. 57 (1956–7), 1. Whether these arguments are limited by the 'politics of death' (N. Walker, *Aggravation, Mitigation and Mercy in English Criminal Justice* (London, 1999), 122) or should be applicable throughout the criminal law is beyond the

stringent limitation upon its acceptance of inadvertence as a basis of criminal liability, the Commission is prepared to accept that a risk of serious injury should suffice. This would involve a broadening of the present law, under which there must be a risk of death.[132]

It follows from the above that the Law Commission's proposals for an offence of killing by gross carelessness can be broadly welcomed subject to three caveats. Firstly, one might want to buttress the above arguments by inserting in a statutory definition that the conduct would need to fall so far below what can reasonably be expected in the circumstances as to demonstrate indifference as to whether death be caused. Such formulations in terms of 'extreme indifference', 'wantonly', 'depraved heart' etc. are commonly found in the United States.[133] However, on balance, such an addition could serve simply to complicate the law—and, if the above arguments are accepted, where the relatively high fault standard advocated by the Law Commission is met, such an inference would be irresistible. Secondly, as mentioned, the risk should be such that *death* would be obvious to a reasonable person in that position. Finally, the Law Commission's partial incorporation of a modified constructive manslaughter into this offence is rejected for the following reasons.

(iv) Killings resulting from dangerous unlawful acts

Under the present law such killings can amount to constructive manslaughter even though the death was not foreseen or even objectively foreseeable. It is this missing link that the Law Commission wish to introduce. Under its proposals a defendant would need to commit a crime *intending or risking some injury* and there would need to be an *obvious risk of death or serious injury*.

Whether the insertion of such a missing link is necessary or, indeed, whether there is a missing link raises a central issue much debated by criminal theorists: to what extent should there be correspondence between fault and resulting harm in the criminal law? Or, to rephrase the question: what weight should be attached to the causing of unforeseen resulting harm?

The literature on this issue is vast[134] and cannot be rehearsed here.

scope of this Chapter. For an argument that such views could have wider application, see C. M. V. Clarkson, 'Violence and the Law Commission' [1994] Crim LR 324. Given its traditional subjectivist stance, such a damage-limitation exercise by the Law Commission is not surprising.

[132] For criticism of the Law Commission's proposals on this point, see Yeo, n. 33 above, 182.
[133] e.g. in Kentucky it is murder when death is caused 'under circumstances manifesting extreme indifference to human life' (Ky.Rev.Stat, s. 507-020(1)(b)). With the removal of the word 'extreme', such a test could suffice for grossly careless killing.
[134] A. Ashworth, 'Taking the Consequences' in Shute, Gardner and Horder (eds.), *Action and Value in Criminal Law* (Oxford, 1993); S. Schulhofer, 'Harm and Punishment: A Critique of Emphasis on the Results of Conduct in the Criminal Law' (1974) 122 U Pa LR 1497; A. Ashworth, 'Criminal Attempts and the Role of Resulting Harm under the Code and in the Common Law' (1988) 19 Rutgers LJ 725; T. Honoré, 'Responsibility and Luck' (1988) 104 LQR 530.

Suffice it to mount one central argument (not considered by the Law Commission in its rejection of the 'moral luck' arguments).

Ultimately, the purpose of the criminal law is to try to prevent the causing of harm.[135] The paradigmatic crime is one where the prohibited harm is intentionally brought about. If no distinction were drawn between causing harm and not causing harm (in, say, attempts), the message communicated would be that the causing of harm was of no moral significance when clearly in terms of social and legal responses, it is of significance. Winch argues that the causer of evil becomes something evil; the causer of death has become something different afterwards, namely, a killer.[136] There is an irrevocable finality when harm, especially a death, has been caused. The defendant has 'brought evil into the world . . . and that evil [cannot] be undone'.[137] The defendant has 'irrevocably engaged herself in the world as a wrongdoer'.[138] The causing of harm arouses extra bitterness and resentment in victims, relatives, and society. The causers of harm feel extra guilt and remorse. The paradigmatic crime involves not just the causing of harm, but that it be intentionally caused. Intending to cause a consequence is generally regarded as the most reprehensible form of fault. Persons' aims or objectives influence our perceptions of them as moral agents and intending to cause a harm is more culpable than merely foreseeing a risk of the consequence occurring (as well as being more dangerous in that intended consequences are more likely to occur).[139]

Within the criminal law there are different 'families of offences'.[140] As already seen in relation to vehicular homicide and corporate killings, the current territory occupied by homicide might embrace more than one such family. However, mostly homicide is an offence of violence where the paradigmatic offence is the intentional causing of death: this is murder. Such a paradigm can, of course, be departed from, but the critical question is: in what circumstances and to what extent? Mandil has argued that, in order to maximize freedom, departures from the paradigm need justification and that such departures should be as limited as possible and should be marked by less liability and/or punishment to emphasize that it is not a paradigmatic case.[141] For example, in cases of attempts where there is no harm,[142] the interests of freedom protected by liberalism insist that the departure be

---

[135] This Chapter cannot explore the role of the criminal law in upholding social values and morality. Arguably, the infringement of such values is also a 'harm'—a harm to society.

[136] *Ethics and Action* (London, 1972), 149–50.

[137] R. A. Duff, 'Auctions, Lotteries, and the Punishment of Attempts' (1990) 8 L & Phil 1, 34. See also id., 'Acting, Trying, and Criminal Liability' in Shute et al., n 134 above.

[138] Duff, 'Auctions . . .', n. 137 above.

[139] See e.g. J. Brady, 'Recklessness, Negligence, Indifference and Awareness' (1980) 43 MLR 381.   [140] See Gardner, n. 98 above.

[141] M. Mandil, 'Chance, Freedom and Criminal Liability' (1987) 87 Col LR 125.

[142] It is unnecessary for present purposes to explore arguments relating to attempts causing second-order harms.

as limited as possible. No diminution from the paradigmatic fault requirement of intention should be permitted. Where no harm has been caused,
one is punishing largely on the basis of the fault requirement and there
should be an insistence on the highest degree of fault, namely intention.[143]

In all cases of homicide the paradigmatic harm requirement, death, is
present. Departure from the paradigmatic fault requirement is permissible
and so reckless killings and grossly negligent killings can be justified as long
as it is emphasized that these are separate and lesser crimes than murder.
The Law Commission is prepared to depart from the paradigm when the
result is one as serious as death and to allow gross carelessness to suffice as
the requisite fault element—but only if there is a 'link' to the resulting harm
(death or serious injury must be obvious). That the defendant must be
'culpable in some way'[144] is indisputable. The critical question in relation
to constructive manslaughter is whether the fault requirement is too far
removed from the paradigm and whether that fault must connect or 'corre-
spond'[145] with the resulting death.

It is my argument that in appropriate cases the requisite culpability can
be found in the circumstances/context in which the defendant acted without any necessary correspondence to the death. The notion that culpability
can be established without the fault element corresponding to the prohibited harm is hardly a novel one in English law. For example, cases on intoxication clearly establish that the requisite culpability lies in the excessive
consumption of drink or drugs. It is blameworthy to reduce oneself to a
state in which one might inflict violence on another; one has made oneself
a 'time-bomb' waiting to go off; if the bomb explodes and death results, a
manslaughter conviction can follow.

However, once one has severed the connection between fault and result,
the problem is one of identifying what sort of fault should suffice for
manslaughter. It is submitted that when death has been caused departure
from the paradigm is permissible as long as the actions are within the same
family of offence, namely violence. The essential point about constructive
manslaughter is that the defendant has chosen to engage in criminal,

---

[143] Horder uses a different argument to reach the same conclusion: in relation to attempts
the 'main role [of intention] is in changing the normative significance of conduct . . . Without
the intention to commit the crime, there is not only no fault; there is simply no wrong' or, he
continues, it 'merge[s] with a different wrong: endangerment'; see J. Horder, 'A Critique of the
Correspondence Principle in Criminal Law' [1995] Crim LR 759, 762. My suggested analysis
would lead to the same result: where there is no harm, allowing recklessness to suffice instead
of intention involves a double departure from the paradigm which (if it is still to be criminal)
must be marked by a lesser offence category than attempt, namely, reckless endangerment, a
common offence in the United States. See K. J. M. Smith, 'Liability for Endangerment: English
Ad Hoc Pragmatism and American Innovation' [1983] Crim LR 127.

[144] Law Commission, n. 4 above, para. 4.38 citing a respondent, John Gardner.

[145] For discussion of the principle of correspondence, see Horder, n. 143 above; B. Mitchell,
'In Defence of a Principle of Correspondence' [1999] Crim LR 195; J. Horder, 'Questioning
the Correspondence Principle: A Reply' [1999] Crim LR 206.

dangerous[146] activity: usually violence. Such a person is deliberately engaging in a morally different course of action compared to those who act lawfully and inadvertently cause death. As Horder puts it:

The fact that I *deliberately* wrong V. arguably changes my normative position *vis a vis* the risk of adverse consequences of that wrongdoing to V., whether or not foreseen or reasonably foreseeable . . . If . . . my unlawful act is meant to wrong V. . . . its deliberateness changes my relationship with the risk of adverse consequences stemming therefrom.[147]

This change in normative position is, of course, morally interesting. But is it enough for the fault element for manslaughter? The answer is yes—provided the change in normative position is one involving an attack upon the victim. The moral quality of a deliberate attack upon a person brings the assailant within the family of violence. A defendant who attacks another and risks injury cannot complain when criminal liability is imposed in relation to injuries—even death—resulting from the attack. Horder distinguishes between 'pure luck' (where a fortuitous result unconnected to one's endeavours occurs) and 'making one's own luck' (where the consequence is directly connected to one's endeavours). Where a death results from an unlawful attack on a victim, the defendant 'by directing [his/her] efforts towards harming V.' is responsible for the bad luck that s/he has created.[148]

Take, for example, the case of *Williams*[149] which is a classic example of the sort of constructive manslaughter objected to by the Law Commission and many commentators. The defendant gave a young woman two pushes and one slap. As a result she fell back, caught her head on a wall-mounted heater, damaged her neck and died. Sacks J., in substituting a sentence of two-and-a-half years' imprisonment, agreed with the trial sentencing judge that this death was 'in a sense, accidental' but stressed that 'we do bear well in mind that this was an assault on a woman' and that he 'set about her . . . with terrible consequences'. Such, admittedly rather generalized, statements are an acceptance of the above proposition that when the defendant, instead of merely quarrelling with the woman as he had been, chose to attack her, he deliberately changed his normative stance to become a violent actor who should bear responsibility for the consequences of his violence. His actions were simply not of the same moral order as those of a person who swears at a woman who in distress turns away and hits her head on a wall-heater and dies.

This line of reasoning, however, suggests that it is only those who attack

---

[146] The requirement of dangerousness is often overlooked in some of the more far-fetched examples of what could possibly constitute constructive manslaughter. See e.g. Law Commission, n. 4 above, para. 4.34 and Mitchell, n. 58 above.

[147] Horder, n. 143 above, 764.   [148] Ibid.

[149] [1996] 2 Cr App R(S) 72.

their victims in the sense of *assaulting* them[150] *intending or foreseeing some injury* who alter their normative position relevantly to bring themselves within the family of violence. From this it follows that not every unlawful act should suffice for constructive manslaughter as it does under the present law (as long as it is dangerous). Accordingly, there should be no liability for manslaughter in some of the well-known cases such as *Newbury*[151] and the drug-injection or drug-supply cases such as *Cato*.[152] Such offenders have of course engaged in actions of a certain moral quality and there might indeed be risks of adverse consequences flowing from their wrongdoing. They could possibly be liable for killing by gross carelessness. But, by not attacking their victims, they have not chosen to embark on a violent course of action. They have departed too far from the family of violence: the connection between their fault and the death is too tenuous.

From this it follows that some sort of constructive manslaughter[153] should be retained but only unlawful acts of personal violence involving at least a common assault with intention or foresight of some injury should suffice. This involves partial acceptance of the Law Commission's proposal that what is required is the commission of a criminal offence intending or risking some personal injury. That criminal offence, however, would need to involve a common assault. However, this approach involves rejecting the Law Commission's 'missing link' that death or serious injury be an obvious risk.

This would be an important restriction on the present law in terms of the underlying principle, but would not have a drastic effect on the actual disposition of most cases. In the previously-mentioned survey of fifty-six manslaughter sentencing appeals, fifty-one of the cases involved the commission of an unlawful act. Most of these involved attacks (kicking, punching, stabbing etc.) which would clearly come within the proposed reformulated offence. However, five cases did not involve an attack amounting to at least a common assault. Of these three would clearly fall within reckless manslaughter or grossly careless killing.[154] However, two cases would not fall within the proposed modified test and would probably not amount to homicide under any of the other species. In *Kennedy*[155] the

---

[150] Gardner argues that an assault is not a crime of violence but rather concerns the invasion of a person's body space ('Rationality and the Rule of Law in Offences against the Person' [1994] CLJ 502). The better view is that as a battery involves force and psychic assault involves threatened force these offences fall within the family of violence.

[151] [1977] AC 500.   [152] (1976) 62 Cr App R 41.

[153] Whether the offence should still bear the name 'manslaughter' is discussed below at p. 164.

[154] *A.-G.'s Ref. No. 68 of 1995 (Dawes)* [1996] 2 Cr App R(S) 358: D. reversed over victim while stealing a car and displayed 'total reckless disregard for the safety of the owner'; *Sogunro* [1997] 2 Cr App R(S) 89: false imprisonment leading to death by starvation amounted to 'gross neglect'; *A.-G.'s Ref. No. 5 of 1995 (Johnson)* [1996] 1 Cr App R(S) 85: supplying methadone: knew of risks of 'serious damage or even death'.

[155] (1994) 15 Cr App R(S) 141.

defendant accidentally dropped a match during a burglary causing a fire and death to the occupant. This unlawful act (burglary) would not qualify as an attack involving at least a common assault and gross carelessness as to death would be difficult to establish. However, in this case the defendant had not brought himself within the family of violence. The connection between the burglary and the death was too tenuous. The death was pure luck as opposed to his having made his own relevant luck. A conviction for burglary only is appropriate.

In the other case, *England*[156] the defendant set fire to a car in the middle of the night without 'contemplat[ing] for a moment that anyone was inside the vehicle'. A young man was asleep in the rear passenger seat and was burnt to death. In confirming a sentence of seven years' imprisonment Russell LJ stressed that: 'People, if we may say so, sometimes tend to forget that the loss of life, however unintended, is a serious aggravating feature of dangerous and unlawful behaviour'. This statement would be acceptable if made in the context of sentencing the defendant for arson, the offence he would be convicted of under my proposal. What is not acceptable is to allow the fortuitous death, which was totally unconnected to the defendant's unlawful act which was an attack on property and not person, to alter retrospectively the characterization of the moral quality of the defendant's action so as to bring him within the violence family. These two cases are the only ones in the survey where the death was genuinely bad luck and a homicide conviction breaches not only the principle of correspondence but, more importantly, the principle of fair labelling.[157]

This proposal to retain a modified species of constructive manslaughter is unlikely to be warmly embraced by traditional subjectivists and/or proponents of the principle of correspondence. However, evidence of support for some form of constructive manslaughter can be found in the views of some expert commentators and in popular opinion and judicial attitudes. With regard to the 'experts', respondents to the Law Commission's Consultation Paper were split in their views with a significant body of support for retention of the present law (or some variety thereof).[158] Popular opinion is always difficult to assess but some guidance can be found in the results of Mitchell's study measuring public perceptions of the gravity of various homicide offences.[159] Of the scenarios presented to respondents, the one regarded as most serious was where a disturbed burglar picked up a nearby ashtray and hit the householder over the head with it—a classic case of constructive manslaughter. The most common reason given for this high seriousness score was 'the fact that the killer was already committing a

---

[156] (1995) 16 Cr App R(S) 777.
[157] The Law Commission's proposals would have a much greater impact in that 13 of the cases surveyed would cease to come within the category of homicide.
[158] N. 4 above, para. 4.36.   [159] N. 58 above.

crime'.[160] The other potentially relevant scenario was one where, in a supermarket queue argument, a man 'gently pushed' a woman who 'unexpectedly tripped and bumped her head against a wall' and, having a thin skull, died. This was, unsurprisingly, ranked low in the order of seriousness because the killing was perceived as 'accidental' and 'unforeseeable'. Mitchell describes this as an instance of the type of constructive manslaughter the Law Commission has recommended abolishing.[161] However, on the facts presented in the scenario it is doubtful whether this would qualify as constructive manslaughter either under the present law or under my proposal. While the push would qualify as a battery it would not be a *dangerous* unlawful act under the present law. And it would not be constructive manslaughter under my proposals because with a 'gentle push' there would not be the requisite foresight of at least some personal injury.

The level of sentences imposed in constructive manslaughter cases tends to suggest judicial support for the continued existence of the offence. Of the fifty-six cases surveyed there were fourteen instances where, had constructive manslaughter been abolished, the defendant could only have been guilty of a lesser non-homicide offence. If sentencing and appellate judges shared the Law Commission's scepticism about constructive manslaughter, one might have expected to find the sentences imposed in these cases to be more akin to those imposed for the lesser offences. Yet the average sentence in these cases was 4.3 years' imprisonment. While it is difficult to draw clear inferences from the length of sentence imposed as this is affected by a variety of other aggravating and mitigating circumstances surrounding the offence and the offender, it nevertheless appears that the fact of death resulting from an unlawful act is regarded as highly significant by sentencers. Even in the *Williams* case, discussed above, a sentence of two-and-a-half years' imprisonment was substituted by the Court of Appeal (from an original five years' sentence) where the only underlying offence committed by the defendant (where the mens rea corresponded with the actus reus) was a battery carrying a maximum of six months' imprisonment.[162]

Finally, the practical implications of a full abolition of constructive manslaughter should not be completely overlooked. Of the thirty-two cases classified in my survey as reckless manslaughter, thirty-one also involved the commission of an unlawful act that would have sufficed for constructive manslaughter and of the nine cases regarded as gross-negligence manslaughter, five involved such unlawful acts. Without the 'easy fallback'

---

[160] N. 58 above, 469. Of course, under my proposal, only the attack and not the burglary would qualify as the unlawful act for constructive manslaughter.

[161] Ibid.

[162] A conviction under the Offences Against the Person Act 1861, s. 47, would, of course, have been possible. However, this is also a constructive crime equally reviled by the proponents of the principle of correspondence.

of constructive manslaughter these cases would have become significantly more complicated and protracted in requiring the requisite recklessness or gross negligence to be proved. There would probably also have been many more appeals on points of substantive law. Such arguments *alone* could not justify the retention of the offence of constructive manslaughter, but assuming acceptance of the earlier principled arguments, the desirability of speed and certainty in the criminal justice system should not be despised.

3. Fair labelling: Nomenclature and Offence Seriousness

The above analysis has concluded, as did the Law Commission, that there should be several separate homicide offences covering what is at present involuntary manslaughter and the vehicular homicide offences. The central reason for this proposal is, as argued above, that the present offence of involuntary manslaughter is too broad and that, in fair labelling terms, offences should be structured to reflect the essence of the wrongdoing involved and to convey the relative seriousness of the offences. In pursuit of this objective, it is necessary, in conclusion, to consider the nomenclature that should be used to describe these offences and to rank them hierarchically in an order of seriousness. This will enable appropriate sentencing maxima to be attached to each offence. It is beyond the scope of this Chapter to suggest precise sentencing maxima.

Under the present law it is extremely difficult to establish any clear hierarchy of seriousness as between the three existing categories of involuntary manslaughter as the length of sentence imposed is strongly affected by a variety of aggravating and mitigating circumstances surrounding the offender and the offence. However, dicta in the cases from my survey and deductions from the facts and sentences imposed suggest that the most serious cases are those where the defendant acted recklessly. This is consistent with the Law Commission's view that its proposed offence of reckless killing should be the most serious, punishable by a maximum of life imprisonment. As argued above, such cases can be the near-neighbours of murder and so it is justifiable that they be treated as the most serious. The Law Commission has eschewed entirely the use of the word and label 'manslaughter'.[163] However, given the seriousness of such offences and given that there is still much currency in the label 'manslaughter', such killings should continue to be labelled manslaughter. This will enable them to be marked out more clearly from the other homicide offences which will not bear this label.

---

[163] This approach is supported by G. Virgo who asserts that 'most cases do not involve anything remotely akin to slaughter' ('Back to Basics: Reconstructing Manslaughter' (1994) 53 CLJ 44).

In my survey the next most seriously regarded cases were constructive manslaughter. If the earlier arguments are accepted, this too is appropriate. The grossly negligent killer is engaged in lawful activities, often simply performing their job.[164] S/he does not recognize the possibility of the consequence occurring. The moral culpability of the constructive manslaughterer is aggravated by the choice to engage in a violent attack. However, the culpability is less than the reckless killer and should be marked by a different label and lower sentencing maximum. This could soften the criticism by those who seek complete abolition of constructive manslaughter. To mark the lesser seriousness of this offence, the label manslaughter is inappropriate. Perhaps something as simple as 'killing by attack' or 'causing death by attack' would capture the essence of the crime.

The least seriously regarded cases in my survey were those involving gross negligence where no unlawful act was committed. Given the lawful nature of the actor's conduct, such a ranking is consistent with the arguments presented above. This offence should carry a lower maximum than 'killing by attack' and there can be little objection to the Law Commission's proposed label of 'killing by gross carelessness'.

Where one should rank the two species of vehicular homicide is problematic. While the context of the killing perhaps suggests a different 'family' of offence from other homicides and therefore no need for incorporation into the above hierarchy, in terms of fault there can be little distinction between those who kill through the dangerous operation of their cars and those who kill with machines, trains etc. Accordingly, there is a prima facie case for ranking such killings on a par with killing by gross carelessness. However, given the extensive usage of motor vehicles in our society and their immense potential for harm to other road-users, there could be important deterrent justifications for an increased sentencing maximum for such killings (compared to killing by gross carelessness). With regard to nomenclature, there can be little objection to the present offence descriptions although a simple name like vehicular homicide, widely employed in the United States, or, to be consistent with the other proposed offences, vehicular killing, could be appropriate.

Finally, corporate killings clearly present a claim to be classed as belonging to a different 'family' of offences. While individual managers can and should be liable in appropriate cases for killing by gross carelessness, the offence of corporate killing can only be committed by a company. Accepting the Law Commission's recommendations, the fault lies with a management failure (as opposed to any individual failure) and it is the company that is punished. Accordingly, the term 'corporate killing' is

[164] If my limitation to violent attacks is accepted, those committing other unlawful acts will fall within the same category as the grossly negligent or careless killer. The point remains that such a defendant is engaged in non-violent unlawful activity where physical harm to the victim is not part of the rationale in acting.

appropriate. The appropriate level of punishment should reflect the seriousness of the offence and therefore fines of an appropriate magnitude, bearing in mind the annual profits made by the company, should be imposed. Further, the law should recognize the potential for a range of other corporate sanctions such as probation and community service.[165] However, as imprisonment is not an option here, it is impossible to rank this offence within the hierarchy of seriousness suggested for the other homicide offences.

E. CONCLUSION

This Chapter has argued that the case for a reform of the present law is overwhelming. The Law Commission's proposals for the creation of several separate offences have, subject to minor criticisms, much to commend them both structurally and in terms of the minimum fault requirement for each offence. Where I radically part company from these proposals is in respect of the abolition of constructive manslaughter. While this book was in production, the Government published its proposals for reforming the law on involuntary manslaughter.[166] The proposals are largely consistent with my argument in this Chapter. Most of the Law Commission's proposals are accepted in toto but the Government 'is less convinced of the merits of [the Law Commission's] argument' for the abolition of constructive manslaughter[167] and concludes that 'there is an argument that anyone who embarks on a course of *illegal violence* has to accept the consequences of his act, even if the final consequences are unforeseeable'.[168] The italicized words coupled with the subsequent definition that the unlawful act must involve the defendant intending or being reckless as to whether some injury is caused[169] are largely[170] compatible with my arguments advanced above. Provided constructive manslaughter is narrowed to bring it within the family of violence, its retention is more than excused by instinct: it can be justified by principle.

---

[165] See J. Gobert, 'Controlling Corporate Culpability: Penal Sanctions and Beyond' [1998] Web J. [166] Home Office, n. 117 above.
[167] Ibid., para. 1.7. [168] Ibid., para. 2.10. My emphasis.
[169] Ibid., para. 2.11.
[170] Under my proposal there would need to be an attack involving an assault. Persons, such as suppliers of drugs, can commit unlawful acts foreseeing the risk of some injury and so qualify for this offence under the Government's proposals. Under my argument there would be no liability for homicide in such a case.

7

Sentencing in Homicide

MARTIN WASIK*

A. INTRODUCTION

The purpose of this Chapter is to assess critically the sentencing principles which are applicable in homicide cases. The main focus is on sentencing for the offence of manslaughter, an area which has occasioned especial difficulty for sentencers. There is no appellate guideline judgment in this area of the law, and judges have from time to time suggested that it is 'impossible' to subdivide the offence and match different classes of manslaughter to appropriate sentencing brackets.[1] The Chapter also considers how the sentencing parameters within homicide might change if the mandatory penalty for murder was abolished. While this may not be a realistic prospect in the short or medium term,[2] it is surely important to retain a vision of what the law of homicide might look like if and when that change eventually does come about. In the absence of any realistic and coherent alternative models for the law to adopt, the status quo may persist for even longer than it otherwise would.

The overall structure of the substantive law of homicide, and issues such as the continuing role (if any) of the partial defences, are questions considered in depth elsewhere in this volume. At first sight it may seem very difficult to propose sentencing guidance for homicide offences without first knowing whether homicide might in due course become a single offence, or an offence which has two, three, or more, legal subdivisions. There is indeed an interconnectedness of issues in this area which makes proposals for reform especially difficult. A suggested change to any one part of the law often sets in train a broader rethinking of all the rest. Despite this undoubted difficulty, however, the sentencing questions which arise in homicide cases do seem likely to remain much the same, irrespective of the formal offence structure which is eventually settled upon, since the general characteristics of homicide cases tend to remain fairly constant over time.

---

* Professor of Criminal Justice, School of Law, University of Keele.
[1] e.g. *Boyer* (1981) 3 Cr App R(S) 35, per Dunn LJ.
[2] Home Secretary Jack Straw said in Parliament on 14 March 2000 that he was 'completely opposed' to abolishing the mandatory life sentence for murder.

In 1998/9, the most recent period for which official figures are currently availabl:, a quarrel, revenge, or loss of temper accounted for half of all homicides committed in England and Wales. Overall, 97 per cent of homicide offenders were male, and nearly two-thirds of the victims were male. Just over half of the male victims, and 69 per cent of the female ones, knew the main or only suspect for the offence before it took place. Even where the suspect was unknown to the victim, just over one-quarter of homicides took place during a quarrel, an act of revenge, or loss of temper, although in one-third of cases the reason for the homicide could not be ascertained. Only 6 per cent of homicides were carried out in furtherance of theft or gain. Homicides where the suspect appeared to be mentally disturbed, or where there was no apparent motive (those killings which are of course the standard fare of detective fiction), comprised only 4 per cent of homicides in 1998/9. The age group most at risk, as in other years, was that of children under one year of age. Those most at risk, apart from infants, were males aged between sixteen and forty-nine. As far as methods of killing are concerned, sharp instruments were the most common weapons. Most other homicides were committed by hitting, kicking, strangulation, and other manual methods, with the use of a gun being relatively rare.[3] These are very similar patterns to those reported by Mitchell,[4] and by Cullen and Newell,[5] in detailed research carried out by them in earlier years.

The ways in which sentencing issues in homicide are *resolved*, however, does depend a great deal on the formal structure of the law. In his writings, David Thomas has shown that the legislative trend towards using broadly defined offences, such as manslaughter, reduces the fact-finding role of the jury, and it places greater burdens on the sentencer at a stage of the criminal justice process where the evidential and procedural rules are much less clear than at the trial. Manslaughter verdicts leave judges with much work still to do. On the other hand, in murder cases, the mandatory sentence means that judges have effectively no decisions to make at all. It is salutary to recall, in the present context, Thomas's remark that 'A reconstruction of the law of homicide must begin with a decision on the nature of the sentencing structure which is to be attached to the offences concerned',[6] so that reform of the substantive criminal law ought to *start* with sentencing considerations, and work backwards from there. While one may not wish to go quite so far in 'putting the cart before the horse', Thomas is surely right to stress the importance of the 'cart' and the 'horse' being considered

---

[3] All information taken from Home Office, *Criminal Statistics for England and Wales for 1998* (2000) (Cm. 4689).
[4] B. Mitchell, *Murder and Penal Policy* (Basingstoke, 1990); id., 'Thinking about Murder' (1992) J Cr L 78.
[5] E. Cullen and T. Newell, *Murderers and Life Imprisonment* (Winchester, 1999), ch. 1.
[6] D. A. Thomas, 'Form and Function in Criminal Law', in P. R. Glazebrook (ed.), *Reshaping the Criminal Law* (London, 1978), 21, 27.

together, as part of one system. Unfortunately it remains the case that new offence-structures are introduced to the substantive law with little thought being given to the sentencing implications. A recent example is the statutory scheme of racially aggravated offences in the Crime and Disorder Act 1998, where a range of differentially increased maximum sentences has been incorporated into the law without any guidance for sentencers as to the implications for punishment.[7]

B. SENTENCING AND THE OFFENCE STRUCTURE IN HOMICIDE

Before turning to a more detailed consideration of sentencing in homicide, two general points might usefully be made at the start. These relate to life sentences, and to offence subdivisions within homicide.

1. LIFE SENTENCES IN HOMICIDE

The number of life-sentence prisoners in the United Kingdom has increased sharply in recent years, with the number of lifers beginning their sentence each year exceeding the number who are released by a ratio of about three to one. The total number of life-sentence prisoners has now passed 4,000, and seems set to reach 6,000 or 7,000 over the next five years or so.[8] Nearly 80 per cent of lifers are serving sentences for murder, while a further 6 per cent received their life sentence for manslaughter, other homicide, or attempted homicide.[9] The prevalent and increasing use of the life sentence in homicide cases transfers much of the effective power to determine sentence length to the executive authorities. This is particularly so where an adult is sentenced for murder. Sentencers have had power since 1965 to make a recommendation in open court as to the minimum period to be served by an adult who receives the *mandatory* life sentence for murder,[10] but this is not binding and in fact gives the court very little influence over the lifer's release date. Release has always been a matter primarily for the executive authorities and the Home Secretary rather than the sentencing court, a state of affairs which has attracted much recent criticism.[11]

On the other hand, in relation to *discretionary* life sentences for manslaughter, and other offences attracting life imprisonment as the maximum penalty, sentencers are now expected to specify the 'relevant part' of

---

[7] See Sentencing Advisory Panel, *Consultation Paper on Racially Aggravated Offences* (reprinted at (2000) 164 JP Jo 156).

[8] Stephen Shaw, 'Foreword' in Cullen and Newell, n. 5 above, vii.

[9] *Prison Statistics England and Wales 1998* (1999) (Cm. 4430), ch. 5.

[10] Murder (Abolition of Death Penalty) Act 1965, s. 1(2).

[11] See e.g. the critical comments of the judges in the Divisional Court in *Secretary of State, ex p. Hindley* [1999] 2 WLR 1253.

the sentence which should be served by the offender before he or she is first considered for release by the Parole Board. Change has come about as a result of criticism of the earlier regime by the European Court of Human Rights.[12] The new arrangements are applicable to sentences of detention during Her Majesty's pleasure, detention for life, custody for life, and where the life sentence is imposed 'automatically' for the second serious offence under the Crime (Sentences) Act 1997, as well as to discretionary life sentences.[13] The current 'sentencing guideline' applicable to all life sentences, apart from the mandatory life sentence for murder by an adult, states that the trial judge should normally specify as the 'relevant part' a period of one-half of the determinate sentence which would otherwise have been imposed for the offence.[14] Appeal may lie against the period specified by the judge in these circumstances.

If the mandatory life sentence for murder was removed, and/or there were tighter restrictions placed on the use of life sentences in homicide generally, then sentencers would establish greater control over custodial-sentence length. To some extent this is happening already, as a result of the various European Court rulings. The current legislative trend in England and Wales, however, is to require the courts to increase their use of inde-terminate sentencing, most obviously with the introduction of the highly controversial 'automatic' life sentence for the second serious offence.[15] The human rights implications of 'automatic' life sentences are coming under intense scrutiny.[16] So is the predominant influence of the Home Secretary in respect of mandatory-life prisoners. Implementation of the Human Rights Act 1998 seems set to force further concessions from the Government, which will have the effect of returning greater power to the courts. Recently, as a result of strictures by the European Court of Human Rights,[17] the Government has announced legislative change to transfer the power to review the 'tariff' imposed in respect of young offenders convicted of murder, from the Home Secretary to the judiciary.[18] The development of more comprehensive sentencing guidelines within homicide would be greatly assisted by further such developments.

---

[12] *Thynne, Wilson and Gunnell* v. *UK* (1990) 13 EHRR 666; *Hussain and Singh* v. *UK* (1996) 22 EHRR 1.

[13] Crime (Sentences) Act 1997, s. 28, replacing the Criminal Justice Act 1991, s. 34.

[14] *Secretary of State for the Home Department, ex p. Furber* [1998] 1 Cr App R(S) 208; *Marklew* [1999] 1 Cr App R(S) 6. Exceptionally, a period of up to two-thirds of the notional determinate term may be fixed.

[15] Crime (Sentences) Act 1997, s. 2; Powers of Criminal Courts (Sentencing) Act 2000, s. 109.

[16] See *Kelly* [1999] 2 Cr App R(S) 176, and the trenchant commentary by David Thomas at [1999] Crim LR 242, arguing infringement of the ECHR, Art. 3 ('inhuman or degrading treatment or punishment').

[17] In *T.* v. *UK* (App. No. 24724/94); *V.* v. *UK* (App. No. 24888/94), 16 December 1999.

[18] Reported in *The Times*, 14 March 2000.

2. Offence Subdivisions within Homicide

Another issue, referred to briefly above, is the manner and extent to which homicide offences are to be subdivided. To take one of two possible extreme positions, homicide might be structured so as to have a large number of subdivisions within it. These might reflect variations in the culpability of offenders, such as premeditation, intent, recklessness, degree of mental disorder, and killing under provocation. They might also reflect other special features of the case such as (perhaps) a particular method employed in the killing, the motivation of the killer, characteristics of the victim, matters relating to the past offender–victim relationship, and so on.[19] In a scheme with a complex structure like this, it would be important that the correct charge (incorporating the relevant alleged aggravating feature, or features, of the homicide) was selected by the prosecutor. The *jury* would have to resolve the issue when an aggravating feature was alleged by the prosecution, but denied by the defence. So, provision would need to be made for the jury to convict for a lesser form of homicide if the aggravating feature alleged in the indictment was not established beyond reasonable doubt.[20] Sentencing guidelines would then be required from the Court of Appeal to cater for each of the subdivisions of the overall offence. Comparison might be made here with the Federal Sentencing Guidelines in the United States. These cater for several sentencing subdivisions within homicide, indicating a prescribed custodial sentencing range for each subdivision.

If, however, we take the other extreme of a single undivided offence of homicide, selection of the appropriate charge would clearly not be an issue. In this scenario the jury's finding of guilt would provide very little factual information for the sentencing judge beyond the bare statement of 'guilty of homicide'. The sentencer, in determining the factual basis for the sentence to be passed, might perhaps proceed by asking the jury for further and better particulars of their verdict. Such an approach has generally been deprecated by the Court of Appeal, on the ground that it risks revealing the fact that different jurors may have reached their verdict by different routes, a finding which might seriously undermine faith in jury decision-making.[21] Despite this, judges still do sometimes ask juries questions of this kind in manslaughter cases. An alternative approach is for the sentencing judge to conduct a *Newton* inquiry[22] to settle outstanding facts which are relevant

---

[19] For examples from different jurisdictions see House of Lords, *Report of the Select Committee on Murder and Life Imprisonment* (HL Paper 78-1 of Session 1988–9), vol. 1, app. 5.

[20] Criminal Law Act 1967, s. 6(2) would require appropriate amendment.

[21] See J. C. Smith, 'Satisfying the Jury' [1988] Crim LR 335.

[22] (1982) 4 Cr App R(S) 388.

to sentence, and on which there is a sharp divergence between the prosecution and defence versions of what actually happened.

It can be seen that the structure of the substantive law of homicide here determines the forum in which a contested issue is to be resolved. Provocation provides a good illustration. Under current homicide law the issue of provocation is left to the jury, so that it decides whether murder, or voluntary manslaughter, has been committed. The judge then passes sentence on that factual basis. If the law of homicide was reformed so that provocation was no longer part of the substantive law, but a matter in mitigation only, it would become an issue for the judge to determine, where necessary by a *Newton* hearing.

It is clear that while a scheme with *many* subdivisions within homicide would protract trials by requiring juries to resolve a greater number of factual questions, a scheme with *no* subdivisions would militate against fair labelling[23] and deprive the jury of the opportunity to reflect widely shared views on the moral differences implicit in different kinds of killings. Some of the defects of the latter approach can be seen in the current English law, and this suggests that *more* subdivisions are needed, rather than fewer. We have noted that judges still find the need to question juries as to the basis for their verdict of manslaughter.[24] Sometimes, when the Court of Appeal comes to review a sentence on appeal, the judges concede that they cannot tell from the record of proceedings whether the defendant was convicted of manslaughter on the basis of an unlawful act, or manslaughter under provocation,[25] or whether the jury found there to have been provocation, or diminished responsibility.[26] These are clear indications that additional grading within the substantive law of homicide is required prior to the court moving to the sentencing stage.

3. A SUGGESTED SENTENCING STRUCTURE

In light of the above, and since the offence category of homicide is a very broad one, it is suggested that for the purposes of the present discussion there should be at least *three* sub-divisions within homicide to facilitate fair labelling, and (perhaps) to provide any partial defences with appropriate lesser crimes upon which to bite.[27] Further, it is proposed that any future offence structure for homicide should distinguish at the very least between (1) intentional killing, (2) reckless killing, and (3) killing by gross

---

[23] G. Williams, 'Convictions and Fair Labelling' (1983) 44 CLJ 85. See further, B. Mitchell, 'Public Perceptions of Homicide and Criminal Justice' (1998) 38 Br J Crim 453.

[24] See *Frankum* (1984) 5 Cr App R(S) 259; *Baldwin* (1989) 11 Cr App R(S) 139.

[25] See *Gunn* (1992) 13 Cr App R(S) 544, where Lord Lane CJ thought it 'tolerably clear' that this was 'involuntary manslaughter not provocation manslaughter'.

[26] *Irons* (1994) 16 Cr App R(S) 46; *Hall* [1997] 1 Cr App R(S) 406.

[27] It is recognized that separate 'fallback' offences, such as voluntary manslaughter, may be created to fulfil this role. See further below.

carelessness, and that the first category should be called 'murder', while the second and third categories should not.[28] It is also suggested that the maximum penalty for murder, and for reckless killing, should be life imprisonment, while the maximum penalty for killing by gross carelessness should be imprisonment for a fixed term, say, ten years. These assumptions are broadly in accord with the existing Law Commission proposals on reform of offences against the person.[29]

It is hard to argue with the proposition that, if the fixed penalty for murder was abolished, that offence should henceforth be punishable with a *maximum* of life imprisonment. There is more scope for argument over the relationship between the maximum for murder and the maximum for reckless killing. It may be claimed, with some justification, that in a hierarchy of offences the relationship between the offences should be reflected in gradations in the maxima. One of the criticisms of the existing structure of non-fatal offences against the person, for example, is that the maximum penalty for assault occasioning actual bodily harm under section 47 of the Offences Against the Person Act 1861 is the same as the maximum penalty for the supposedly more serious offence of wounding or inflicting grievous bodily harm under section 20.[30] It seems legitimate for courts to assume that the sentencing levels for offences which carry the same maximum penalty should be broadly similar, and the Court of Appeal has sometimes made this point expressly.[31] The argument is less strong, however, where the two offences which are being compared both carry life as their maximum. While one can accept that, in general, determinate sentencing levels for reckless killing would be somewhat lower than those for murder, there would certainly be examples of both offences where the criteria for imposing a *discretionary* life sentence would be made out. The modern test for the imposition of such a sentence is whether the offender represents a serious danger to the public, and whether that state of affairs is likely to continue for an indeterminate period of time.[32] The Law Commission was unable to decide between a maximum sentence of ten years or fourteen years for the proposed offence of killing by gross carelessness, though it probably leant to the former view. The problem is that the existing structure of maximum penalties is so ramshackle that it is not difficult to highlight apparently irrational comparisons with other offences.[33]

---

[28] Contrast the different approach taken by William Wilson in Chapter 2, above.

[29] Law Commission, *Legislating the Criminal Code: Involuntary Manslaughter* (Law Com. no. 237) (1996).

[30] A. Ashworth, *Principles of Criminal Law*, 3rd edn. (Oxford, 1999), 326.

[31] e.g. *Jones* (1990) 12 Cr App R(S) 253 on the appropriate sentencing bracket for the offence of administering a noxious thing with intent under the Offences Against the Person Act 1861, s. 24.

[32] *A.-G.'s Ref. No. 32 of 1996* [1997] 1 Cr App R(S) 261; *McPhee* [1998] 1 Cr App R(S) 201.

[33] Is 10 years an appropriate ceiling for this offence when e.g. handling stolen goods and cultivation of cannabis both attract a maximum of 14 years on indictment? See Law Commission, n. 29 above, paras. 5.46 *et seq.*

C. The Sentence For Murder

1. Current Sentencing Practice

As explained above, the period served in custody by an offender sentenced for murder is largely determined by the executive authorities, but with the opportunity for a degree of judicial input. Before imposing the mandatory sentence of life imprisonment and deciding whether to make a recommendation as to the minimum period to be served, the judge will go through a process akin to the sentencing exercise for other offences, considering reports and listening to a plea in mitigation.[34] Minimum-period recommendations are actually made in only a minority of murder cases, around 10 per cent. The recommendation may itself be for *life*[35] where, in an exceptional case, that is the period necessary to serve the requirements of retribution and general deterrence.[36] Otherwise, it will be for a fixed term of years. The idiosyncratic nature of this process means that there are no sentencing guidelines for the offence of murder. Since the judge's recommendation is not binding on the Parole Board, there is no right of appeal against it,[37] and so there is no case law as to what an 'appropriate' recommendation for a given murder case might be. It was said in one case[38] that a recommendation should not be made for less than twelve years, but this may misrepresent the law.[39] It does seem strange that a judge, having presided over a murder trial in which there are exceptional mitigating circumstances, cannot signal this by recommending a short minimum period. Aside from the recommendation under the 1965 Act, however, in *every* murder case the sentencing judge is required to indicate in writing the 'tariff period' which in his view is necessary to meet the requirements of retribution and deterrence in the case. This report goes to the Lord Chief Justice, who records his view, and thence to the Home Secretary, who may set a higher or lower tariff than the judges.[40] Once the tariff has been communicated to the prisoner, it may only be varied upwards at a later date in very exceptional circumstances.[41]

---

[34] *Todd* [1966] Crim LR 557.

[35] Notwithstanding the fact that, logically, life cannot be a *minimum* period. The Criminal Law Revision Committee, 12th Report, *The Penalty for Murder* (1973) (Cmnd. 5184), para. 34, suggested that in a case of exceptional gravity the judge should say that there is no minimum period which can be recommended.

[36] Cullen and Newell, n. 5 above, 22, state that there are 26 current lifers in this category. A recent example is Dr Harold Shipman, convicted of the multiple murders of patients. See further L. Blom-Cooper and T. Morris, '"Life" until Death: Interpretations of Section 1(1) of the Murder (Abolition of Death Penalty) Act 1965' [1999] Crim LR 897.

[37] *Leaney* [1996] 1 Cr App R(S) 30.   [38] *Flemming* [1973] 2 All ER 401.

[39] See the discussion in *Archbold* (London, 2000), para. 19-96.

[40] *Secretary of State for the Home Department, ex p. Doody* [1994] 1 AC 531.

[41] *Secretary of State for the Home Department, ex p. Pierson* [1998] AC 539.

If the fixed life penalty for murder was abolished, what would be the appropriate sentencing range for that offence thereafter? Little assistance on this point can be derived from current practice. The simplest approach would be to take a group of offenders sentenced to life imprisonment for murder and to ascertain the periods of time actually served by them before release. In one case in 1996 the Court of Appeal noted that the average term served by lifers was '. . . currently . . . about fourteen years . . . equivalent to a determinate sentence of twenty-one years . . .'.[42] There are problems with this line, however. Firstly, the notion of an 'average term' may be very misleading, concealing a wide and perhaps highly skewed range around that average.[43] Secondly, as explained above, the duration of a mandatory life sentence is effectively determined by the executive authorities. They may take into account a range of considerations beyond the facts of the murder itself, having to do with perceptions of risk of reoffending, fear of public reprisals against a lifer after release, and 'public confidence' in the criminal justice system generally.[44] Actual release dates, then, may well be misleading as to the *relative seriousness* of particular murder cases. An alternative would be to examine periods recommended by judges under the 1965 Act.[45] This would give a better indication of relative seriousness, but its value would also be limited. As we have seen, recommendations are made in only a minority of (perhaps unrepresentative) cases, and judges in murder cases are apparently not informed of recommendations given by judges in other murder cases.[46] In contrast to recommendations under the 1965 Act, however, 'tariff periods' are set in *all* murder cases, through the process involving the trial judge, the Lord Chief Justice, and the Home Secretary referred to above. Tariff periods would probably provide the most useful and comprehensive guidance available on the relative seriousness of different murder cases. They are not routinely made public, but are sometimes released to the press in cases attracting particular public interest. The tariff is now always disclosed to the prisoner, and can be found in the early-release dossier, so in principle could be catalogued by officials or by researchers.

There are one or two other pointers to what might be seen as the

---

[42] *A.-G.'s Ref No. 33 of 1996* [1997] 2 Cr App R(S) 10, 17, per Kennedy LJ.

[43] The average term served by life-sentence prisoners has increased significantly over the years. In 1979 it was 9.1 years, in 1989 it was 12 years, and by 1997 it was just over 14 years: Cullen and Newell, n. 5 above, 21.

[44] *Ex p. Doody*, n. 40 above; *Ex p. Hindley*, n. 11 above.

[45] Valuable information about recommendations in murder cases made in the years between 1965 and 1975 may be found in A. M. N. Shaw, 'The Penalty for Murder and Judges' Recommendations' (1976) 15 How J 31. The author found that recommendations were being made in less than 10% of murder cases, but that the majority of recommendations were for periods of 15 and 20 years, with 25, 30, and 35 years being reserved for particularly heinous killings.

[46] According to Lord Windlesham, 'Life sentences: The Paradox of Indeterminacy' [1989] Crim LR 244, 255.

appropriate sentencing bracket for murder cases. One could, for example, examine the case law on offenders sentenced for *attempted* murder, or for inflicting grievous bodily harm with intent, under section 18 of the Offences Against the Person Act 1861. Without the intervention of good fortune or prompt medical intervention, many of these cases would have fallen to be sentenced as murder. Thus, one can find comments by judges in the Court of Appeal that a particular case was, on its facts, 'almost murder'. In *Thomas*,[47] for example, the offender, after a drunken quarrel with her cohabitee, poured petrol over the victim and set her alight, causing 50 per cent burns and requiring skin grafting and extensive surgery. Lawton LJ commented that:

In really bad cases of causing grievous bodily harm with intent it is often a matter of chance that the victim does not die . . . If the victim does not die because of superb surgery and medical treatment, then the offence is within touching distance of murder . . .

There remains, however, an unquantified gap between the appropriate sentence for an attempted murder and the completed act, or between a section 18 assault which does, or does not, cause death. It is, of course, a highly arguable point as to how much additional time needs to be served by an offender to mark the fact that it is 'often a matter of chance' that death *has* occurred in these circumstances. This general issue is considered further below. In one case involving sentencing for attempted murder, the Court of Appeal rejected as 'completely unrealistic' an argument by defence counsel designed to compare the sentence for the attempt with a recommendation which a judge might have given if the victim of the attack had died.[48]

Another approach would be to examine cases falling at the top end of the manslaughter range where, again, one can find comments by judges that the case was 'almost murder'.[49] This is perhaps a more reliable guide to the appropriate determinate sentence for murder since, unlike attempted murder and wounding with intent, the actus reus of manslaughter and murder is the same, the main variable between the two offences being the offender's culpability. Indeed, it is possible to find groups of cases where the facts are substantially the same, but where some have been sentenced as murder, and some have been sentenced as manslaughter. This divergence arises in consequence of changes over the years to the meaning of 'intention' in murder, and the consequent adjustment of the borderline between the two crimes.

Compare the following two cases:

---

[47] (1985) 7 Cr App R(S) 87.
[48] *Al-Banna* (1984) 6 Cr App R(S) 426; an argument based on 'a number of cases in a schedule prepared by the Criminal Appeal Office'.					[49] See *Palma*, n. 52 below.

Hyam[50] (petrol poured through letter box and ignited the house of a woman against whom D. had a grudge; intended victim escaped but two daughters of the intended victim died). D. convicted after a trial; law reports of the appellate hearings in the Court of Appeal and the House of Lords give no indication of any minimum period having been recommended by the trial judge.

Nedrick[51] (paraffin poured through letter box and ignited the house of woman against whom D. had a grudge; fifteen-year-old child of the victim died in the fire). D. convicted after a trial, where the murder conviction was quashed on appeal and manslaughter conviction substituted, sentence of fifteen years.

with

Palma[52] (petrol poured through letter box and ignited the house of a man against whom D. had a grudge; son of the intended victim died in the fire). The Court of Appeal said that it was 'astonished' that the prosecution had accepted a plea of guilty to manslaughter, and that this was 'as bad a case of manslaughter as it is possible to have, short of murder', the prison term of twelve years was upheld.

and with

Archer[53] (material soaked in petrol, set alight and pushed through letter box of a house where Ds mistakenly believed a person against whom they had a grudge to be living; one of the occupants of the house died and a second suffered extensive burns). Court of Appeal upheld one sentence of twelve years and reduced the other sentence to eleven years to reflect the different stages at which the Ds had pleaded guilty.

Again, however, a comparison between the sentences passed for murder and manslaughter must be carried out with great care. It might be assumed that, aside from cases such as these lying close to the murder/manslaughter border, offenders convicted of murder will ultimately serve a longer term in prison than those convicted of manslaughter. In fact, however, *discretionary* lifers on average spend *longer* in custody than mandatory lifers, with 17.4 per cent of the former serving over fifteen years in prison, compared to 11 per cent of the latter.[54] At first sight this looks rather odd, but the apparent anomaly is surely explained because a life sentence for manslaughter requires a finding by the court that the offender will continue to represent a risk to the public for an indefinite period, while a life sentence for murder, being mandatory, will include many instances where the offender represents little or no future risk.

---

[50] [1975] AC 905.   [51] [1986] 3 All ER 1.
[52] (1986) 8 Cr App R(S) 148.   [53] [1998] 2 Cr App R(S) 76.
[54] Cullen and Newell, n. 5 above, 21.

An examination of the sentencing patterns for homicide in other jurisdictions might also be helpful, at least in identifying considerations which
underpin the distinctions between different grades of homicide.
Jurisdictions which recognize several subdivisions in the offence would be
most helpful here. It must be recognized, however, that different countries
have quite different sentencing conventions, and that this will crucially
affect sentencing brackets and starting points. In Spain and Italy, for example, the homicide of a *near relative* is regarded as a separate and aggravated
form of the offence,[55] but no such distinction is drawn in English law and
it does not seem to have been argued that familial killings should be set
apart in that way. A number of other jurisdictions subdivide the offence of
murder, reserving the most severe sentences for cases in which particularly
reprehensible *motives*[56] for killing have been established, or where the
killing has been carried out by particular *means*, such as by shooting, or by
frightening a person to death.[57] Some jurisdictions give considerable weight
to the fact that the killing was done in the course of committing another
specified offence,[58] or was a *provoked* killing, while others seem to regard
this as less significant.

The various considerations referred to in the last few paragraphs would
provide some pointers in designing a sentencing framework for murder but,
again, they are of limited value. If the fixed penalty was abolished it would
fall to the Court of Appeal to draft sentencing guidelines for murder as a
matter of urgency, and the Court would best start with a more or less clean
sheet. The Select Committee of the House of Lords was very concerned that
the '. . . abolition of the mandatory sentence would present peculiarly difficult sentencing problems for the trial judge . . . [b]ecause there are no precedents to guide the judge in imposing a determinate sentence for murder'.[59]
With respect, however, the Lord Chief Justice was surely right when he said
in evidence to the Committee that, in his view, the provision of sentencing
advice in murder cases would create no special difficulty.[60] It would be a
challenging task, certainly, but inherently no more difficult than the drafting of sentencing guidelines for other offences. It is worth noting that under
recent legislation the Sentencing Advisory Panel would be closely involved
in assisting and advising the Court of Appeal in the formulation of the new
guidelines.[61] The Panel's involvement in this area of sentencing might be
seen as particularly appropriate, given the public interest which would be
bound to surround the abolition of the fixed penalty for murder, and the

[55] House of Lords, n. 19 above, app. 5.
[56] Or, indeed, for random motive*less* killings.
[57] Canadian Criminal Code, s. 222(1)(d).   [58] Ibid., 230.
[59] N. 19 above, para. 113A.   [60] Ibid.
[61] The Panel is established under the Crime and Disorder Act 1998, s. 81. As to the duty of
the Court of Appeal to issue sentencing guidelines and to have regard to the views of the Panel;
see s. 80 of the 1998 Act.

Panel's statutory responsibility to consult widely before issuing its advice to the Court.

2. TOWARDS SENTENCING GUIDELINES FOR MURDER

Currently, the basic sentencing structure in the Criminal Justice Act 1991 does not apply to murder.[62] If the fixed penalty was abolished, the 1991 Act, appropriately amended, would presumably henceforth apply to murder as it does to all other offences. Then, an offender would fall to be sentenced for murder either on the basis of the seriousness of the offence (under sections 1(2)(a) and 2(2)(a) of the Act), or on the basis of the requirement of public protection following commission of a violent or sexual offence (under sections 1(2)(b) and 2(2)(b)).

While all cases of murder would qualify as 'violent offences' under the latter provision,[63] it is submitted that the former provision is the one which would normally be invoked in murder cases. A discretionary life sentence cannot be imposed on the gravity of the offence alone, but only on public-protection grounds.[64] The sentencing court should turn to the latter provision only where, exceptionally, a longer-than-normal sentence (or a discretionary life sentence) is required to 'protect the public from serious harm from [the offender]'. This phrase is to be construed as a reference to '. . . protecting members of the public from death or serious personal injury, whether physical or psychological, occasioned by further such offences committed by him'.[65] Most murderers represent a low risk of repetition of violent or sexual reoffending. Home Office figures show that there is an extremely low reconviction rate for murder of those who have already been convicted of murder. Of those convicted of murder between 1988 and 1997 only ten (or 0.6 per cent) had a previous conviction for murder, while another twenty had a previous conviction for manslaughter. Although the figures do not reveal the number of offenders convicted of murder who go on to commit other serious violent or sexual offences, it can probably be inferred that only a small proportion of those convicted of homicide in fact represent a significant threat to the community.[66]

In drafting sentencing guidelines for murder, therefore, the first task would be to identify a number of sentencing brackets within that offence, based on *offence seriousness*. The second task would be to identify gradations of seriousness within those brackets (aggravating and mitigating factors affecting offence seriousness), and the third task would be to take

---

[62] Criminal Justice Act 1991, s. 1(1); Powers of Criminal Courts (Sentencing) Act 2000, s. 79(1).

[63] For the definition, see s. 31(1) of the 1991 Act, and s. 161(3) of the 2000 Act.

[64] *Meek* (1995) 16 Cr App R(S) 1003; *Robinson* [1997] 2 Cr App R(S) 35.

[65] Criminal Justice Act 1991, s. 31(3); Powers of Criminal Courts (Sentencing) Act 2000, s. 161(4).   [66] See also Cullen and Newell, n. 5 above, ch. 1.

account of matters of personal mitigation. Fourthly, regard would then need to be given to other considerations which would cut across those basic divisions, such as: (a) the appropriate use of longer-than-normal sentences and discretionary life sentences in those cases where a continuing substantial risk to the public *was* established; (b) the use of hospital orders where it was apparent that the offender required treatment rather than punishment;[67] and (c) cases where the offender would attract an automatic life sentence on the basis that the homicide was the second 'serious offence' of which he had been convicted.

Offence divisions within homicide derive from the fact that the actus reus is the same throughout the offence categories. What varies through these gradations, therefore, is the degree of culpability of the offender. Herein lies an important difference from other sentencing hierarchies, such as those involving non-fatal violent offences, sexual offences, or drug offences, where both harm *and* culpability vary as one moves through the offence gradations. Within the category of murder, it has often been suggested that one might wish to draw a distinction between *premeditated* and *intentional* killings. This is an important moral distinction, and it is one which ought to be recognized in the law, if not by different offence labels (as is done in some other jurisdictions), then by different brackets within sentencing guidelines for murder. Premeditated killings are regarded as the most culpable of all killings in that they involve a calculated decision by D. to take life, whilst the latter may result from the formation of a more transient, or fleeting, intention to kill.

(i) Premeditated killing

In English law we are not accustomed to working with the concept of premeditation, as opposed to intent. What, in addition to intent, does premeditation require? In the United States, premeditation marks the distinction between first and second degree murder, but the term has proved difficult to define. The main issue is the length of the period of deliberation involved. According to LaFave and Scott,[68] 'Perhaps the best that can be said of premeditation . . . is that it requires that D. with a cool mind did reflect, at least for a short period of time before the killing' but the authors refer to cases where premeditation has been found in a 'brief moment of thought' or a 'matter of seconds'. They recognize that the distinction between first and second degree murder may be in danger of breaking down, and commend other judicial authorities which have insisted on proof of 'prior calculation and design'. It does seem that killings involving only short periods of reflection are better treated as 'intentional killing' rather than 'premeditated killing', reserving the latter for cases in which there is

[67] Criminal Justice Act 1991, s. 4; Powers of Criminal Courts (Sentencing) Act 2000, s. 82.
[68] W. R. LaFave and A. W. Scott, *Criminal Law*, 2nd edn. (St Paul, MN, 1986), 643.

clearly shown to have been calculation and planning.[69] It is suggested, then, that a premeditated killing must involve forethought, or planning. It entails a degree of cold calculation which excludes it from the more typical murder case which arises from an argument or brawl.

It is anticipated that when sentencing for *premeditated killing*, the court would be dealing with cases:

(a) where the killing has been planned and carried out by D. in a ruthless, 'professional' manner. The Court of Appeal indicated in one case involving the attempted murder of the Israeli ambassador in London, the victim having been shot in the head and left with permanent grievous injuries, that sentences in the order of thirty to thirty-five years are appropriate for 'political murders or attempted political murders of this sort';[70]

(b) where D. has killed V. intentionally in the course of committing another crime, whether gratuitously, or in a deliberate attempt to avoid detection for that other crime;

(c) where D. has tortured or otherwise cruelly treated the victim in the course of killing them, over and above the violence necessarily involved in the offence itself; and

(d) where D. has revenged himself upon V. Often this will amount to premeditated killing, but there will be some cases (such as so-called 'cumulative provocation') where D. has killed in understandable resentment at earlier ill-treatment by V. There would probably be general agreement that such cases should not remain within the category of premeditated killing, but should still come within intentional killing or be dealt with separately under specific provocation or diminished responsibility provisions. This is considered further below.

Relevant *aggravating factors* would include:

(i) where the killing was carried out for the payment of money or the promise of such payment;

(ii) where the offence was racially motivated;

(iii) where V. was targeted as being vulnerable;

(iv) where there was a high level of planning by D;

(v) where D. forearmed himself with a weapon;

(vi) where extensive and/or multiple injuries were inflicted on V;

(vii) where D. returned to kill V. after targeting V. on a previous occasion or occasions;

(viii) where more than one life was taken;

(ix) where V. was a police officer, prison officer, or other public servant;

---

[69] Canadian Criminal Code, s. 231(2): 'Murder is first degree murder when it is planned and deliberate.'   [70] *Al-Banna*, n. 48 above.

(x) where the offence was committed while D. was on bail; and
(xi) D.'s previous convictions and failures to respond to previous sentences.

Relevant *mitigating factors* would include:

None.

Also relevant as *reducing sentence*:

D.'s timely admission of guilt.

Personal mitigation would include:

 (i) D.'s genuine remorse; and
(ii) D.'s clean record and good character, although not a matter of great significance here.

(ii) Intentional killing

Within the sentencing band for *intentional killing* would be included a wide variety of cases where, although the murder was not planned in advance, it took place in circumstances where D. is clearly shown to have used violence with the intention to kill. Also falling within this category would be cases where D. is shown to have intended to cause serious injury to V, being aware at the time that such harm may result in V.'s death. In these cases the formation of the necessary intention may have been fleeting, or have occupied only a matter of a few seconds.

It is anticipated that when sentencing for *intentional killing*, the court would be dealing with cases:

(a) which might be seen as 'typical' murder cases, arising in the context of a quarrel or fight; and
(b) other, less typical cases, but which are characterized by an intention to kill or cause serious personal injury.

Relevant *aggravating factors* would include:

  (i) where the offence was racially motivated;
 (ii) where D. forearmed himself with a weapon;
(iii) where V. was targeted as being vulnerable;
 (iv) where D. used a weapon to inflict injury;
  (v) where extensive and/or multiple injuries were inflicted on V;
 (vi) where D. returned to kill V. after targeting V. on a previous occasion or occasions;
(vii) where more than one life was taken;
(viii) where V. was a police officer, a prison officer, or other public servant;
 (ix) where the offence was committed while D. was on bail; and
  (x) D.'s previous convictions and failures to respond to previous sentences.

Relevant *mitigating factors* would include:

(i) a significant degree of provocation by V; and
(ii) overreaction by D. in self-defence.

Also relevant as *reducing sentence*:

D.'s timely admission of guilt.

Personal mitigation would include:

(i) D.'s genuine remorse; and
(ii) D.'s clean record and good character.

Before leaving the topic of sentencing for murder, it may be helpful to indicate a number of matters which, it is submitted, should *not* be regarded as having a significant impact on the sentence to be imposed, whether for premeditated killing or intentional killing. They may be termed *neutral factors*. These would include:

(i) whether the death has been caused by a positive act, or by an omission;
(ii) (apart from where specified in the aggravating circumstances in the guidelines) the identity[71] of the victim, or the previous relationship between the offender and the victim;
(iii) (apart from where it reflects on matters of culpability referred to above) the nature of the weapon[72] which was used to kill; and
(iv) representations made to the court by the relatives of the deceased victim, whether these are designed to encourage the passing of a more severe, or a more lenient, sentence.[73]

D. The Sentence for Manslaughter

No *general* sentencing guideline has been issued by the Court of Appeal for manslaughter. This is highly unusual for an offence which carries such a high maximum penalty, and which comes before the Court of Appeal so regularly on appeal against sentence. One reason for this is undoubtedly the considerable breadth of the offence and the range of factual circumstances in which it may be committed. As Lord Lane CJ said in one case:[74]

Of all the crimes in the calendar, the crime of manslaughter faces the sentencing judge with the greatest problem, because manslaughter ranges in its gravity from the borders of murder right down to those of accidental death.

---

[71] Targeting of a vulnerable victim is an aggravating factor.
[72] The use of poison to kill the victim would e.g. almost always evidence premeditation.
[73] See *Nunn* [1996] 2 Cr App R(S) 136; *Hird* [1998] 2 Cr App R(S) 241; *McCourt v. UK* (App. No. 20433/92) 15 EHRR CD 110.
[74] *Walker* (1992) 13 Cr App R(S) 474, 476.

While this is certainly true, offence breadth alone does not explain the paucity of appellate guidance. Drug trafficking, robbery and rape are all broad offences, but these are areas in which the Court of Appeal has managed to generate guideline judgments. In manslaughter the problem is not just about breadth. It also derives from the unsatisfactory compendious nature of the substantive law. Quite different legal entities are here gathered together under one umbrella and, although linked by the causation of death, the culpability element varies widely from one form of the offence to another. In provocation cases, for example, the defendant is shown to have had the mens rea for murder, whilst in other manslaughter cases a high degree of negligence is enough to convict. In some examples the defendant knowingly runs the risk of causing the victim's death, but in others he has foreseen no harm to the victim at all, so that culpability falls far short of the tragic outcome. What is clear is that these widely varying forms of manslaughter cannot possibly be accommodated within a single sentencing guideline. Subdivision of the offence for sentencing purposes, despite judicial pronouncements to the contrary,[75] *is* possible, indeed it is essential, if progress is to be made.

1. CURRENT SENTENCING PRACTICE

It emerges from the Court of Appeal authorities gathered together in David Thomas's *Encyclopedia*[76] that different sentencing brackets have developed where the court is sentencing for different forms of manslaughter, even though these profiles are not linked within any overall sentencing structure.[77] Thomas has subdivided *involuntary* manslaughter cases according to the following categories:

(1) manslaughter arising out of disputes and fights;
(2) manslaughter by stabbing;
(3) manslaughter involving the use of a firearm;
(4) manslaughter in the course of a burglary;
(5) manslaughter in the course of a robbery;
(6) manslaughter of a young child;
(7) manslaughter caused by setting fire to buildings, etc.;
(8) reckless manslaughter;
(9) manslaughter by injection of drugs;

---

[75] In *Boyer*, n. 1 above, 35, Dunn LJ said that it was '. . . impossible to subdivide the offence of manslaughter into different categories and say that any particular sentence is appropriate for any particular category of offence'.
[76] *Current Sentencing Practice*, B1-1–B1-3, adopted by Law Commission, n. 29 above, app. B.
[77] See further M. Wasik, 'Form and Function in the Law of Involuntary Manslaughter' [1994] Crim LR 883.

(10) 'other forms' of manslaughter, a section comprised of two cases involving the commission of manslaughter in the context of sexual activities, and

(11) manslaughter involving the use of a motor vehicle.

It is not clear whether these categories are meant to reflect significant moral distinctions, or whether they are merely sub-headings to reflect frequently recurring factual situations. There has been no endorsement of these categories by the Court of Appeal, but the authoritative nature of Thomas's work, and the regularity with which it is referred to by the higher courts, suggests that his classification has at least an unofficial standing.

To judge from the cases reported by Thomas, involuntary manslaughter arising from category (1) in disputes and fights generally attracts sentences in a lower range of two to four years, and an upper range of five to eight years. The lower range is appropriate where typically the offender has struck the victim a single blow, but death has resulted unexpectedly because the victim has struck their head on the pavement or some other hard object. The higher range is appropriate where the attack has been more sustained, such as where it has continued once the victim is on the ground, and particularly where there has been the use of a weapon, or kicking as well as punching. One difficulty which has beset sentencing in manslaughter cases is the appropriate balance between an offender's culpability and the resultant harm. This issue has always been controversial,[78] and there is inconsistency in the sentencing cases. Earlier decisions took the line that, where there has been an assault by D. upon V, the case should be sentenced in much the same way irrespective of whether V. sustains only minor injuries or, through mischance, meets with death. In *McNamara*[79] the Court of Appeal stressed the need for the courts to '. . . disassociate the fact of death from what the offender did to bring it about'. This case was, however, disapproved in *Ruby*,[80] where Lord Lane CJ said that:

In these cases there is an element in the sentence which represents the fact that death has ensued. It is not proper for the Court to treat a case where death results from an unlawful blow, simply on the basis of an assault committed under section 20 of the Offences Against the Person Act 1861.

The line adopted in *Ruby* has generally been followed in recent years in an attempt to give appropriate weight both to the offender's fault *and* the stark and inescapable fact of the victim's death. This is, of course, a practical though rough compromise, reflecting the nature of an offence which, in some of its forms, 'grossly exaggerates the amount of culpability, producing an extreme form of constructive liability'.[81]

---

[78] There is a substantial academic literature. See e.g. J. Gobert, 'The Fortuity of Consequences' (1993) 3 CLF 1; and A. Ashworth, 'Taking the Consequences' in S. Shute, J. Gardner, and J. Horder (eds.), *Action and Value in the Criminal Law* (Oxford, 1993).
[79] (1984) 6 Cr App R(S) 356.   [80] (1987) 9 Cr App R(S) 305.
[81] Ashworth, n. 30 above, 307.

In categories (2) and (3) the use of a lethal weapon such as a knife, or especially a firearm, takes the case into a somewhat higher sentencing bracket. Stabbing cases seem typically to be in the range of five to eight years, which is much the same as the upper range for category (1). If a firearm has been used to kill, however, sentences between six years and twelve, sometimes fifteen, years have been imposed. The exact sentence often turns on the extent to which the offender has armed himself in advance of the killing. Cases on manslaughter committed in the course of carrying out a burglary, robbery or other offence now stress the fact that, in concordance with the decision in *Ruby*, the sentence must be higher than would have been imposed for the burglary or robbery standing alone, even where the death was almost accidental.[82] Killing in the course of a burglary attracts sentences in the range of six to ten years, though where the victim was elderly and vulnerable the sentence may be twelve years or more.[83] Killing in the course of an armed robbery is marked out as more serious still, attracting sentences in the range of twelve to fifteen years.[84] For manslaughter of a young child the sentencing range is a wide one, probably from around two years up to eight years,[85] depending on whether the child has died as a result of a single incident or from repeated abuse, and to some extent taking account of personal factors relating to the offender.

Manslaughter under provocation, and manslaughter under diminished responsibility, are recognized as providing fairly discrete areas for the purposes of sentencing. In typical cases of manslaughter by provocation the Court of Appeal has traditionally approved sentences in the range of five to eight years.[86] More recently, however, somewhat longer sentences have been signalled, in the region of ten to twelve years, where there has been provocation but where the offender has forearmed himself and has almost invited a confrontation, or where the case is close to a revenge killing.[87] There are also instances of lighter custodial sentences being substituted on appeal, and it is recognized that community sentences, or even conditional discharges, have been passed by sentencers for some domestic killings

---

[82] See *Paget* (1982) 4 Cr App R(S) 399, where in the course of a robbery the offender struck the victim so that he fell and hit his head. A post-mortem showed that the victim's skull was 'fairly thin'.

[83] *Harwood* (1985) 7 Cr App R(S) 362; *Brophy* (1994) 16 Cr App R(S) 652.

[84] *Tominey* (1986) 8 Cr App R(S) 161; *McGee* (1993) 15 Cr App R(S) 463.

[85] *Tickle* (1990) 12 Cr App R(S) 395 suggests a normal range of 3–7 years.

[86] *Light* (1995) 16 Cr App R(S) 824, per Lord Taylor CJ: 'the majority of cases . . . show a sentence of seven to eight years for manslaughter of a spouse when provoked'. *McMinn* [1997] 2 Cr App R(S) 219, per Staughton LJ: 'one rarely sees sentences of more than seven or eight years for manslaughter by provocation'.

[87] *A.-G.'s Ref No. 33 of 1996*, n. 42 above, per Kennedy LJ: 'Where an offender deliberately goes out with a knife, and uses it to cause death, even if there is provocation he should expect to receive on conviction in a contested case a sentence in the region of 10–12 years.'

involving cumulative provocation.[88] In manslaughter by diminished responsibility the sentencing profile is different. One leading decision[89] explains that sentencers in such cases need to consider first whether, in the light of the offender's mental disturbance, a hospital order or a life sentence is appropriate. If not, custodial sentences in the range between three and six years seem to be the norm. Again, as with provocation, exceptional mitigation will sometimes be reflected in a very short custodial sentence, or a community disposal. If there is a common thread running through the provocation and diminished responsibility sentencing cases, it is the frequent appellate references to the need for punishment to reflect, on the one hand, the loss of life and, on the other, the extent of the offender's *reduced* or *residual* culpability for the killing. In provocation cases the culpability will be greater where the defendant was already harbouring a grudge, if he was forearmed, and if there was time to 'cool off'. In diminished responsibility cases sentencers try, in the light of medical evidence, to make an assessment of the extent to which the depression or other condition from which the defendant suffered actually limited their responsibility for the killing.

2. TOWARDS SENTENCING GUIDELINES FOR MANSLAUGHTER

The Law Commission has proposed that the offence of *involuntary* manslaughter should be divided into two, with reckless killing in the upper band and killing by gross carelessness in the lower band.[90] The existing variety of involuntary manslaughter known as voluntary-act manslaughter would be abolished. Reckless killing would be committed where a person causes the death of another while aware of a risk that his conduct will cause death or serious injury, and it is unreasonable for him to take that risk. Killing by gross carelessness would fit below reckless killing, and would be committed where a risk that the defendant's conduct will cause death or serious injury would be obvious to a reasonable person, the defendant was capable of appreciating the risk at the time, and that his conduct fell far below what could reasonably have been expected of him in the circumstances.

Subdividing the offence of manslaughter into two or more offence bands, arranged hierarchically as the Law Commission has proposed, would be an important step towards the production of comprehensive sentencing guidelines for manslaughter. A hierarchical arrangement of offences is much more conducive to the development of sentencing guidelines than the

[88] *Gardner* (1993) 14 Cr App R(S) 364, where the Court of Appeal varied a 5-year sentence on a woman suffering from 'battered women's syndrome' in consequence of years of abuse and violence from her husband, to a probation order.
[89] *Chambers* (1983) 5 Cr App R(S) 190. [90] Law Commission, n. 29 above.

current manslaughter umbrella, under which shelter a diverse group of wrongs with little sentencing correlation amongst them. We can expect that, were this scheme to be implemented, different sentencing regimes for the two offences would emerge much more clearly than is the case under the present law of involuntary manslaughter. With the abolition of unlawful-act manslaughter, the most acute cases of mismatch between offender culpability and resultant harm would be removed, since the definition of reckless killing links the defendant's fault more closely to the prohibited consequence of death. Familiar issues of proportionality in punishment would dominate in the sentencing of reckless killing, but killing in cases of gross carelessness would attract other concerns as well. Culpability might be relatively low, and there would often be substantial mitigation and remorse. But there has still been loss of life and, not infrequently in such cases, several or many lives may have been lost. The court might nonetheless prefer to disqualify the offender from a position of authority or trust, and impose other remedial and educative measures, rather than pass a prison sentence.

The Law Commission proposals relate only to involuntary manslaughter and, therefore, do not consider how the issues of provocation and diminished responsibility might function within the proposed hierarchy of homicide offences. There seem to be three options for accommodating these issues. The first is to provide that provocation and mental disorder short of insanity should henceforth simply be matters relevant in mitigation. This would be a tacit recognition that the principal rationale for their existence as distinct defences has always been the fixed penalty for murder, and that the removal of that penalty would logically signal their demise as well.[91] The second option is that provocation and diminished responsibility might continue to operate as partial defences, but within the new offence structure. The main purpose of this would be to avoid unfair labelling. So, for example, where a jury found that an offender charged with intentional killing had been provoked to kill, this would result in a conviction for the next lower available homicide offence, in this case reckless killing. This outcome might seem rather artificial, however, since the definition of reckless killing hardly seems apposite to cater for provocation cases, an example of inappropriate labelling. The third alternative would be to have a distinct fall-back offence to cater for cases in which one of the partial defences had been accepted by the jury. The fall-back offence would play a similar role to voluntary manslaughter in the existing law, and it might be renamed 'killing under provocation' or 'killing under diminished responsibility', as appropriate. Alternatively, if the term 'manslaughter' did not figure in the names of the new substantive offences, it might be retained specifically for this limited purpose.

---

[91] C. Wells, 'The Death Penalty for Provocation?' [1978] Crim LR 662, and the same author's contribution to this volume, Chapter 4 above.

(i) Reckless killing

It is anticipated that when sentencing for *reckless killing*, the court would be dealing with cases:

(a) where the defendant, for whatever reason, has knowingly exposed someone to a high risk of death or serious personal injury, such as by fire-raising (the four cases listed above, including *Hyam*, are examples), or by sending an explosive article through the mail;

(b) where a person in the course of their employment, in a situation carrying important responsibility for the well-being of others, such as a doctor or a train driver, has knowingly run a serious and unacceptable risk of causing death or serious personal injury; and

(c) where the defendant, together with another person, has engaged in behaviour which the defendant knows to carry a high risk of serious personal injury, and which has resulted in the death of that other. An example is *Pike*[92] where D. administered a chemical to his sexual partner which he knew could cause loss of consciousness and in fact caused death.

Relevant *aggravating factors* would include:

(i) a [high] level of awareness on D.'s part that he was taking a [gross] risk of causing death or serious physical injury;

(ii) where D. had been aware of a continuing risk of death or serious personal injury for a period of time, but failed to take positive and appropriate steps to counter that risk;

(iii) where the taking of the risk by D. represented a significant breach of trust or abdication of his responsibility;

(iv) where the offence was racially motivated;

(v) where V. was targeted as being vulnerable;

(vi) where D. forearmed himself with a weapon;

(vii) where D. had targeted V. on a previous occasion or occasions;

(viii) where more than one life was taken;

(ix) where V. was a police officer or other public servant;

(x) where the offence was committed while D. was on bail; and

(xi) D.'s previous convictions and failures to respond to previous sentences.

Relevant *mitigating factors* would include:

(i) where D.'s awareness of the risk of death or serious personal injury was only a fleeting one; and

(ii) where V. consented to the risk.

---

[92] [1961] Crim LR 114.

Also relevant as *reducing sentence*:

D.'s timely admission of guilt.

Personal mitigation would be:

(i) D.'s genuine remorse; and
(ii) D.'s clean record and good character.

(ii) Killing by gross carelessness

It is anticipated that when sentencing for *killing by gross carelessness*, the court would be dealing with cases:

(a) where D. has been engaged on a course of conduct and has negligently created a risk which causes death (an example is *Morgan*[93] where a train driver with an excellent driving record inexplicably passed yellow and red signals and collided with another train);
(b) where D. has been engaged on a course of conduct and has created a risk which he has then negligently ignored, and which causes death (an example is *Kennedy*[94] where D, in the course of a burglary at night, carelessly started a fire; he left the scene and one of the occupants of the house was killed);
(c) where D. is the manager of company which organized outdoor activities for young people, but did so to a deplorably low standard and failed to conform to health and safety regulations. An example is *Kite*;[95]
(d) where D. and another person have engaged in conduct which obviously represented a risk of death or serious injury. An example is *Williamson*[96] where the defendant and partner practised mutual partial asphyxiation to heighten sexual sensation. Other examples are *Billia*[97] and *Clarke and Purvis*.[98]

Relevant *aggravating factors* would include:

(i) a gross departure by D. from the appropriate standard of care;
(ii) where the failure is part of a pattern of dereliction of duty on D.'s part; and
(iii) where more than one life has been lost;

Relevant *mitigating factors* would include:

---

[93] (1990) 12 Cr App R(S) 504; 18 months, with 6 to serve and the balance suspended, reduced to 4 months to allow D.'s immediate release ordered on appeal.
[94] (1994) 15 Cr App R(S) 141; 8 years reduced to 6 years on appeal.
[95] [1996] 2 Cr App R(S) 295; 3 years reduced to 2 years on appeal.
[96] (1993) 15 Cr App R(S) 364; 4 years reduced to 3 years on appeal.
[97] [1996] 1 Cr App R(S) 39; 9 years reduced to 5 years on appeal.
[98] (1992) 13 Cr App R(S) 552; 5 years reduced to 3½ years on appeal.

(i) where D.'s failure is best characterized as stupidity (as in *Lamb*[99]), or a lapse of attention; and

(ii) D.'s own personal characteristics which mean that D. would find it very difficult to comply with the requisite standard of care.

Also relevant as *reducing sentence*:

D.'s timely admission of guilt.

Personal mitigation would be:

(i) D.'s genuine remorse (often a characteristic of such cases, given that the disastrous consequences will not have been foreseen by D); and

(ii) D.'s clean record and good character.

In parallel with the guidelines in relation to premeditated killing and intentional killing, above, the following factors should *not* be regarded as having a significant impact on the sentence to be imposed. They may be termed *neutral factors*. These would include:

(i) whether the death has been caused by a positive act, or by an omission;

(ii) (apart from where specified in the aggravating circumstances in the guidelines) the identity of the victim, or the previous relationship between the offender and the victim;

(iii) (apart from where it reflects on matters of culpability referred to above) the nature of the weapon which was used to kill; and

(iv) representations made to the court by the relatives of the deceased victim, whether these are designed to encourage the passing of a more severe, or a more lenient, sentence.

E. Conclusions

This Chapter has probed a number of aspects of sentencing in homicide, but it has been only a partial exploration. It has left out of account, for instance, sentencing for offences such as causing death by dangerous driving, or aggravated vehicle-taking resulting in death. Nor has it had anything to say about the important and topical issue of corporate killing. The focus has been on the offences of murder and manslaughter, and an attempt has been made to break new ground by considering the sentencing parameters likely to emerge in the event either of the abolition of the mandatory penalty for murder, or the reshaping of the law of involuntary manslaughter. It is clear that the current scene is dominated by issues surrounding life sentences, although in the next few years these will be subject to increasing challenge on human rights grounds. There is an urgent

---

[99] (1967) 51 Cr App R 417; 7 years reduced to 2 years on appeal.

need to reverse the trend towards increasing reliance on life sentences. We need to return to the principle that '. . . life imprisonment . . . must only be passed in the most exceptional circumstances . . . for offenders . . . who are in a mental state which makes them dangerous to the life or limb of members of the public'.[100] The Chapter has also stressed the importance of the structure of homicide offences to the development of rational sentencing principles. It has been argued that the principled development of sentencing guidelines requires the avoidance of overly broad offences. Such offences fail to make explicit the moral distinctions which should be reflected in the law, and they lump together very different forms of conduct under a single, misleading, offence label. Sentencing coherence in homicide, it seems, depends upon offences being arranged hierarchically, and with gradations within those offences being clearly based upon the different degrees of offender culpability for causing death.

[100] Per Lord Lane CJ in *Wilkinson* (1983) 5 Cr App R(S) 105, 108.

Index

Index